If You Say So

Copyright © Michelle Herman 2025

First published by Galileo Press in March 2025
ISBN 978-0-913123-51-5 (deluxe paperback)
ISBN 978-0-913123-50-8 (paperback)

Publisher's Cataloging-in-Publication data
Names: Herman, Michelle author.
Title: If you say so / written by Michelle Herman.
Description: Aiken, SC: Galileo Press, 2025.
Identifiers: LCCN: 2025933534 | ISBN: 978-0-913123-50-8 (paperback)
Subjects: Ballet—United States. | Loss (Psychology). | Authors, American—20th century—Biography. | Essays. | Family & Relationships / Death, Grief, Bereavement | Performing Arts / Dance / General | Pets / Essays & Narratives
Classification: LCC PS3558.E63 I4 2025 (pending) | DDC 814/.54—dc23

Cover and interior design by Adam Robinson
Back cover photograph by Leiland Charles © 2025
Cover and interior art by Glen Holland © 2025

Portions of this book first appeared, in different forms, in *American Scholar*, *Columbus Monthly*, *Creative Nonfiction*, *Edible Columbus*, *Epiphany*, *The Keepthings*, *Michigan Quarterly Review*, *seedfall*, *Slate*, and *The Sun*.

If You Say So

Michelle Herman

GALILEO PRESS
South Carolina

Also by Michelle Herman

NONFICTION

Like A Song

Stories We Tell Ourselves

The Middle of Everything

FICTION

Close-Up

Devotion

Dog

A New and Glorious Life

Missing

FOR CHILDREN

A Girl's Guide to Life

For Judith Schwartzbaum

and all the Flowers

Contents

1
Armed	1
In the Body	21
On Balance	35

2
Starting & Stopping	53
Gone	73
Daily Papers	85
Like an Egg	103
Sea-Change	117

3
Old House	129
Animal Behavior	151
If You Say So	205

1

Armed

Picture this: twenty-four masked people in a field, every one of them—every one of *us*—decked out in variously whimsical homemade costume armor. I have a computer keyboard hanging from its knotted cord around my neck—it dangles just below my waist in an approximation of a knight's plackart—and tied around my waist by *their* cords are two computer mice I've painted, as I've also painted the keyboard's keys, with many shades of glittery nail polish. I'm wearing my mother's white gloves from the fifties and a silver Miss America–style sash that says MAMA in purple sewn-on letters (made for me by my daughter); there's a flexible aluminum dryer vent on my right arm, wrist to elbow, and a stuffed snake coiled around my head, which also features a number of hornlike silver spikes made of aluminum foil protruding from my piled-up hair. Strapped on my back is a knapsack filled with half a dozen more, much bigger, stuffed snakes, their heads and tails poking out from the knapsack's incompletely closed front flap. The snakes, like the nail polish, once belonged to my daughter, whose enthusiastic permission to discard everything she left behind in her childhood room when she first left home for college—snakes, snowglobes, schoolwork, trophies, beauty products, etc.—has not persuaded me to do so.

I'm not the only one whose costume armor includes a child's castoffs. Kendra is wearing bits and pieces of her kids' old Halloween costumes (Mighty Morphin Power Ranger, Flapper Girl); the scarf Danielle has tied around her waist is imprinted with dragons and belongs to her six-year-old, Myriam; and Laura S has a bandolier made of the cardboard inner tubes of toilet paper that's studded with her children's toys from fast food restaurant meals, birthday goodie bags, and dentist awards. Also, I am pretty sure the multiple tutus around Stacie's neck belong to River, her three-year-old, but she hasn't said so and I haven't asked. I haven't asked about the shiny, pastel-colored plastic streamers that hang from her arms to the ground, either. It's hard to talk to anyone who's not positioned directly to the left, right, in front of, or behind you (it's hard enough to have a conversation with someone six feet away; at double or triple that, masked and outdoors, there's no point trying). But the truth is, it doesn't matter, because there's only so much time to talk anyway when we meet up in the field on Sundays.

We're making a dance film in the time of the pandemic, and every minute is precious. We've only got these three hours once a week, and it's turning cold. In fact it's already cold: it's early November and it has started to snow.

When we first began meeting in the field, after six months of rehearsing virtually, we were overdressed for the weather, sweating under our armor, dog-panting behind our masks. One Sunday in October, an hour into rehearsal, I thought I might be about to faint. "I think I need a break," I called out. I could hear how shaky I sounded, so I let myself sink slowly to the grass to keep from toppling over.

The snake around my head was cinched too tight that day across my temples. I was wearing a black jumpsuit over a black long-sleeved leotard under my armor, and the temperature was hovering around eighty; the sun was relentless in the shade-free field as we moved through the choreography again and again.

I'm the only one who ever came close to fainting. I don't know why. I'm not even the eldest of our troupe—there are half a dozen people who are older—and my armor isn't the heaviest or the most constricting. Perhaps the others are more stoic. Or more easily embarrassed (if they felt like they might faint, they'd keep it to themselves and take their chances). To be honest, I had tried to tough it out: I'd been dizzy and lightheaded for a good ten minutes before I said anything.

Over the three-month period of in-person rehearsal and filming, there ends up being just one Sunday when there is perfect weather for dancing outdoors in Columbus, Ohio. "That was a great day, wasn't it?" we say for weeks afterwards. But even on the not-great days, even in the rain, or under a blazing sun, or when the wind is so strong that parts of people's costumes fly away—or on the cold November Sunday when it starts to snow as soon as we are in position in the field—we are happy to be there. It's our only reason to go anywhere.

It was not supposed to be this way. Nothing was supposed to be the way it was that fall.

The plan had been to begin rehearsal in spring 2020, in the studio, for a dance performance in the summer, one that would occur in the usual way—in person, in a theater. More than forty of us—mostly amateur but unusually dedicated dancers—were going to participate. Some of us had been among the ten who'd been involved in the first project of this kind two years before, when Russ Lepley, one of our dance teachers, had come up with the idea of recasting on us the contemporary piece he'd created that spring for six professional dancers. At that point, the dance company he and his spouse, Fili Pelacchi, had founded in Columbus was almost a year old, as was the studio they'd opened with the mission of teaching adult beginners to dance. What they'd had in mind when they left the contemporary company they'd been dancing with in Munich, armed with nothing but their savings and the daring plan to start a small upstart dance company of their own in the U.S., was that the studio would support their fledging artistic venture.

And at first that was how it was: there were two separate entities, each with its own purpose. The company, Flux Flow Dance Project, performed the work Russ choreographed, and the steady stream of adults who showed up for classes at the Flux Flow studio kept the company (and Fili and Russ themselves) afloat. Some of those adults were true beginners, like I was, and some, like my new friend Judith, had been dancing for years at other studios. Some had been through serious ballet training as children and into their teens but had stopped dancing long ago and were starting over, this time at a studio whose motto was "come as you are" (where no one cared about how big or small their bodies were or how they wore their hair or where they *had* hair, and where they could dance in baggy shorts or pants and T-shirts—*or* leotards and tights—or tutus, for that matter). Some had started dancing as small children and had never stopped, had kept taking classes all through college and in grad school and had found a new dance home at Flux Flow studio; some were former dance professionals who'd been sidelined by injury or circumstance (parenthood, geography, age, size, health, finances, a dance job that had evaporated) or who'd simply had it with the dance life and all of its attendant miseries, but wanted (still—or, more often, again, and after a long break) to dance for the joy of it.

Russ and Fili welcomed all of us, and treated all of us the same way. They gave us their full attention; they treated us as if each movement we made mattered. As if *we* mattered. We were honored, dazzled, thrilled—we were irresistibly drawn to come back day after day.

Judith called us a cult (but that was her mordant sense of humor: she was also the one who once said, in a ballet class, during barre—in response to Fili's exhortation to pay more attention to the inside leg than the working, outside leg—"If God wanted us to pay attention to it, he wouldn't have called it the inside leg"). It was true that we were as devoted and hard-working as actual disciples—so that when Russ and Fili raised the possibility of making that first piece for us to dance in public, it wasn't as surprising a development as it might have been. To the ten of us who volunteered to do it, I suppose it seemed like the inevitable outcome of the hours and effort we had already put in. And for Russ and Fili, setting choreography on us—ages twenty-two to over seventy, tall and short and fat and thin, and more than half of us with not even a year of dance classes behind us—was a chance to break free of the supposed norms of dance performance, to put into practice in their art what they'd come to believe (what they could *see,* each day in the studio with us): that different kinds of bodies and movement experience made something happen in dance that lifelong training in "the right bodies" did not.

Thus began the collaboration of company and studio, which over time would blur the differences between the two. In some of our performances—that first one, for instance—our piece was on the same bill as the company's; in others, we danced alongside—or served as the corps de ballet for—the members of the company. For some, and for parts of others, it was us alone onstage.

Or—in this newest piece, as it became clear that the original plan would have to be scrapped—us alone in a field, our faces covered, our bodies armored.

Carolina is wearing a colander on her head and there are multicolored paper chains and strips of fabric wrapped around her chest and legs. Judith has stuck toothbrushes and bottles of mouthwash into the many pockets of what must be a fishing or hunting vest, and everything else she's wearing is leopard-patterned: hat (a shower cap), mask, gloves, scarf, shoes—even the duct tape that secures the toothbrushes and mouthwash. Charity's armor is all cardboard and metal—thick silver wire springing from her head along with the inner tubes of paper towels, kitchen implements of every kind hanging from her cardboard breastplate.

We thought we'd be back in the studio in a few weeks, that by midsummer we would be onstage. We convened for our first virtual rehearsal midday on March 17, each of us holding a spatula and a pot lid—the glimmer of an idea that was the piece's starting point, a child's version of a sword and a shield.

Every time we start a new performance project, Russ will bring the seed—sometimes a seedling—of an idea to the first rehearsal. Then he begins to move and we watch and imitate him. We ask questions, *he* asks questions. We try the phrase again. He makes adjustments, adds, subtracts. Another phrase is made, and then another. Soon he'll stand back and watch us move through everything we've got so far, with Fili leading us this time—the two of them talking all the while: "What if we tried this instead?" "What if we did this and *then* this, twice?" "Oh yes, that's nice" or, "No, let's let that go."

I am reminded, every time, of writing a first draft of a new essay or story. I have an idea (maybe no more than a fragment of an idea)—maybe an image or a feeling or a half-formed thought—but I don't know yet what I want to do with it. I set out not knowing where I'm going, but I have to trust myself. I know that there's *something* that has brought me to the page.

Twice a week, Tuesdays and Sundays, we log on to Zoom and raise our spatula swords, swing our pot lid shields. We sway and spin, bend low, raise ourselves up on our toes. We advance and retreat, fall forward and lift ourselves, draw our shoulders and our heads back. We whip our spatulas through the air and bellow and duck behind our potlids or hold them just above our heads as if they are umbrellas. We crouch, scanning the horizon. We make ourselves as big as we can. And then we make ourselves small.

As the dance takes shape, it gives shape to our lives, too. Seeing one another twice a week, even as small squares on our computer screens, going through Russ's familiar warmup, step-touch through shaking every part of ourselves, then settling in to review everything we have so far, then leaning in to the screen to watch as Russ shows us the new movement he has worked out since our last rehearsal, then trying it ourselves as he talks us through it—this is something we can count on when there is so little else that can be counted on. I feel anchored by this project. I feel as if, without it, I would float off into space.

The structure steadies me, as does being part of a community—for although I am at home (and soon I will stop going anywhere, even out for groceries), I'm working with so many of my friends *toward* something. It isn't clear yet what it is, what form it will ultimately take, or how the different parts of it will fit together. *We* are together, though. We're counting on each other to keep showing up.

We dwindle, though, inexorably, as the weeks and then the months pile up. Exhausted, stressed, pulled in too many directions by work from home and children at home, or panicking because of lost work, or having grown too anxious to commit to something that is stretching on for so long with so nebulous—with *no*—endpoint, some of us bow out. We lose Heather, a physical therapist, to the needs of her young children and the demands and strain of her work with frail clients who have to be seen in their homes. We lose Harry to his worry about spending so much time away from his postdoc research on food cultures of the contemporary Mediterranean, and Karina to her worry when *her* postdoc, in plant molecular biology, ends and she is desperate to find a way to extend her visa so she won't have to return to Brazil. We lose Natalie, we lose Cheryl, we lose Lisl.

But for those of us who stay, the project is ballast—or an axis to revolve around. That the project has no end in sight *helps* me: it mirrors what's happening beyond the project, what's happening to everyone, except that *this* is interesting and inspiring, rigorous and difficult and fun. It keeps me putting one foot in front of the other as I do my best to go about the rest of my life, all of it so much diminished and constrained and wrong.

I don't sleep, and there are days when I can't write—days when I can't read. My daughter, Grace, 500 miles away, confesses that she'd had the virus and had kept it from me, dodging my phone calls and texts when she was at her sickest, telling me the truth only now that she is on the mend (not wanting to worry me, my friends say when I tell them, but I know that what she'd feared was that I would freak out, jump in my car, and drive to New York City at the peak of the pandemic there). My students are falling apart. I do what I can to try to help them hold themselves together—nothing works.

I hold *myself* together dancing. I concentrate on this: swinging my spatula-sword, my pot lid-shield, in a choreographed battle against an invisible enemy. And I'm part of an army fighting it. I am not alone.

I sometimes wake up in the middle of the night and feel my hands twitching—I've been swinging my sword and shield in my sleep. I remember this from the last project, the way the choreographed movements I was practicing again and again would get under my skin, into my bones, be with me all the time, no matter what I was doing. No one had told me this (but then I'd never asked): how when you're making a dance piece, the movement you've learned becomes a part of you, so that even when you're not moving you can feel the movement just under the surface of everything else you do.

※

For my sixty-fifth birthday, in March 2020—less than three years after I had started dancing—I planned a big party. I invited all of my Columbus friends (which meant, in the main, by then, my dance friends). It was going to be a "piano bar" cocktail party on a Sunday evening. We'd all dress up, drink martinis and boulevardiers, eat fancy *hors d'oeuvres*. One of my graduate students, Molly Brown, was going to play; my friends would be able to request songs and sing them.

Molly came to my house several times in the weeks leading up to the party so that we could practice a few jazz standards we'd picked out for me to sing—I wanted to be well prepared for my own party, and although I'd been singing all my life, lately it had taken a backseat to work and dance (something had to go). Charity and I had met with Molly too, to practice the song we were going to sing together—one called "The Grass is Always Greener," from the 1981 musical *Woman of the Year*, in which two women argue over whose life is better, each (a "newswoman" and a "housewife") insisting that the other's is. And I had suggested to Fili, who also sings, that we tackle Sondheim's "Not While I'm Around" from *Sweeney Todd* together (*Nothing's gonna harm you/not while I'm around*).

I cancelled the party on March 12, three days before it was scheduled to happen. The sheet music for the duet version of the Sondheim song had just arrived. Fili and I hadn't even had a chance to sing it through together once.

On March 9, my actual birthday, a Monday, I had celebrated in my friend Cheryl's backyard hot tub with five other friends—she had declared that I couldn't let the day pass without at least a small celebration. I'd known Cheryl, a massage therapist, for twenty years, and when I first started taking ballet classes I suggested, during a massage, that she join me at one. Now she too takes classes regularly.

Three other dance friends—Russ, Fili, Judith—were in Cheryl's backyard with me on my birthday. I invited two non-dance friends: Nick, a writer, and Nicole, a psychologist. The seven of us just barely fit into the hot tub. We drank French 75s, ate take-out Chinese food, and sat inches from each other, sweating and laughing and talking in the thrashing water. The day was cool, but surprisingly not very cold—it is usually very cold on my birthday. When we'd had enough hot-tubbing, Cheryl brought out a pile of thrift store fancy dresses she'd collected over the years, and Judith and Russ and Fili tried them on, modeling them for us—clothes to wear to the piano bar party. Before we left Cheryl's house, I hugged everyone. They all hugged one another.

This was the day, I now know—surely I wasn't aware of it at the time—that the first three people tested positive in Ohio. But it isn't as if we didn't all know by then that the pandemic existed. I remember that we talked about it. I know that the evening before, I went out to dinner with my husband, a rare occurrence for us (he's a painter who tends to work nights and sleep during the day, so at my dinnertime he's having breakfast—but also he isn't interested in food, except, he says, as "fuel": he says he doesn't understand the *point* of restaurants), and besides that, he'd suggested it himself, which made it feel especially festive. I remember that I brought hand sanitizer and Clorox wipes, that Glen and I cleaned our hands after we touched the restaurant's door handle, then the menus, then the pen supplied for signing the credit card.

But the next day, with some of my closest friends, it never occurred to me—to any of us—not to hug, not to climb into hot water together and squeeze close so that we could all fit. We shared a meal without thinking twice about it. We passed champagne glasses to one another.

None of us were sick, so what was there to worry about? It wasn't as if we were around strangers.

That was what we thought—it was what most people thought—on March 9, 2020.

If we were careful when we were out and about, we were all sure (weren't we all sure?) we would be—everything would be—all right.

◦◦

That May, George Floyd was murdered. Black Lives Matter protests bloomed across the country. We stopped rehearsing. Many of us were at the protests every day, and those of us who were too fearful of contracting the virus to chance being in a crowd had no heart for rehearsal anyway—none of us could imagine swinging make-believe weapons and protective gear just then. But it wasn't long before Russ suggested that we use our rehearsal time to come together, to sit and talk over Zoom. And soon we were up on our feet again, because *talk* is not how Russ processes the world or makes sense of his own thoughts and feelings. It was a relief to all of us to move again, to absorb what was happening and what we were making of it *without* words.

As we grieved and raged, Russ made new movement for us, and by the time we took up our spatulas and pot lids once more, the piece itself had changed. It changed the way any work of art does when it's being made over a long period of time, as life unfolds and makes its way into it. As the ground shifts and shifts again under one's feet.

In flux, we kept on. Whatever else was happening—and so much was happening—there was still this, every Tuesday, every Sunday.

All summer long, it was how I knew what day it was.

And in between the two weekly rehearsals, I kept practicing. Or dreamed myself practicing. Swing, swing, swing, and step and turn, lift, down, down again, and now around. Again. Again.

◦◦

Gail's an occupational therapist. Danielle, an anthropologist by training, is a lecturer at the university; last year she taught ten classes in seven different departments. Sherry's a middle school teacher.

Carolina, a classicist, is fluent in ten modern and five ancient languages.

Nancy is a retired social worker. Holley is a speech-language pathologist. Natasha, a Russian émigré, does something I don't understand having to do with "comprehensive intellectual property analysis" (I've asked her to explain it and she says, "No. It's too boring to explain").

In the field, on Sundays, in the midst of the pandemic, we are nothing else but dancers.

It's impossible to *be* anything but dancers—impossible to think of anything but the choreography we've been working on for so long by now. Impossible to worry about anything, to feel sad or angry or afraid. We have to concentrate on what our bodies are supposed to do, the shapes we're making with them, what shapes we'll be making next. We have to concentrate on what the people nearest us are doing, to make sure we're all doing it at the same time.

It was a revelation to me when I began dancing—the way everything that wasn't dance would vanish, the way all that mattered was keeping my legs turned out, one hand light on the barre, the other sweeping through the air as gracefully as I could manage. And my épaulement—the position of my head and neck and shoulders.

That all around me there were other people doing the same thing at the same time did not cross my mind at first. I was thinking too hard about what I was doing, what I needed to try harder to do, what I wanted to be able to do next time, to take in my surroundings. But the first weeks passed, and then the first months passed, and the efforts of everyone around me became *part* of what quieted everything outside the studio and everything else inside me. They became part of what I did, part of what I was. I moved through ronds de jambe and fondus with Judith and Lindsey and Rian and Mal and Tamie and Natasha and the others. All of us together. All of us in it together.

We are lying on the cold ground, writhing, because Russ has flipped a piece of the choreography and has us doing it lying down. We look like—we feel like—bugs trying and failing to get up after being knocked onto our backs.

This would be fine—we are all used to doing this sort of thing by now—but, as I have said, it has begun to snow.

Snowdrops are falling into my eyes as I lie on the ground, six feet away from Danielle, who, besides her daughter's scarf imprinted with dragons, has an air filter tied to her back, a heart made of red-and-white striped straws attached to her chest by a safety pin, and a hat that's actually a camping pot. Six feet away on my other side is Jenny, whose armor is made of plastic bags and soda cans.

I can't feel my fingers—I'm not wearing warm gloves; I'm wearing the pearl-encrusted white gloves that are part of my costume.

I close my eyes so that the snow falls onto my eyelids instead of into my eyes, which is a little better. I am trying to decide if what we are doing makes us more or less like professional dancers. I make a mental note to ask Russ or Fili later.

We've been thrashing and twisting on the snowy ground for an hour when he gives us a break to get warm. We scramble to our feet, run to the pile of coats, put them on as well as we can over our costumes. We wrap scarves around our faces. All of us are miserable, but until Charity says, "Guys, we can't do this. We need to tell them to let us go home," it has occurred to none of us that this is a possibility.

Natasha's armor is made of used plastic bottles she has cut in half, connected with key rings, and sprayed with metallic paint. "It feels very protective," she tells me. Brad has made his out of brown felt lavishly embellished with metallic emblems (some of which, it takes me a few weeks to notice, are Stars of David) and from which he has affixed a variety of kitchen utensils—they clank when he walks. His headpiece turns out to be a repurposed helmet from when he was in a local production of *Shrek*. Laura W has toilet paper rolls and canning jar rings strung on rope wrapped around her torso and a hairpiece made of wine corks.

Nancy's armor includes a puppet she'd used in her therapy practice with children and is otherwise made of bubble wrap, reinforced by twin mini-colanders from microwavable meals—one bright red colander over each breast. Pat's chest is protected by a roasting pan.

Dian, who is from China and is an actual dancer—she graduated in the spring with her MFA in dance from Ohio State—has made her costume armor entirely of gauze, except for the headpiece, which looks like a halo.

The city of Columbus shut everything down on March 22. My own life had been shut down for over a week by then. The day I cancelled my birthday party was also the day Fili and Russ decided they would close the studio and move their classes online.

My university's spring break came and went and was extended by a week as administrators scrambled to figure out what to do—and then classes resumed, and those of us who taught them were given no direction except that they would have to be taught virtually for the rest of the semester. One of the students in my undergrad class had to teach me how to use the university's Zoom account (for the first session after we switched over, she was the one who created the link and hosted the meeting). By the end of the semester, like everyone else, I was adept at creating and hosting Zoom meetings. I was using Zoom not only to teach and advise and attend meetings and conduct thesis defenses but also to talk to friends I hadn't been in contact with for years. Before the novelty of Zoom wore off (and, also like everyone, I retreated from doing anything on Zoom except what *had* to be done), Danielle's six-year-old daughter taught me how to change my background. When I grew bored of outer space and the beach, I added my own and used them for teaching and for meetings: a stock photo of a disco and one of the Brooklyn Bridge; a photo I'd taken in the dance studio, my dance friends stretching at the barre or chatting with each other; a photo of Freud's office in London, featuring the couch on which his patients had lain during their analysis, that I'd taken myself at the Freud Museum when I was on sabbatical in London.

And then I tired of Freud too and returned to my own living room, to real life, as background.

⚜

Almost everything Jovita is wearing was a gift, she says: folkloric shoes from Spain and a handmade, crocheted googly eye hat—both gifts from her sister—and a fanny pack, a gift from her parents. The keffiyeh around her neck and shoulders—"to try to make them look bigger," she explains—was a gift from an Iraqi veteran. She's also wearing swim goggles.

Tamie has made chaps out of hundreds of strips of different kinds of fabric and a breastplate out of beer caps; her headpiece is a three-foot-tall upside down hat from which she has hung long ropes that swing when she moves.

Jane is wearing a large quilted pillow with openings she's cut into it for her head and arms. Her twin sister Annie has wrapped herself in scarves and reflective duct tape. Gail has a curtain rod—with curtains—across the back of her shoulders.

For several weeks, we shoot the part of the piece that involves eight-foot poles we hold between us as we dance in pairs. It's the first time we've paired off and danced with the poles between us instead of imagining the holding of one end of an imaginary pole, imagining a partner at the other; for the first time, we fully understand which way to turn *around* the pole. Directional positioning is the hardest thing to convey over Zoom: which corner to point our bodies toward, which way to turn them, which corner to be facing *after* the turn.

Charity and I pair off in the field, the pole between us. For part of the pole dance, we are meant to face each other, one end of the pole held up by my shoulder, the other by her hip; at other times, we are both facing forward, the pole balanced between our palms. There is a part of the dance when we are both facing right, one end of the pole digging into the small of my back. In other parts we are connected sternum to sternum, hip to hip, belly to belly.

Russ asks us to try some different ways of being attached. I put my end of the pole into my hair, which is coiled in a thick bun on top of my head, but when Charity and I begin to move, it falls and smacks my face. "Okay, let's not do that," Russ says, as gently as it's possible to say something when speaking through a megaphone. It's the only way we can hear him when we're spread out across the field.

I put the pole in the center of my chest. Charity's end is just below her heart.

"I wouldn't touch you with an eight-foot pole," someone inevitably jokes. But it isn't really a joke at all, is it? Not now. Not for a long time.

I find myself thinking more and more about the invisible enemy we are fighting. It started off seeming obvious enough (so obvious I wondered if it might be a little heavy-handed)—our pathetic, even childish, efforts to fight and protect ourselves from the enemy we couldn't see. But the metaphor begins to shape-shift as we move from rehearsing into filming, then as filming progresses, week by week. Russ has us each begin parts of the choreography at different times. He has us "break" the choreography (making it wilder, more desperate). He has us slow it down and speed it up at points we choose ourselves. He has us tearing off parts of our armor and flinging them away, making a mountain of our castoff armor.

It's impossible not to think about what it is we have been arming ourselves against—about the many thing, all the things, we all arm ourselves against.

As we near the end of filming—the only time most of us see anyone in person anymore—I think about loneliness: what I have been arming myself against all my life. Long before the lockdown that made *lonely* everyone's chronic condition—that made it concrete, visible, unavoidable—it was the way I understood myself. It's the way I've understood myself since I was three or four years old.

For a long time this was a source of shame. It seemed to me everyone else knew how *not* to be lonely. I was wrong about this— does it not go without saying that I was wrong?—but I was past middle age before I understood that.

I am lucky in so many ways. My daughter survived the virus in those early, pre-vaccine days. I was able to keep myself safe—to stay locked up in my house, to order groceries and anything else I needed online—without worrying about losing my job. It was easy to keep my husband safe, too (Glen is always sheltering in place: his painting studio is steps from our back door). My teaching salary and benefits supported us both, and I was able to pass my stimulus checks on to my daughter, who couldn't work for months. My elderly mother was safely tucked away at my brother's house in New Jersey, leaving her own apartment in Manhattan empty for a year, and was still able to pay her rent, since she was determined to return to it. If she'd run out of money—if she ever runs out of money—my brother is in a position to take care of her.

We all are college educated. I live in a house. I can afford to pay my mortgage.

And we are white.

I recite all of this to myself sometimes at night when I can't sleep. I count my blessings. I don't call them "blessings." I don't believe in blessings. I call them luck. My father dropped out of high school. He sold insurance to support us. My grandparents escaped pogroms. We nearly lost my mother to the crushing depression she suffered in her twenties and early thirties and again when I was in *my* twenties. We all made it out okay.

And we all made it through the pandemic—those of us who were still here when it began (my grandparents gone, my father gone).

There's no reason for anyone to care about a privileged white woman whose life has been made better, made less lonely, made more meaningful, through dance—an art, an occupation, that came into her life only in her sixties. Whose experience of a global pandemic was eased and steadied by a dance project. Who, in the midst of a worldwide crisis, found order and peace and what my grandmother would call *koyekh*. Strength.

That's what I am thinking now that I am writing about it. But writing about it—writing about everything—is how *I* process what I'm feeling. The irony of my life is that writing is such a lonely activity and yet it's the activity that has kept me company practically my whole life. It's what I reached for as a lonely child—my mother behind a closed door, my grandmother warning me not to trouble her. It's what I buried myself in throughout my teens and young adulthood. It was a way of being lonely *for a reason.*

I didn't know that finding my way toward dance would make me feel less lonely than I ever had before. It's not that I've outrun or outfoxed my loneliness. It's not that I've fixed it (as I used to believe that each new boyfriend would fix it, or each new best girlfriend, or motherhood). My loneliness is like a dog that lies sleeping beside me as I go about my life. The way Ella, the rescue puppy I adopted four months into quarantine, would lie beside me while I wrote, all day long any day I wasn't Zoom-teaching a class or attending meetings. When the puppy woke up, she demanded my attention, and I'd give it to her.

My loneliness demands my attention too. I tend to it the best I can.

The way dancing concentrates me, the way there is room for nothing else because my mind is so fixed on the movements of my body—the movements of my body and the bodies around me—is still part of the joy of dance for me. Even in a field on a bitterly cold day, in an absurd costume, a mask covering half my face, the whole world beyond that field uncertain, dangerous.

It is a temporary vanishment, to be sure. But it's something I keep with me all the rest of the hours of the day, the week, the months that just keep stacking up.

The weary twenty-four of us who have remained are ready for the project's end. We know we'll miss it, but we're ready. That's how it goes, I've learned—something else no one ever told me about making something that's meant to be performed. That by the end of the process one is eager to be done with it … and still it's awful to be done with it. Even if it has gone on for so long it's become exhausting, boring—how one longs to be done with it!—once it's over, one longs for it. For the camaraderie, for the routine, and for the movement too. For each specific movement, and for the whole of it.

I cannot believe I will never make those particular movements again. I know them so well, and yet I know I will forget them, just as I've forgotten all the other choreography in all the other pieces we have made.

I know too that even when I have forgotten them, I will still miss them.

This is something else I've learned, so late in my life, through dance. That forgetting doesn't mean the end of missing. Forgetting doesn't arm one against loss or against longing.

I try to remember that. I try to remember everything.

In the Body

I cried during my first ballet class.
    Not because I didn't know what I was doing (although I *didn't* know what I was doing) or because it was too hard for me. Or because I was embarrassed or frustrated or wanted to flee. I'd been prepared for all those possibilities.

But I'd told myself it wouldn't hurt to try taking a ballet class—that it would be stupid not to, and how lazy would a person have to be not to try just one class if it were held on the very block on which that person lived?

The studio was on the former site of a health-food co-op, a beloved neighborhood institution that had been there since my daughter's childhood. I had liked the co-op too, but I had been bemused by the neighborhood-wide mourning when it closed. I'd lived in the neighborhood since 1989, long enough to remember all the other tenants of that space over the last three decades—an Asian grocery store, a Christian Science reading room, a camera shop. It didn't seem to me to be a tragedy that the co-op had been replaced by a dance studio. I was just glad it wasn't a coffee shop.

Coffee shops and microbreweries had been springing up all over Columbus. Soon, I thought, every last resident would have their own special place to have a beer or a latte.

My neighborhood, South Clintonville, once inhabited by the blue-collar middle class—plumbers, electricians, contractors—had somehow become charming and desirable to young people with jobs in the arts, in tech, in the nonprofit world, or at the university. For years I had been the lone college professor on my block—I'd been the only writer in the neighborhood; Glen, the only artist.

Now people made happy jokes about South Clintonville. They called it the Williamsburg of Ohio.

I suppose this might have pleased me, or at least amused me, if I had been up to it. I wasn't.

I walked the two hundred and forty-five steps from my door to the door of the dance studio—the same two hundred and forty-five steps that Grace had walked to the co-op (the only place she was allowed to walk to on her own as a small child) to pick up a quart of milk, a bottle of tamari, a bag of brown sugar—feeling grim and anxious.

I had to get some exercise, I knew. Most days, I sat all day long—sat for sixteen hours, and then went to bed. I felt guilty about not taking better care of myself. My father had been sedentary all his life, and I'd fretted over it and chided him about it. Now he was gone, and in the three years since his death I'd gained a lot of weight.

But at the same time I felt guilty about *caring* what I weighed. I felt guilty caring about how I looked. I refused to even consider "going on a diet." I'd been on diets almost my whole life, just as my father had. By now I hated the idea on principle. I also hated it because I knew how miserable it would make me, and it seemed to me I couldn't afford to be any more miserable than I already was.

I had just returned from a sabbatical that had jolted me awake to the many ways my job as a professor had ceased to be a source of fulfillment, much less joy, for me. I still liked being in the classroom with my students, still liked talking with them, advising and mentoring them, but this had become a smaller and smaller part of what I was paid to do. I was dreading going back to work.

And the loss of my father still felt fresh to me. I still woke up every morning feeling crushed and flattened by it. And I missed my daughter, with whom I had just spent more time than I had in years: I'd finished my sabbatical with a month at my mother's place in New York, where I'm from and where Grace had moved after her college graduation. Grace and I had dinners out, with and without her grandmother. We met for drinks and karaoke in the East Village and went to the theater and took the kind of interesting, long, rambling walks that could not be taken in Columbus. We sat talking for hours in her apartment in West Harlem or in my mother's living room in Yorkville. Now I was back home, without her, missing her.

I was glad that she was launched—living her own life, surrounded by friends in the city she'd been aimed at like a missile practically since birth. She was newly in love, too. And the theater company she'd founded had made a beautiful, strange, thrilling show that summer on Governors Island (I'd taken the ferry out to see it four times). I was proud of her, excited for her. But I couldn't seem to get used to not being a *daily* sort of mother anymore. Now that she was out of school, I didn't even have the illusion that she considered our house in Columbus home. "She has a new 'permanent address' to fill in on forms," I told my friends, saying it as if it were a joke, as if I didn't find it unbearably sad.

My bulwark during those first Grace-has-left-home years had been the family dog, and she had died the year before, after a brutal four months during which I had done everything I could to keep her comfortable and safe and feeling loved.

I had been counting on a friend—my best friend for a long time—to help me through what I had known would be a rough stretch, just as I had helped her through one of her own a few years before. But she had let me down. The friendship had ended bitterly.

And so I walked into the studio, that the first time, feeling wretched. Guilty, anxious, lonely. Heartbroken. Grief-stricken. Lost.

I took off my shoes and added them to a small pile of other people's shoes under a long shelf. The space had been thoroughly, dramatically renovated. The co-op had been dark, a jumble, every inch crowded with jars and bags and bins and boxes, the aisles so narrow you had to turn sideways if two people were in the same one at the same time. The studio was white, bright, spare. I tried, but I could not remember what had been where during the co-op's seventeen years in this spot.

I felt uncustomarily shy as a beautiful young person welcomed me, apologizing that there would be so few students—only three of us—and noting that they had just opened and were still "figuring things out."

The other two students were a girl who couldn't have been more than sixteen and a woman not much younger than I. Fili, the teacher, who had been the one to greet me, put on pop music and said, "Let's start by facing the barre, feet in parallel position." We began our first pliés, Fili talking all the while about what our bodies were doing, what we might consider thinking about, how we might imagine the wall in front of us as a window we were gazing out of.

I was relieved that neither of the others seemed to know any more than I did, or to be any more adept at executing any of the movements Fili so carefully described and demonstrated, offering each of us gentle corrections. And oh, how patient Fili was with us, talking us through the positions of the feet and the arms as we made our way through our first barre routine together.

I'm not sure exactly when I started crying, but it couldn't have been much more than ten or fifteen minutes into class. Fili didn't say anything. It was *hard*, what I was trying to do, but I wasn't crying over that. I was crying because it was beautiful. Because it was beautiful and *I loved it so much*. Because I felt (against any expectation, against logic) a glimmer of how I had felt when I'd held Grace in my arms for the first time, a sense of *Oh, how I have missed you! Where on earth have you been? I've been waiting for you all my life.*

I didn't know why I felt this way about extending my right foot, which I was simultaneously turning out and pointing as hard as I could, while at the same time concentrating on the muscles of my left leg—the "standing leg," Fili called it, and I thought, *It's nice that I've got a leg to stand on.* This made me laugh. And then for no good reason Fili laughed too, as if they'd heard what I was thinking.

Two days later, I was back. This time I felt weirdly confident. Walking in, saying hello to Fili—it already seemed familiar, an old habit.

There were twelve of us in class that afternoon, all adults this time. As we stood facing the barre and pliéd, Fili talked us through the muscles we were engaging, coaxing us through each slow movement.

I had never before concentrated so intently on doing something with my *body*. When we rose up on our toes, I thought hard about the way my muscles wrapped around my leg bones, about the "attraction" of my heels toward each other and at the same time toward the wall I was facing — which wasn't a wall, I was reminded, but an imaginary window I was to gaze out of. My eyes filled again. Fili came by and murmured, "Think of the little light in your chest," and somehow I understood what that meant. I don't know how. I let the light shine.

I took a class that Saturday, then again on Sunday, and on Monday. I took two classes back-to-back the following Wednesday, one with Fili and then one, my first, with Fili's husband, Russ. "Lead with your heart!" Russ called out as we ballet-walked across the room. "Don't look down! Step into the water!"

I came back, day after day. I tried Fili's contemporary dance class (about which I can now remember only that early in the hour Fili had all of us pause to hug one another hello, and instead of this feeling idiotic, as I would have sworn it would, it was lovely). I took Russ's contemporary class. I tried a contact improv class. I took "dance karaoke," for which Russ choreographed a simple movement for every word of a pop song, and I thought my brain would explode—there were so *many* "simple" movements. How was I to remember them? In Fili's jazz class there was just as much to memorize, and the movements were more complicated: I couldn't figure out how to remember what the phrase was (step front, step back, step ball change, bring the leg around, then turn—or step back, step front, step ball change, *then* turn and at the same time bring the leg around?) *and* make an effort to do any of it well.

But something was happening. In ballet, even when I couldn't remember a pattern at the barre or the rules for some specific port de bras—the carriage of the arms—I could sometimes do it anyway. It was as if my body knew before my mind did. Then, just for a moment, I would feel my body and my mind working as one, communicating and cooperating with each other.

I had never experienced such a thing before. During the brief periods of my life when I had exercised, I had always turned *off* my mind in order to attend to my body. And I'd always wanted the activity to be fun—otherwise, how would I get through it? It was hardly ever fun.

Dance was fun (sometimes it was fun), but from the start it was the *work* of dance that appealed to me. I was accustomed to mental work, but in ballet I found what seemed to me an extraordinary twist: I was living that mental work *in my body.*

In my body—with which, even more remarkably—I was making art.

For a long time I'd hardly felt as if I *had* a body. What I had was a container for my mind. I was aware of my body only around matters of sex—when it seemed useful to have one—and when I was annoyed or angry or disgusted with it, which was often. I was forced to be aware of it too when it so often, inconveniently, failed me: the tendonosis in my wrist and forearm thanks to overuse of trackpad and mouse; repeated back injuries, thanks to sitting hunched over the keyboard; so many sprained ankles ever since I'd sprained one for the first time on the first day of junior high school—falling down the stairs, my dress flying over my head.

The only other time my body had impressed itself upon me was during my pregnancy, when, unlike many women, I was madly in love with it. That remains the only time I have ever examined myself in a full-length mirror without any clothes on and regarded myself as frankly gorgeous. I stood naked in front of the mirror every day, admiring my pregnant body. I had never considered my body especially useful before, beyond its use as an irritating container for what I thought of as my "actual self." But now that body was profoundly useful. And the overall shape of it, the wide hips and protruding belly and big soft drooping breasts, looked exactly *right* for once, exaggerated and necessary and important. I felt as tenderly toward it as I did toward the baby it was housing.

And I remember that after my daughter was born, I—*like* every other woman I have ever talked to about this—felt alienated from the body, the container, that the baby had left behind.

In ballet, my body is not a container. In ballet, there is no separating the body and the mind. I *have* to think hard to create the shapes, to make the movements, of ballet. Even standing still in first position—which to the observer doesn't look like anything at all—requires the engagement of muscles that will not turn on without my express command, muscles that do not engage reflexively the way my muscles do when going about ordinary tasks. There is nothing ordinary, nothing of the day-to-day, about ballet.

And then there is this: almost from the start I saw that ballet would fulfill a longing I'd had as far back as I could remember, a longing that accounts for the pleasure I take in hosting and leading a Passover Seder, although I am a firmly nonbelieving Jew; a longing that expresses itself in how much I envy my poet friends their sonnets and villanelles and ghazals. It's a need for something that is formally specific, codified, part of a long tradition—something that not only has history but that has not changed much over time. It now seems to me surprising that I *hadn't* known how much I would love making movement that so many had made before, movement that would be recognizable in previous centuries and centuries to come—and that would become mine as well, simply by my own attempts at thoughtfully performing them. Like a Seder, like a villanelle. But with my body. *In* my body.

In ballet, Fili would say, *you are a fairy-warrior. On the outside you are floating and light, and on the inside you are like iron.*

I was sore all the time, but I kept going back. I iced my calves and ankles, my lower back, my knees. I took baths in Epsom salts. The soreness should have dampened my spirits, but instead it made me smile. Being sore *meant* something. I thought about the pain of labor, all those years ago, and how I'd gotten through it only by reminding myself, in an increasingly hysterical mantra, that this wasn't ordinary pain—it was pain with a purpose, pain that was getting me something I wanted. Not like any pain I'd ever had before. Pain with a reward at the end of it. Pain that was worth it.

But after every class, those first weeks, I was exhausted physically from attempting all the balances, from swooping forward and around in the still unfamiliar movement of a rond de jambe (and what were my arms supposed to be doing while my leg was sweeping through a circle?) and mentally worn out from thinking, trying to remember, counting. Being in my body was hard work. I'd had no idea.

When it's hard, Fili told us, *we tend to push, but what we need is to pull back and let it flow. Keep the quality and the connection instead of using force.*

Ballet is not for everyone, I know. To enjoy practicing ballet, you must enjoy doing the same things over and over again (and only sometimes—even rarely—doing them any better than you did the last time). In a ballet class, one feels, always, as if one were *preparing* for something. And for most people, it's preparation that leads to nothing except more preparation.

And in ballet, unlike most other areas of life, "preparation" itself is an art form, or at least it is to me. I have never stood at the barre and done a tendu—the apparently simple act of extending the working leg along the floor until only the toes remain there, as the other leg remains *apparently* still—that I have not taken great pleasure in. I have never—not even in that first class—done a *tendu* thoughtlessly. And even after hundreds of thousands of tendus at the barre, I am still concentrating hard on each one. There would be no point in doing them at all if I were only going through the motions.

And here is a curiosity: by definition, the forty-five minutes or so I spend at the barre, the first half of every ballet class, is literally a period of "going through the motions"—that is, moving through a set of prescribed physical activities—but that phrase, which itself means "thoughtlessly, automatically," is the opposite of what is being done. Even as these "motions" become second nature, as by this time so many of them are to me—the lift of the kneecaps, the wrapping of the muscles of the thighs around their corresponding bones, the lifting without clenching of the buttocks, the rotation of the arms, the visualization of the invisible strings (this one from hand to knee, drawing the knee up as the arm comes around; this one connecting the heel to the opposing shoulder) and of the body's spirals and the "little light" in the chest—they still require focus, care, intention. No matter how familiar ballet gets, it remains unlike breathing or walking or what happens when we sit down or stand up. In ballet, there is sort of tuning the mind in to the place on its dial that monitors the body's placement and carriage. It's like the difference between talking and singing—the difference between talking and singing *well*. That elevation of the ordinary. That leaving behind of the everyday.

You are a martini glass, Fili would tell us as we lifted into arabesque on relevé.

With each return to sous-sus from passé: *Slide your foot into the boot the other foot is already wearing.*

In *an extension à* la seconde, *Set your leg on the shelf.*

The other regulars and I traded cheerful complaints about our aching calves, our backs, our brains, our ankles and feet. I'd bought a pair of ballet shoes, but I didn't like them. We inspected one another's shoes and gave advice as if we knew what we were talking about. We promised ourselves that if we did *more* ballet, our feet and ankles would grow stronger and stop hurting.

"You're getting better," Fili would tell me after a class, and when I said I didn't think I was, they would tell me one or two things I had done that day that I hadn't been able to do the day before.

Everything is connected, Fili insisted. *Everything you do is informed by what you have done before.*

Search every moment for what is there. Especially in the pauses, you have time to find something new, the next thing.

I had to take a break from dancing in mid-August for a trip to see my in-laws in Georgia. For once, I was looking forward to it. Glen and I had bought Grace and her then-boyfriend, Nathan, a pair of plane tickets so they could meet us there, and I was thrilled to have the chance to spend some time with them. Grace was eager to show Nathan the place that had so enchanted her in childhood—the house her grandfather had built himself, the pine woods around it.

One day we went fishing. Well, I sat on the grass and read Tessa Hadley's short stories while the fishing went on. I kept thinking about ballet. I kept thinking about how it felt to lift my arms into second position and rotate them. I put my book on the grass and did it, right there. How satisfying it was, this new feeling in my body. I was surprised by how eager I was to get back home, even though my daughter wouldn't be there, even though there'd be no dog to greet me as if I'd been gone for years. I couldn't wait to get back to ballet.

Imagine you are in a toaster—as we rose from plié to relevé, then lowered to plié again.

Make sure not to touch either side.

And always, every day: *Reach, reach. Reach far in all directions. You are Leonardo's L'uomo vitruviano.*

Did I think of dancing as a cure for what had been ailing me? I don't think so. I knew I was ailing, but I never stopped to think that dance might help—that dance *was* helping—me recover. I'd spent a lot of time that year thinking about failed relationships and disappointments, loss, and grief—the reckonings of late middle and early old age—but it did not dawn on me that I had reached a pivot point. That I was in need of, poised for, a big turn in my life.

Even the sabbatical I took was not my own idea. It was my daughter's. She pointed out that I hadn't given myself any time to grieve or rest after my father's death—that I had thrown myself, first, into dealing with the aftermath of it, and then into my teaching and administrative work, filling every minute as I charged ahead, refusing to delegate anything to anyone. I was acting like my father, she implied. "It's not sustainable," she said. "It worries me."

We were in a restaurant in New York, out to dinner with my mother and my brother and Hula, my friend of going on forty years, when Grace made this pronouncement. I'd come to the city for a long weekend to celebrate my birthday—a big one, my sixtieth—and the waiter had just brought a giant plate of cotton candy for dessert, which had made me laugh. Now everyone sat silently as my then-not-quite-twenty-two-year-old daughter lectured me about my life.

"You always say there's no one to pick up the slack if you take time off. But haven't you noticed that literally no one else cares about this? Everybody else takes their sabbaticals as soon as they're eligible to. Everybody else takes time off whenever and however they can. You're the one who picks up everybody else's slack."

Well, that was the problem, I told her. I was the one who could be counted on. That was why I *couldn't* take time off.

"No, Mama. The problem is that this is how you think about it. If you're not there, somebody will have to step up. And even if they don't, it's not your job to worry about that."

Wasn't it? I thought.

"Seriously, Mama, does anybody else wait *twenty years* between sabbaticals? You've already lost two you were entitled to."

She had been paying closer attention than I knew. I was surprised. And impressed. And also (a first) cowed.

"You have got to start taking care of yourself," she said sternly. "Promise me you will."

I promised. And then, I guess, I did.

Commit to the transitions, Fili said. *Even though they are not the highlights, they are the platform for the highlights.*

Glen and I went to London, where we rented a flat belonging to an old friend who, by excellent coincidence, was on sabbatical himself, spending the year in New York. I finished a draft of the novel I'd been working on for nearly a decade. Glen filled a stack of sketchbooks. I explored London, did my writing in the British Museum, and saw friends—some I'd first met when they'd passed through Columbus at some point and with whom I'd stayed in touch over the intervening years, and one friend I'd met during my first year out of college and hadn't seen since the eighties, when he moved abroad. I hadn't realized how much I'd missed spending time with him.

I loved everything about being in London, which very quickly felt like home. If Grace hadn't been in the U.S., if there were no reason to believe that someday I would be a grandmother, I found myself thinking, I would *move* to London. I'd retire as soon as I was able, pull up stakes, relocate.

When we returned to the U.S., Glen got on a flight to Columbus and I stayed on in New York with my mother. I was in no hurry to get back. A job I no longer loved was waiting for me. As was a city I had *never* loved, where my once-best friend and I were not on speaking terms. My daughter was an independent adult who had little (it seemed like no) need for me. My dog was gone. My father was gone.

But the month ended. I went home.

And started dancing.

The dancing didn't always go smoothly. I continued to forget combinations at the barre. I continued to trip over my own feet as I danced from the corner, though I had ceased to dread it—I had come to look forward to it as a chance to try out what I had been practicing at the barre.

Once, I cried in class not because I was moved but because I was ashamed—I'd stumbled badly halfway through a pirouette. Fili ran up to me, put their arms around me, told me I was beautiful, told me everything was fine. "Don't worry," Fili said. "It just takes time."

Build a solid structure, and then find the open spaces where you can experiment, be yourself, and make it your own.

With stability comes freedom. If you are strong in your center, the rest can move freely around it.

And: *No matter what happens, stay in it. Even if you forget or make a mistake, keep moving.* "Here I am!" *Own it. And then find your way back in.*

One evening, as I danced from the corner—balancé, balancé, tombé pas de bourré, piqué arabesque, failli—Fili called out, as I lifted into the piqué arabesque for the third time, "Michelle, other arm!" and I switched arms, from right out to right up, from left up to left out. And then Fili called out: "Oh! Michelle, other *leg!*" And so I switched legs too: left leg in arabesque, not the right one.

And I didn't cry. I laughed. Because I was so happy. Because I *could* have been embarrassed but I wasn't. Because I didn't care that I'd made a mistake—two mistakes. Because I had the rest of my life to get it right.

On Balance

Yesterday was a good balance day. I knew it would be, too, just minutes into class. I was *solid*—solid and light, both at once (the peculiar paradox of a balance in ballet—or, really, just one of the peculiar paradoxes in ballet). My back felt strong; my shoulder blades, drawn back and low, were the places wings would have been attached—if only I had wings. (I could picture them, though: enormous, thickly feathered, gray and white—who knows why?—and brushing the floor behind me, rising with my arms as they moved into fifth position.) My feet felt strong, for once, too—my feet are my weakest link, but today it was as if they had roots deep below the marley floor. And my legs! Knees lifted, muscles drawing outwards. Planted, steady. And yet I was floating—up and up, weightless, beyond gravity.

Rooted and floating. That is the confluence I am forever chasing.

Ballet is a study in mixed metaphors. Grounded *and* buoyant. Solid and fluid.

Strong and soft. Exacting—*precise*—and flowing.

Press down and rise at the same time. Descend and lift.

The oppositions of ballet, which once bewildered me, have come to be a part of why I love it so. Nothing else I do embodies so much oxymoronicity (and ballet is so serenely contradictory, I now find it impossible not to be charmed by it). What remains confounding to me is the uncertainty of ballet—the zigzag of failure and success, not only from day to day but from one hour to the next, and from right to left. It happens *while doing the exact same thing* multiple times in a row. (The first pirouette, of a series of three, en dehors from fourth position, might be perfectly sound—and so might be the third—but the second one will fail, and *how can that be?*)

I have never been able to be sure I will not fall out of a turn, or if I will tip dangerously forward during a no-barre shift from coupé to passé. I cannot predict whether a piqué arabesque will be graceful or ludicrously clumsy.

You'd think the ups and downs of the writing life—not to mention the ups and downs of life itself—would have taught me about unpredictability. Uncertainty. Instability.

But it's ballet that's teaching me at last to live with the not knowing. Not knowing what will happen *and* not knowing why it doesn't happen when it doesn't, why it does happen when it does.

Why wonder? I remind myself.

It's a question I have never asked myself before.

Ballet has also taught me to make peace with my own limitations. Nothing else I've ever practiced has done that. In ballet, what choice do I have? I'm not strong (I have never been strong, not even in my youth). I have the built-in limits of my physiology: my archless feet, the angle of my natural turnout, the fact that if I try to bring my feet to sixth position—close together and in parallel—my knees smash together painfully. And I began ballet too late to ever master certain skills. I shall never be en pointe. I shall never achieve flight in grand allegro. (And the day I execute a promenade correctly, I believe the studio will close, as if for the observation of a national holiday.)

But ballet has made me curious instead of frustrated or angry or despairing about my immutable limitations. I'm interested in how they work; I'm interested in finding strategies I might make use of to accommodate them.

I've learned to set modest goals (two pirouettes in a row, now that I can do one reasonably well—on some days, anyway), as well as goals that would seem to be modest (a true, deep, grand plié in first and fifth positions) but are not modest at all—not for me—and which I am aware I may not live long enough to meet.

But I can try.

Ballet is humbling. It's exacting. It is thrilling—sometimes frightening. The other night, dancing across the floor, we were to land a pirouette in arabesque—that is, with one foot on the floor, the other leg turned out and extended, with a pointed foot. It's a common enough step but one that I'm afraid of—afraid to land without both feet to catch me, afraid I'll fall so hard I'll hurt myself. And so, at the end of every turn, I balked at the last second, landing in a grounded fourth position. *Next time*, I thought.

Ballet makes me optimistic.

It fills me with joy, even when I'm struggling. *Fills* me, truly. It flows through my bloodstream—it's as if I've been injected with it, straight into a vein.

If I were to say *and that's why I dance*, I would not be lying.

But I also dance because it gets me up on my feet after a long day of sitting—thinking, typing, reading—and it turns out (and really, who knew?) my body needs to get up and move for a few hours every day.

Before ballet, I had complained for years, for decades, about how I couldn't seem to get myself into a "fitness routine"—lamenting that I knew I should, but, oh, how I despised even the *words* "fitness routine." I despised each word separately and I despised the two together even more. I also hated the phrase "working out" (a perversion, it seemed to me, of the excellent verb "work"). If I could become *fit* by *working*—like my ancestors, the peasants, did—I'd be fine with it.

That was what I said. But my great-grandfather Shepsal was a barrel-maker; my great-grandmother Menukhe was "a businesswoman" (this according to my grandmother, whose own great-grandmother, Ruchel—who famously lived to a hundred and thirteen—was a baker). These are the only three ancestors I know anything about on my mother's side. On my father's side, I know about only one, my great-grandfather Joseph, a tailor. None of these are the kinds of jobs, as far as I can tell, that keep a person especially *fit*.

The last time I'd moved my body daily was during the two years before my daughter was born. That was when I learned to swim, at thirty-five. Learning to swim seemed like a fluke, or even a miracle—I had never expected it to happen. I was pleased enough, excited enough, to want to do it every day.

I didn't swim well or even efficiently (I never quite got kicking figured out, and I swam excruciatingly slowly, a mile in just over an hour), but for a couple of years I did it faithfully. And then I was pregnant, and soon my pregnancy had taken over my body, and it seemed that I could not have been all that attached to my daily slow mile in the pool, since pregnancy was all it took for me to give it up. And once I wasn't pregnant anymore, I had a newborn baby to take care of, and a full-time teaching job and books to write and so on—and now, more than three decades after I stopped swimming, it is almost as if I had never learned how.

The time before *that* that I exercised daily was when I was in my twenties, living in a fifth-floor walkup on the farthest-east end of East 78th Street in Manhattan. Instead of a shower, it had a tub on clawfoot legs in the kitchen (the toilet was behind a curtain, in a perplexingly short hallway), and my parents gave me the birthday gift I'd asked for, a membership to a gym on the corner of 76th, just so I'd have a nearby place to shower.

But I was too embarrassed to walk past all those women in shiny Lycra and leg warmers and hightop Reeboks, take a long shower, and leave. So I began taking an aerobics class every morning before my shower. After a while I added yoga, too—to cool down after aerobics, before showering. And then, as long as I was there—why not?— three times a week I did the round of Nautilus machines.

This also went on for two years, until I left New York for Iowa City, for grad school, where I lived in a whole, if tiny, house, and had my own shower. I never once considered going to a gym.

In the three decades that followed, I tried vigorous, Western-style yoga; I jogged five or six slow miles, three times a week, on a treadmill at Planet Fitness; and once, for seven months, when Grace was in elementary school, I had a Curves membership (which entailed descending into a dark, windowless room and making a thirty-minute circuit of alternating purple equipment and jogging squares).

I dieted, too. I've been on all the diets every other woman of my generation who isn't "naturally thin" has, starting with the Stillman Diet when I was a 130-pound teenager wishing to be a 115-pound teenager. I cycled through Weight Watchers, Jenny Craig, Atkins, and even the Suzanne Somers diet (a complicated system of food combinations a poet and professor friend surprisingly recommended—which was why I tried it, although it was every bit as silly as you'd think). For a whole year I was on the Always Hungry? diet that a doctor named David Ludwig promised would end dieting forever even as weight dropped off effortlessly (it did not).

But well before my first diet, I was **aware** of dieting. I was pretty sure I should be doing it myself once I found out that a girl in my sixth grade class, Bobbi Shamah, was on a diet, because I was fatter than Bobbi.

My size has fluctuated over the years (I once got painfully skinny after a major heartbreak, and I dropped a lot of weight when I was a nursing mother; I worked hard to lose forty pounds the year before Grace left for college—it took the whole year—then gained it all back over two or three months, three years later) but for most of my life I have been on the low end of fat. When I was a child, my mother took me shopping in the "chubby section" of Alexander's department store in downtown Brooklyn; as an adult, I've most often been "small fat" (in the words of fat activist Aubrey Gordon) or what the writer Roxanne Gay calls "Lane Bryant fat."

And so, for me, one of the paradoxes of ballet is supremely personal.

To be a ballet dancer has always required a specific type of body. Girls who love ballet, who have practiced it since they were young children and have become accomplished dancers, have been discouraged from continuing if they have the "wrong" bodies for it. And so many of those whose bodies were deemed "right" for ballet, who did go on to have professional careers, have been badly damaged by ballet's traditional, rigid—cruel, unforgiving—standard of beauty.

Yet my own dedicated practice of ballet—at my age, as an amateur—has allowed me *for the first time in my life* to appreciate, admire, and celebrate my body for what it can do if I give it a chance.

Ballet has granted me the wisdom—and the grace—to care less about my fatness than I ever have before.

I'm grateful I did not discover ballet as a child and come to love it as I do now. I would have been crushed to learn, as I surely would have, that ballet was *not for me*.

But for four or five years, beginning when I was five or six years old, I took *modern* dance class after school one afternoon a week at the Marjorie Mazia School of Dance in Sheepshead Bay. Like legions of other little girls in Brooklyn, most of us second-generation Americans (our parents, scratching their way into the middle class, the children of the Eastern European immigrant Jews who arrived in the U.S. not long after the turn of the century), my best friend Susan and I walked hand in hand to Marjorie's studio, four blocks from the building where we both lived, and then up a flight of creaky stairs, to change into our black leotards and spend an hour being fully in our bodies. How delighted I was by what my "chubby" body could do in that mirrored room I flew through.

I don't remember when or why I stopped taking class with Marjorie. It might have been when I was eleven and we moved half a mile away—too far to walk by myself, and I suppose I was reluctant (or not allowed?) to take the bus or subway unaccompanied, and there was no one available to take me. But it may just have been because I felt I'd aged out—the presumably more mature pleasures of junior high school beckoning (I was wrong: there were no pleasures, only pain). But it's also possible I quit before that, if my friend did—because I did whatever Susan did, I so admired her. (I have a vague memory of her "moving up" to classes at the Neighborhood Playhouse—which could not be walked to from our building—so that she could take classes in acting and voice as well as dance. My parents would have found this overkill and would not have allowed it.)

I should not have stopped. I loved taking class with Marjorie. I loved Marjorie herself (as everyone who knew her did, I think). She was beautiful and kind, charming and glamorous, endlessly patient and pleased with us. She wasn't like any other adult, and her studio wasn't like anywhere else.

Opening that door on Sheepshead Bay Road was like having special knowledge of a *secret* door, surrounded as it was by the storefronts that made up our everyday lives: the pizza place; the candy store; the newsstand where, after dance class, Susan and I would be allowed to stop in and buy comic books (we'd each have been given a quarter, and the Archies and DC Romances we favored were twelve cents apiece); the "appetizing store" with Sam behind the counter, where we bought bagels and lox on Sundays; the pharmacy we called "Doc's"; DuBarry's jeweler, where my mother took me to get my ears pierced (right after Susan got *hers* pierced) even though my father had said no—the only time I can recall that she ever defied him; the handbag store where my mother and grandmother shopped.

Through the secret door and up the steps, then through another door, and there it was: another world, the world that Marjorie presided over. One she seemed to have made just for us.

Marjorie was in her late forties then, her hair already silver. I remember thinking she was very old—old *and* glamorous, a pairing with which I'd had no experience. She had danced with Martha Graham; she'd been married to Woody Guthrie—these were the real-world things we all knew about her. We knew two of her children: her daughter Nora was the "big girl," five years older than I, who danced at the front of the studio, so we could follow her, and Marjorie's son Arlo was the sullen teenager who would sometimes sit in a corner with a book. And we knew Woody was famous, but most of us knew nothing about him other than "This Land Is Your Land" (which we sang in school, after "My Country 'Tis of Thee" and "America the Beautiful"). Of Martha Graham we knew nothing at all, but when Marjorie spoke of her, we nodded solemnly. We could tell that we *should* know.

Woody Guthrie had been Marjorie's second husband. By the time she was my teacher, they were long divorced, I knew, but I also remember being told (by an older, wiser child who took class with me) that she'd *had* to divorce him, because he was very sick and she couldn't afford the cost of his care, that in order for "the government" to take over the expense of his long hospitalization, it was necessary for them to divorce; I even remember wondering if such a thing could be true. I learned much later that it was. When Marjorie died, in March 1983, and I read her obituary in *The Times*, not only was this reported but another rumor I'd heard as a child was confirmed: that even after their divorce she'd remained devoted to him. "I never really divorced him in my heart and in my actions," she had told an interviewer six years before her death. And after his death, through several subsequent marriages, she became devoted to the cause of curing Huntington's, the disease that had killed him. She became an activist, eventually convincing Jimmy Carter to form a Presidential Commission to study Huntington's, which she headed, and lectured medical students about the disease; she worked with the National Committee for Research in Neurological and Communicative Disorders and became a member of both the New York State Commission on Health Education and Illness Prevention and the state's Genetic Advisory Committee. (Some of this I didn't know until *now*, doing research to fill in the gaps of my understanding of who she was.) As a principal dancer with the Graham Company, she danced in "Primitive Mysteries" and "Appalachian Spring," among other masterpieces of the thirties and forties. She was also the first member of the company to be granted permission to teach Graham technique outside Martha Graham's own school. One of her earliest students was Merce Cunningham.

I knew almost none of this. Even so, when one of my teachers in elementary school assigned the writing of a *Reader's Digest*-style "Most Unforgettable Character I Ever Met," it was Marjorie I wrote about. And long before I started dancing again, a good fifty years after I last set foot in Marjorie's studio, I thought of her far more often than makes sense. I could—I *can*—see her clearly in my mind, in her long green wrap skirt tied at the waist over a black long-sleeved leotard cut low in the back. Her silver hair, her elegant bare feet. I can still hear her telling us to dance "like a candle's flame," or like the branches of a tree when the wind blows through them. Or like ponies, or like kites on a long string. Like clouds.

Telling us to take up space. To be joyful, to be bold.

Her studio was the only place where I *was* joyful and bold as a child. Where I felt I could take up space.

As it happens, today too was a good balance day. They don't often come two days in a row, and I was so surprised, I made a sound (*ah!* perhaps, or just a gasp, or I might have said *oh my*) after I rose to my first relevé in passé—the coda to ronds de jambe—and stayed there, suspended, grounded. I made my surprised sound, and the people around me laughed. It was good-natured laughter—it is always good-natured laughter in this studio. And they all knew what had surprised me. We all know each other—at least we know each other's dance-selves—very well.

I was perfectly balanced for what seemed like a long time. I didn't falter until Leiland, who was teaching, called out, "Very nice, Michelle!"

The spell was broken. I tipped sideways. I had to grab the barre to keep from falling.

Balance, it must be said, has never been my strong suit.

I have other strengths, however. I am remarkably flexible (but then I was born that way, so I am wary of taking credit for it). And I have a flair for drama (possibly ditto).

Fili says I am a "romantic" dancer. Sometime too romantic. Sometimes I am *all* theater (or, as Fili likes to pronounce it, **tee**-uh-tuh, a cross between the English **thee**-uh-ter and the Italian—Fili's native language—**tee**-a-tro). All theater, no technique—eyes closed, arms adding flourishes that have no place in any of ballet's port de bras. But sometimes I lean into the drama without losing precision. Without sickling (toes curving inward, heels dropping back) or splaying open my ribcage or bringing my shoulder back with my arm or turning my whole self from side to side … or rolling back on my feet or looking down—or looking *up*—or skipping first position on my way through a series of fast ronds de jambe, or locking my hypermobile knees.

Sometimes I am beautifully theatrical while remembering everything else: I sweep from allongé to the floor, diving deeply (while lifting!) to a place inches beyond my feet, brush the floor with the backs of my hands, sweep up and take a breath, and (ah, **tee**-uh-tuh) arch back (back and back and back—my upper back is one of the places I am most flexible) as I lift up. *Cambré back, one of my favorite things. Not my very favorite thing—my very favorites at the barre are fondu and adagio.*

On a good day—and today was a good fondu day too—my bent working knee in tandem with the plié of my standing knee form the most satisfying diamond of white space, and when the leg extends and straightens—at precisely the same instant that I rise from the plié—my hip stays put (trembling perhaps, but not hiking up). It strikes me that fondu, or melting, is not at all what I experience (what anyone experiences?), executing it. The melting is what an audience is meant to perceive. Adagio (sometimes known as adage—the former Italian, the latter the French adaptation) is about the viewer's perception too. The word means leisurely, at ease, relaxed. But there is nothing relaxed or at ease about the slow, graceful path through cou-de-pied, through passé, through attitude, into a full extension of the leg—not for the dancer. Or at least not for this dancer. I am working too hard, both physically and mentally. I am most certainly not at *leisure*. (But how I love working hard in this way! In adagio, joy flows through me so intensely I sometimes find myself in tears.)

The dancer's experience so different from the experience of the dance-observer—another paradox of ballet? Perhaps not—perhaps this is an irony.

A paradox is a clear contradiction. Irony is a mismatch between what occurs and what's perceived.

Paradox: While a professional ballet dancer's life is one of great imbalance, with little time for anything but the work of dance—little of a life outside of it—what ballet has given *me* is a whole world outside my work, a whole world outside the world inside my head.

Irony: As I become a better dancer, I am ever more aware of what I'm not yet doing very well. Thus, the more gracefully I execute a combination, the more work I recognize still lies ahead.

A balance is not a pose, Fili is forever telling us. *Let it breathe, let it live. You are not a statue.*

As soon as my first class was over, I signed up for an unlimited-class monthly pass, automatically renewable at the start of every month. It has been renewed more than ninety times since then.

Even during lockdown, Russ and Fili didn't miss a single class. When it became clear they'd have to close the studio, a week before Ohio's stay-at-home order was issued, they locked the door and the next day began to teach online. For all the months that followed, when I didn't leave my house, I still danced every day but Friday. I turned my study into a makeshift dance studio, arranging computer monitors around the room so I could see whoever was teaching from whichever direction I was facing. It was easy to give up my study, since during lockdown I found that I preferred writing with my laptop on my lap, sitting in the living room or, even better—if the weather was anything less than terrible—outside on my front porch, where I could see some of the world passing by.

And then I'd go upstairs to dance.

Ballet is as absorbing in its way as writing is. Ballet cannot be danced with half a mind. (It sometimes seems to me that I could use an extra half-mind to keep track of everything I need to think about at once.)

Practicing ballet has calmed my nervous system, made me slow down and pay attention in a way that could not be more different from the way I pay attention to the sentences I write. It refocuses me, reminds me that there's more to life, and more to me, than what I write and how it is received. It brings more beauty and grace into my life, so that the hard parts feel less hard.

And it gives me something to look forward to. At the end of my writing day, whether it's gone well or badly (and whether I've had good or bad or no news from the outside world about something I've already written), I know the studio is waiting for me. That my dance friends will greet me warmly, that we'll all be glad to see each other, and that our teachers will be just as glad to see us all. That they'll take us through the familiar beats of barre—pliés and tendus through grands battements—and then we'll leave the barre for adagio and tendus in the center, then dance from the corner across the floor in diamond-shaped groups. Everything we're asked to do will be a little different from what we did yesterday and what we will do tomorrow, but will also be, in so many reassuring ways, the same. Fili will urge drama, "passion, feelings, and emotions!" and will sing the piano music (higher up the scale than seems humanly possible) and speak nonsense that we understand because we've been together for so long—jokes of language that have been codified, that no one thinks twice about (*from the corner* long ago became *zhe corner* and then *zhe zhe corner* and now is only *zhe zhe*; grand battement is *grand bizhbizh;* and *smoosh* and *pichaquoo* have no English—or Italian—equivalents), or use shorthand for a metaphor last fully invoked years ago (*in the toaster*, Fili will call out, or *jelly walls*). Russ will punctuate the demos of his combinations with sounds invoking how they feel (*ahhhh* and *whoosh* and *fwack-aha! Wah-wee!*), tell us to soutenu into attitude with "no fussing about," and speed-speak his instructions when repeating them (moving apace, comically, like a 10x-sped-up video). Leiland will sing his counts and sometimes his instructions too, use a playlist of Disney songs or Broadway or movie musicals (and periodically declare, "I'm getting emotional!" when a balleted-up piano version of a song from one of his favorite movies—*The Sound of Music*, the Lady Gaga version of *A Star is Born*, *The Wizard of Oz*—comes on) and pause between every song and combination at the barre to look heavenward while humming tunelessly, sketching out with one outraised finger what he means for us to do.

I remember very little of the movement from Marjorie's classes, but I remember how it made me feel. And the way opening the downstairs door, squeezed between two shops, felt like magic—the way that door seemed the entrance to another world, a world in which everything that weighed on me fell away for a time: my mother's debilitating depression, my father's bursts of fury, the constant arguments between him and my grandmother over which one of them was to blame for it. My isolation all week long among the girls in my class at school. How excluded I felt from their fun, how undesirable I seemed to be to them, how desperately I wanted to fit in with them. How baffled I was about how I might accomplish this.

Beyond that door, up that flight of stairs, there was only dance, and for an hour, once a week, I understood myself in a different way. And I was *happy*.

The studio I dance in now is also an outlier on an otherwise quite ordinary street, this one lined with wood-frame houses built, like mine, at the turn of the twentieth century.

But in the midst of them: a portal.

Six days a week (only because the studio does not offer ballet on Fridays*), I spend hours focused on the shapes I make and how I make them. I can hardly believe I am able to make these artful, interesting, *difficult* shapes with my own body. *My* legs, *my* arms. My hands, my back, my feet.

---

* Although, full disclosure, I am in the studio on Fridays too. For yoga.

When I roll up to demi-pointe and feel the clicking into place—the stacking of my bones, the wrapping of the muscles in my legs, shoulders broad and down, every part of me engaged, every part of me in cooperation with each other part—it's like a good conversation among a large group of friends, people who have known and loved each other for a long time, who've found a subject all of them are interested in. They know how to talk to one another without anybody cutting anybody off mid-sentence, without any of them dominating the whole conversation, without any of the quieter ones ever being left out.

Six days a week.
You'd think it was my job.
It *feels* like a job. Not in the sense that anything about it is unpleasant, that it ever feels like drudgery, but in the way that waking up each morning and going to
work isn't a matter of choice (or, rather, it was once a choice—to take *that* job—but after that it's nothing more than what one *does*).
This is how I feel about writing, too: that I chose it long ago, that it isn't a choice anymore. It is only what I do.
I tried to stop writing once. I was feeling brutally discouraged, and I thought: Why do I keep at this? What makes me think I have to? I don't *have* to. I could choose not to, couldn't I? Each day as I picked up a book to read or set out for the garden or played the guitar or piano, I wondered what it would it be like to make that choice, to never write again.
I did not find out. I couldn't stop—that was what I learned that summer. I began writing as if in secret (in secret from myself!). On scraps of paper. On the flyleaf of the book I sat on the porch reading.
And so I gave up on giving up.
It is not a coincidence, I think, that this was the summer that I "found" ballet. That I began writing again in earnest halfway through that summer, at the same time I started dancing. And that I haven't thought once about quitting since then, although nothing much has changed—nothing much except that now I dance.

I almost never go out anymore—to dinner, to parties. I guess that's one other thing that's changed (although I never was a go-out-every-night type; still, I used to meet up with friends two or three times a week). This is not only because I spend so much time in the dance studio (although it's true it's hard to make plans with me, as I won't skip a class); it's also because my need for a social life is now mostly fulfilled by the studio. The ten minutes of talk before and after class, the moments during class when we all laugh together at a joke that someone's made or groan about a combination, the brief whispered conversations while we wait in line to cross the room, seem to be all I require (and possibly all I can tolerate) after a day alone with my work.

That it took me this long to find the perfect balance between alone and not, writing and not, sitting still and not, is too bad, I suppose, but I don't waste time thinking about that. I'm just glad I have it now, glad I found it before it was too late.

One Sunday afternoon, as we balanced in attitude, Fili said, "Imagine hands placed here, lifting you up and holding you there"—and I was able to do that, able to imagine those hands and feel myself lifting higher out of my own legs, balancing, it seemed to me, both higher and longer than I ever had before.

It was not the first time I had made the shape I was seeking to make. It doesn't happen every day, but it happens—and every time it does, it is a kind of holy experience. At such moments, I am perfectly in balance. I am at one with myself, body and mind.

Not posing. Breathing. Solid and light, both. Poised for the next thing.

2

Starting & Stopping

1

I started smoking cigarettes because of a boy—because I was painfully, pointlessly, in love with a boy who had lost interest in me after a few attentive months, and because the girl he had decided he liked better smoked.

The girl was called Dawn. The brand she smoked was Eve.

This is a true story—I haven't changed the names. Though I can see now that they sound made up.

The boy's name, more prosaically, was Russell. Decades later, I learned (from him, in one exhausting, out of the blue phone call) that he had not been sober "even for a day" since he was thirteen—that is, that he had been high "you know, pretty much all day" every day for two years even before I first laid eyes on him in tenth grade; he'd been high all day every day for over forty years.

He was sober then, the day he called me. He was sober because he had been arrested for prescription fraud (he was a dentist, like his father; he had inherited his father's practice). For years he had been writing prescriptions in his patients' names and filling them. Getting sober was a condition of his not going to prison.

It strikes me now, as it did not on the day he called, years ago now, that the phone call might have been intended to be an amend.

If it was intended as such, it was a failed one. He spoke of a vague sense of remorse, but only in passing, without identifying what it was he had regrets about. Mostly he told a long tale of woe, the particulars of which included a house fire in which his girlfriend and his dogs were killed, but his ex-wife, who was living with them, managed to escape. He had lost everything: his beloved and his dogs, his home and all its contents. His license to practice. He was now living in the house in which he had grown up, the house I remembered. His mother, still alive, had decamped for Florida.

I believe it's possible that he retained no memory of how he'd treated me—that he could not have made amends even if he'd wanted to, because he had no idea what he ought to be sorry for. I didn't tell him. I was quiet, letting him tell me his sad story, not saying anything when he expressed his outrage that anyone imagined he'd been reckless with his patients ("I'm so used to being high, it didn't matter—I did my job well"), offered sympathy for the loss of the girlfriend, the dogs—I am good at sympathy—and listened as he reminisced about his parents, about "the old days."

I don't know whether he is sober still. It's nothing to do with me. I'm already resentful that he's taken up this much room in the story—the stories—I set out to tell here, just as he took up so much room, almost all the room, in my life for most of high school and for some time after.

Just as he takes up, still, too much room in my memory. He sometimes shows up, over half a century after I met and fell in love with him, in my dreams—that boy who treated me so roughly in some ways I still won't, can't, talk about.

2

I stopped smoking, too, because of a boy—a man, by then. I was thirty, in my first year of grad school. The man was someone who loved me and was kind to me. *A good man*, I often said. I said it with wonder. It seemed to me a happy accident (some days, even, something of a miracle) that I had found myself in such a relationship. Things had not gone so well over the fifteen years before him. I congratulated myself on my sanity, my newfound maturity, my luck.

Isaac was in med school. He read good books for fun and had a sense of humor. He could dance. He could even cook. He was younger than I was but more mature, more grown up than anyone I knew, in fact.

I trusted him. I was able to rely on him in ways that felt unfamiliar—or, rather, that only felt familiar when I thought back to my early childhood, to my father, my maternal grandparents.

At twenty-six, Isaac was the eldest of eight kids. When I met him, he had been the legal guardian of the three youngest—teenagers, two girls and a boy—for six months. Those three, plus three others (all of them, that is, except for one, the next-eldest), lived together in a house Isaac had bought in Omaha, the nearest good-sized city to the farm they'd lived on all their lives, and which he was renovating for them. That was all Isaac told me at first: that their mother had died, that he'd bought a house in Omaha for the kids to live in, that he was overseeing all the work on it—not to mention the lives of six of his siblings—mostly by phone from 250 miles away. And also that their father had abandoned them—the wife, the eight kids—over a year before. That the parents had come to the U.S. from Cuba in the "brain drain" following the revolution. He told me the rest only after we'd been dating for several weeks: that his mother had been killed in an arson fire, that the fire had been set by a fifteen-year-old boy, that the boy was angry because the youngest of the sisters had been forbidden to date him.

Isaac's real name isn't Isaac. His is one of only two names I've changed in this book, and I've changed his to protect his privacy, particularly around this horrific episode in his family's life; if I still feel protective of him, it's because he earned it—he deserves it.

I quit smoking because he told me to. It was early in our relationship, even before he had related the terrible story of how his mother had died. He told me—bluntly, sadly, yet somehow also matter-of-factly—that he could not keep seeing me if I kept on smoking. It was not a threat—a trick to make me stop. I knew he meant it. (Already

I knew that much about him, that he said what he meant.) When he told me he would not be able to be with me if I smoked, I knew too that it was not because the smell or taste of cigarettes repelled him (although I imagine they must have) or because he thought it was an ugly, stupid habit (although of course it was), but because he would not consider binding up his life with someone who was likely to die early.

Isaac had no interest in dating as an end in itself: his life was too complicated, he was stretched too thin, for that. If there was no possibility that our lives would eventually be bound up, there was no point in our continuing to be involved—I knew that was the way his thinking went. But there *was* such a possibility. Already so much of our conversation was about his sisters, for whose sake he'd bought the house exactly where he'd bought it, so that they'd be in walking distance from the Catholic school they'd been commuting to before. Already I had met them, when they'd driven back with him to Iowa City on a school break after one of his trips to see them; already I loved them. Already the next-to-youngest, who was fifteen, had confided in me about a boy she liked; already I'd taken the thirteen-year-old bra-shopping. Things were getting serious, fast. There was no other way for things to be under the circumstances. If we were dating, we were serious about each other. And if we were serious about each other, I had to stop smoking. By then, fifteen years after I'd started, I was up to three packs a day.

(I have never half-assed anything, not once in my whole life.)

3

I knew better than to think it was Dawn's smoking that attracted Russell, that made him like her more than he liked me. I knew better than to think if I smoked too, he would suddenly be charmed by me again, as he had seemed to be when we first met. I suspected, even then, that what had driven him away was my devotedness, my too-focused attention on him. But I also felt (*knew*, I would have said then) that I wasn't pretty enough. Wasn't thin enough. Definitely wasn't cool enough. I wasn't cool at all. I pretended to be, but I knew I wasn't fooling him. Maybe I wasn't fooling anyone—I worried about that. I talked too much and didn't talk about the right things.

I might have been smart (oh, I knew I was smart). I might have been (yes, even then) a writer, with many, many pages—with entire manuscripts—hidden in boxes under my bed, and other pages I was willing, sometimes eager, to let other people see. I might have had an analytic turn of mind, a pretty singing voice, a kind heart full of empathy for virtually everyone—but none of these gifts were of interest to me, not then, not when they had no market value. They had no market value in high school in Brooklyn in 1970.

But like high school kids everywhere, anytime, I did what I could to appear more valuable. I dressed the way the girls I most admired did, the way my idols (Laura Nyro, Grace Slick) did: in skirts that dragged along the ground, in shawls and peasant blouses and bell-bottom jeans covered with leather patches and embroidered flowers, in halter tops that were just scarves tied at the neck and waist. In my regalia, I cut classes to walk with a pack of kids, some of whom never seemed to enter the school building at all, to the nearby luncheonette that we had designated as our place, and where we did nothing more than stand around desultorily talking just as we'd been doing on the sidewalk in front of our school.

I made an effort is what I am saying—I made the concerted effort that I hadn't made (that I had not known how to make) in junior high to fit in, to find and keep my place among the group I'd chosen (or that had chosen me, or that I'd fallen in with—I will never know). My only two friends from junior high were at a different high school. It seemed to me that I could start over here. I could be anyone I chose to be.

But I felt like a fraud. I didn't want to cut classes. I had always liked school, liked learning things. And I hated getting high. Itt made me anxious, even more self-conscious than I was un-high. I cut classes and got high anyway. There was nothing I would not have done, I think, not to be alone. And it worked: I wasn't. I had friends. First Gary, then Ronnie. Then Dale, Elyse, Billy and Leslie, Steve and Rhonda. Robby. Marty. Vicki. Lisa. Suddenly I had a *lot* of friends. And there were others who were not my friends, Bobby D and Charlie and the other Billy and Felice and Jill and the two Sharons—I can hardly believe that I remember all their names, that I can call up in my mind what they all looked like—but with whom I tried even harder to be the girl *I* looked like.

And, that autumn of 1970, there was the girl named Dawn. I don't think I ever spoke to her. I studied her, though. She was younger, thinner, prettier. Even at fifteen, I was made miserable by *younger, thinner, prettier*. I watched her at parties and on the steps and sidewalk outside school: a fragile-looking girl with a short artful mop of brown hair, expertly black-rimmed eyes, sharp hipbones on display above the band of her Seafarers. Even now I see her sitting on somebody's bed, at somebody's party, holding between the V of her slender fingers the long, slender cigarettes she smoked with the ring of flowers printed on them.

4

Isaac's telling me that I had to quit smoking almost certainly would not have worked if I hadn't already been trying to. I'd even already quit for real once (that is, for longer than a few days), months before I'd left New York for Iowa, but I'd started up again within the first few weeks of starting grad school. We all smoked in grad school in creative writing in the mid-eighties. We smoked while we wrote, and we smoked while we workshopped the stories we had written (there were metal ashtrays in the classrooms); we smoked after workshop as we debriefed in the bar. We smoked at the dinner parties a group of us took turns hosting, and at the much bigger parties for the very famous writers (who also all smoked) who'd come to town to give readings.

Still, I hated that I smoked. I hated that I'd started at fifteen—I was *furious* with myself for having started because of a boy. Because of *that* boy, in particular. I'd been trying to quit for years. I must have quit a hundred times by then, thrown out my pack of Marlboros, gone a miserable day or two without, and then, frantic at one or two

AM, rushed out to buy a pack just so that I could smoke one (*one last one!* I swore) and give the pack away. There were always people smoking as they walked down Christopher Street, where I lived then. I'd try to pick out someone who looked as if they could not afford to buy their own, but in a pinch I'd go for anyone: I'd hand off the pack of Marlboros and say, "Please, take it—I just needed one, I'm quitting." The smoker would smile and thank me, wish me luck. I was so broke then, this was a real sacrifice—buying a whole pack just for one cigarette, charitably donating the pack. One last time, I thought, every time. And every time, I meant it—I was really, truly done this time.

But I wasn't done until Isaac told me that I had to be. It's the thing I'm third-most grateful to him for, after his offering me a sort of relationship and a sort of love I didn't think was possible for me, and his introducing me to the idea of being essential—indispensable—to others. (I knew about *trying* to make myself indispensable; what I learned was what it was like to actually be of use, what it meant to be responsible for anyone beside myself.)

I don't know which of these comes first and which comes second—it varies, depending on the day I'm thinking about it. The latter prepared me for motherhood; the former prepared me for a reasonably healthy marriage, one over three decades old by now. Although it must be said that, after Isaac, I backslid for a time, relationshipwise. Still, it was the memory of loving him—and of being loved back in the way he had—that helped me right myself after two men in a row who treated me as if I were disposable, if not quite as badly as (or if not in all of the particular bad ways that) Russell had, which represents slow progress of a sort.

What I am fourth-most grateful for—I might as well mention it while I'm on the subject—is that Isaac taught me how to drive. It was his birthday gift to me when I turned thirty, before we'd even started dating. I'd known him for three months, and this did not feel like a gift at first. I thanked him for the offer, which he made in writing, in the birthday card he gave me at the party I'd thrown for myself, but gracefully (I thought) declined. I was a New Yorker, after all, only temporarily living in Iowa. Driving was not a necessary life skill for me, I explained. Also (although I didn't tell him this) I was afraid.

But he insisted. Driving was a useful and important life skill for everyone, he said—a skill all adults who were physically able should be in possession of. "Besides, who knows?" he said. "You might not be a New Yorker forever."

He was a persuasive (or maybe just a stubborn) person. I learned to drive.

Along the way, we started dating. He was still teaching me to drive—we were nearly done; I was set to take my driving test the next week—when he told me the full truth about his mother's death. I was at the wheel, practicing non-city driving for the first time as we set out on a camping trip, and I crashed the car.

It was a freak accident. Fresh gravel had been laid but not yet leveled on the two-lane country road we were on, and a tree branch hidden under the fresh gravel caught in the car's steering column. We went off the road and flipped into a ditch—we landed upside down, unhurt (I'd been driving well under the speeding limit) but for the gashes on Isaac's arms after he smashed and climbed out of the passenger side window so that he could come around to my side of the car, because when we stopped moving, upside down, and he asked me if I was all right, I was in shock and couldn't answer. All the stuff we'd packed for camping had crashed through the wall of the trunk and into the car, filling the backseat and all the space between us up in front. He couldn't see me, couldn't get to me, without coming around from the outside.

It had been his mother's car. Still, he said, "It's only a thing." I remember that he said this again and again, while I wept about it. "We're okay, that's all that matters. *Things* can be replaced." He said this in exactly the way he had told me I had to quit smoking, the way he'd told me driving was a necessary life skill, the way he'd convinced me that camping would be fun.

5

Russell drove a powder blue Jaguar V12 convertible his parents had given him for his birthday. It wasn't long before he totaled it, though, just as he destroyed the motorboat they gave him—he couldn't seem to take care of anything. Strangely enough, I have no memory of riding in that car with him, though I remember the car itself perfectly. I do remember riding in the boat. He was reckless behind its wheel. Sometimes he let me steer—I didn't have a clue what I was doing. I couldn't swim, either. But we never, not once, wore life jackets.

This is almost embarrassing—all of it is—as metaphor.

6

By the time Isaac moved to Omaha to start his residency in internal medicine, I was a good enough (if just barely good enough) driver to make the four-hour trip on my own. And so I did it nearly every weekend in my second year of grad school.

In Omaha, I stayed in the house he was still renovating. I learned that *things* mattered to him after all—that he had filled the house with furniture and bric-a-brac that hadn't been destroyed in the fire, that he'd done all he could to restore the furniture that had been damaged but not ruined. He'd bought many more things, too, things meant to replace what had been lost. He made every effort to find things that looked exactly like what they had had before.

I had a room to myself—a small room, the guestroom. But I was the only guest.

I wrote sitting at his desk, in the study he'd carved out for himself in the house. I read curled up on a blue velvet loveseat in the room they called the family room. I took the girls out shopping for new clothes and out to lunch. I had a hand-me-down car of my own by then—it had been my mother's, then my brother's, then my sister-in-law's, and then my father paid someone to drive it across the country to me. It was a 1977 Caprice Classic, pale blue like Russell's Jag, already on its last legs.

When I was there on weekends, it was like we were playing house. I was Wendy in *Peter Pan,* playing at being a mother even though I wasn't old enough to be the mother of these children. Some of the older siblings had moved into their own apartments nearby, but they still came home for dinner most nights. When I was there, we all cooked and cleaned up together. Afterwards, I'd have long talks, separate talks, with each of them about whatever happened to be on their minds.

Once I had graduated and decided to join them in Omaha, renting my own little house halfway between the hospital and the big house where Isaac and his family lived, I stepped up my role. Nights when he was on call, the youngest of the sisters, now fifteen and with a "boyfriend" of her own (they weren't exactly dating, since their in-person time together was always in the company of all of us), would stay at my house, where I had a guestroom just for her. I'd cook the kinds of meals I thought a mother would (meat loaf and mashed potatoes, spaghetti and meatballs) and let her talk on the phone to her boyfriend all she wanted as long as her homework was done. She would fall asleep while talking to him, the long phone cord stretching from my bedroom into hers. I'd go in, late, and gently pull the receiver out from under her and kiss her forehead. I'd marvel over how young and how innocent she seemed, given what had happened to her. I'd marvel over how young she seemed compared to myself at that age. It was a different place, of course, and a different time—Omaha in the late eighties might have been another era on a distant planet from the Brooklyn in which I had been a teenager in the late sixties and early seventies. I wanted to be sure the worst was in her past, wanted to help keep her safe, to help her grow up strong and confident. That I had the chance to also belongs in the top five things for which I am still grateful to Isaac.

We didn't have a lot of time alone together, but I'd known that before I'd joined him, joined them all, in Omaha. I had a book, my first, to finish writing. He had a grueling residency to complete. We both filled our days with work. In the evening, when he wasn't on call, sometimes he would stop in and have dinner with me before he went home; more often, I'd go home with him and we'd make dinner there. I had come to love those family dinners—I had never *had* family dinner before. Growing up, meals in my family had been catch-as-catch-can.

I understood that, for Isaac, his family came first. He had told me early on that this was how it was. I also understood that after that came work. So I already knew I was in third place. But if his tenderness toward me and the romantic gestures he surprised me with, the vacations we took whenever he had time off—vacations we planned together and he paid for—*and* the role I'd found in the constellation of his family, constituted third place, I was fine with that. I had my work, too. Which, for me, came first, I told him. He would have to come in second.

That was how I wanted it to be. How I thought it should be.

I had a lot of thoughts, back then, about how things should be.

7

When I think of myself at fifteen, deciding to start smoking, and the seriousness with which I took that decision (I bought a pack and smoked every cigarette in it, walking up and down the street around the corner from where we lived, smoked one after another, making myself sick, in my determination not to look like an amateur when I smoked for the first time in public)—I think of that girl with pity, with grief. How white-hot with need she was! And there was Dawn—that other, younger girl. Thin, the way my sad girl-self wanted so much to be. And so cool and confident. Just as Russell was. I marvel over this as I look back, marvel over so much unearned confidence. How was it that it came so easily to some of these children, and not at all to me?

Their certainty that they deserved to be admired seems as absurd as my conviction that I wasn't lovable.

This will come as no surprise to any woman my own age: that when I look at the few photographs I have of myself at fifteen or sixteen, I cannot imagine how I could have longed to be thinner or prettier than that beautiful girl, caught off guard by her little brother taking photographs for a school project. That I was too self-conscious to pose for a camera, to allow myself to be the willing, conscious subject of a photograph, seems a quaint notion now—as much so as the pink Princess phone in my room, at which I was forever staring, willing it to ring, willing it to be Russell.

Even at the time, I was ashamed of studying Dawn the way I did. I believed that she was stupid, and not because she was two years behind me in school but because she sounded stupid when I eavesdropped on her conversations. She might have *been* stupid, for all I know. Her drug of choice was "downers," and I saw her at parties weaving, sometimes collapsing in a heap. I listened to her slur her words. And still, I studied her.

I'm not sure she knew who I was. And why would she have? I was inconsequential to her.

I concluded that it was her lack of interest in him, in conjunction with her prettiness, that interested Russell. Or perhaps it was no more than a successful pretense of a lack of interest. I couldn't tell the difference and it seemed to me that he could not have either. And it didn't matter anyway. I could not even pretend to be disinterested—I would not have known where to start. I could not be other than I was: consumed by longing; longing personified. I grasped at straws. The straws, this time around, were cigarettes.

Later, when Russell and I did get back together—when, although he never really gave up chasing other girls, I earned, at last, the position of his real girlfriend—it was because I'd been as stubborn and as patient as Isaac would turn out to be years later. I played the long game, and then the summer before senior year, I had a lucky break: he came down with mono. Everyone he knew, both the girls he fooled around with and the boys he got high with, deserted him. Not me. I visited him every day. We played cards and board games and fooled around—sexually, I mean—and I told him I didn't care if I got sick. (I didn't get sick, which was surprising.) And just as I'd hoped would happen if he only paused long enough to really look at me—to look inside me, to see who I was—I somehow made him fall in love with me.

After that we were together. He was nicer to me for a while, though not consistently. And in what seemed at first to be the pinnacle of our romance, his parents sent us on a trip to Europe. It must have been a high school graduation gift for him (and—or—a wish to get him out of their hair for a while, because he was a handful, wrecking cars and boats, getting arrested for possession, dealing pot out of his basement room). I had already graduated six months early, desperate to get out of high school, where I'd been so unhappy; eager to start college, where I had the idea everything would change.

Nothing changed.

I wasn't quite seventeen, commuting from home to Brooklyn College by bicycle or bus. That first semester I hardly paid attention to my schoolwork. My real life was with him. I spent every minute that I could with him, in his basement in Mill Basin or his upstairs bedroom, where I'd spent so much time during the mono summer.

And then in Europe, things went awry from the start. Things happened that I still can't talk about. Some things happened that had happened before, but that I hadn't understood as terrible—as terrible as they really were—and, even in Europe, I did not quite understand how bad they were. Everything, I see now, was much worse than I thought it was at the time that it was happening.

And this is hard to think about, because I understood even then that much of what was happening *was* bad. I was seventeen that summer and somehow I didn't have the words for some of the particular awfulness. But I know that on the flight home I refused to sit with him, that for a period of time I wouldn't speak to him.

But then I did. I smoothed things over. I told myself I couldn't help it. He went off to college on Long Island and we talked on the phone nightly. I begged him to come home on weekends and sometimes he did. The ashtray in my bedroom overflowed with cigarette butts. I smoked as soon as I woke up each morning. I smoked while I studied—tried to study, half of my attention miles away, with him, torturing myself about what he might be doing and with whom. I smoked entire packs of cigarettes while we talked on the phone.

I smoked instead of eating, too. And I did get thinner, thinner than I needed to be. I remember being very hungry when he came home for his visits. Sneaking cookies into the bathroom at his parents' house, eating them in secret.

8

My father forbade me to go on that trip to Europe, and I went anyway. I said, "You're not paying for it, you can't stop me."

He smoked when I was very young. By the time I was a teenager, it had been years since he had quit. I don't know when he started, but by the time my mother met him—on his seventeenth birthday—the habit was well established. It may be that he was roughly the same age when he began as I was, when I did.

And he must have been about the same age when he quit, too. My mother says he couldn't have been too much more than thirty. Which would make me five. I have clear memories of him as a smoker, though. I remember him telling me to get him his cigarettes when he was in the bath and had forgotten them (how he'd hold his book modestly over the part of him I was not supposed to see). I'd bring him his pack of Chesterfields and the mosaic tile ashtray I'd made for him myself.

I don't know how he managed to quit. I know my mother would not have told him she was leaving him if he didn't. My mother was meek in those days. She would not even have been able to fake that sort of sternness. She was soft-voiced. She was sad—more than sad. Depressed. Her depression is all mixed up with this memory, because she tells me that it was the first psychiatrist she and my father consulted who got him to quit smoking. "He said, 'Don't you want to see Michelle grow up?'"

"And that worked?" I ask her.

"I guess so," she says.

Chesterfield was James Bond's brand. Was that why he smoked them? He loved James Bond. James Bond, Sherlock Holmes, Al Jolson—an odd trinity of heroes, fictional and real. If I thought hard about it, I could probably figure out something important about my father based on how much he idolized these three. But it's smoking I want to talk about, not Dad. Not now, not this time.

9

Chesterfield—like Marlboro, my brand—was marketed to men. Eve was aggressively marketed to women. But then it was a brand designed for women, meant only for them, like Virginia Slims (which had come first, designed to capitalize on "women's liberation"; nobody I knew smoked Virginia Slims—Virginia Slims were for our mothers' generation). Both the package (soft, obviously) and the cigarettes within it were imprinted with elaborately drawn flowers; on the package, a Keane-eyed, long-necked Eve herself was buried to her naked shoulders in a whole *jungle* of flowers. And while I studied/admired/envied/hated Dawn and the Eve in her slender fingers, when I decided to start smoking, I knew better than to buy a pack of Eves—knew I wasn't an Eve sort of girl. I didn't even have to think about it before choosing Marlboro, the brand all my friends smoked. The cool, mostly white, kids. The cool Black kids were mostly cool in a different way, and their brand was Kool. (The tough kids, all of whom were white, smoked too, but I never got close enough to them to know what they were smoking. I gave a wide berth to the football players and cheerleaders, too. These were Black kids *and* white kids and they were a breed apart from us, the hippie kids—more alien to us than even the tough kids in their scowls and leather jackets. I don't know what brand of cigarettes the football team and their cheerleaders smoked. For a moment, working on this essay, I thought of asking them—I'm now Facebook friends with some of these former kids—but it turns out that even after more than fifty years I'm still a little bit afraid of them.)

I remember that a couple of renegades among my crowd—Billy, and Bobby D (who was so cool he seemed practically asleep as he rocked back on his heels on the sidewalk in front of the school, and the truth is I don't even know if he was still *in* school then, if he had dropped out or possibly graduated: I never once saw him enter the building)—had chosen a brand of their own: Billy, I recall, smoked Parliaments; Bobby D, I'm almost sure, smoked Winstons.

After I smoked that first pack of Marlboros—the whole pack, practicing so that when I lit up in public for the first time I'd look like a pro (like a Chesterfield smoker, it occurs to me now: Chesterfield's advertising slogan in the forties, when my father first started smoking, was "the brand preferred by professional smokers")—I smoked Marlboro for close to a decade. When I started worrying about my smoking, in my mid-twenties, I tried to taper off with various low-tar brands, starting with Marlboro Light, then working my way through the many others: Merit, Vantage, Carlton, True Blue, Now). For a while, in the late seventies, I smoked Jakartas, clove cigarettes (I thought they were better for me; I was wrong). Later, during one of the periods when I was trying to quit, I followed the advice of the American Cancer Society, and along with wrapping up my pack of cigarettes with rubber bands, to make it difficult/annoying to get into, and writing down what time it was and how badly I needed to smoke each time I braved that rubber band gauntlet, I switched brands with every pack I bought. Thus, in the early eighties, I smoked Winston and Tareyton and Parliament and Kent and Lark and even, rebelliously, unfiltered Camels. I smoked every non-mentholated brand there was except for Chesterfield (which I must have avoided because I associated the brand with my father, with whom I was angry in my twenties). Smoking was supposed to be less appealing if the cigarettes didn't taste exactly as expected.

This didn't work on me. Smoking was always appealing. That was the thing. I hated that I smoked. But I loved smoking.

10

It's been forty years now since I stopped smoking.

It's been forty years since I started driving, too.

I'm tallying things up. I'm counting, keeping track.

More than fifty years have passed since I took that trip to Europe—half a century! That makes it sound like history, when everything about that summer is still so surprising and so painful to me when I think about it. But maybe I'm misusing the word *history*. Maybe history can always be surprising, painful; maybe the passage of time means nothing much. Or nothing at all.

At fifteen (and sixteen and seventeen) I loved that boy, Russell, so immoderately. I loved him for reasons that make no sense to me now. And yet I can recall clearly what it felt like to be in love with him. That desperate, out-of-control, helpless feeling I called love but am sure, as I look back, had little to do with love. I don't have to look all the way back to Russell to see that. I would feel the same way again later, again and again, with other boys and men. I would feel it with, *for*, the man I started seeing right after—days after—Isaac and I parted ways. That was a calm, tearful, peaceful breakup, a breakup we'd been heading for without either of us knowing it, when at last we both understood that there was not a way to compromise on what we wanted from our lives, what we wanted for our futures. That he would not be happy married to someone who felt as I did about her own work, living in a city, stopping at just one child. That I would never want to have the six or seven or eight children he so longed for, raise them Catholic, live in rural Iowa.

11

The man I fell in love with after Isaac was much smarter, more sophisticated—on the surface a much better match for me than Russell had been years before. But like Russell he was charmed by me and then abruptly wasn't, and like Russell he made use of me when it pleased him, discarded me and picked me up and then discarded me again. For years, in my dreams, I conflated the two of them. I would wake up not knowing which one I had dreamed about, and only slowly realize it was both of them, mixed up together.

It took me much longer to give up allowing men to treat me badly than it took me to quit smoking. I was searching for a reason—a good reason, a better reason than "because I'm doing myself harm." Between Russell and the good man I eventually married there were far too many who were awful. Awful to me and also objectively awful, although I didn't see it that way at the time. I don't even want to name them. Like murderers whose photographs non-tabloid newspapers refuse to print, I am afraid they might enjoy what passes for celebrity. I don't want to give any of them the satisfaction of knowing how much harm they caused me, how much harm they helped me cause myself. Would it give them satisfaction? Perhaps not, perhaps they'd have regrets. But I doubt it. If they had any regrets, they would have made amends by now.

12

Isaac had more imagination about my future than I did. I'd had trouble (in fact I was incapable of) imagining a life for myself other than the one I had already had. But somehow I ended up not returning to New York to live and work as I had planned, somehow I ended up in the Midwest forever, teaching at a university. For years I still thought I'd go "home" after a while, that this arrangement, despite being a tenure-track arrangement, was only temporary.

Isaac, who went on to become the country doctor he had hoped to be, raising his six children on a farm in Iowa, was right about the useful skill he'd insisted that I learn, of course. The Ohio city I have lived in all these years has a population of a million, but it's an ordinary American city, a middle western city—the kind of city in which it is very hard to live unless you drive a car. I don't know how I would have managed, particularly with Grace when she was a child, if I hadn't learned to drive. I don't believe I ever would have, either, if he had not insisted. Just as he'd insisted that I give up smoking.

13

I still dream of smoking. These are good dreams. I wake up longing for a cigarette, even after all these years. But then the longing passes—it was only a remnant of dream-longing.

I am not the sort of person who could smoke a cigarette occasionally, I know that. I have friends who can, who can smoke a single cigarette, or even two or three, at a certain kind of party, drinking, dancing—it's part of a night of hedonism. And then the next day they are back to being nonsmokers. If I smoked one cigarette, I would instantly start smoking again, I know this about myself. And so I haven't smoked one since 1985.

In my dreams, though, sometimes, I am that sort of person. I am smoking, but I know it's temporary. They're dreams in which *I'm smoking now, but perhaps tomorrow I won't be*. I'm enjoying every minute of it. I've smoked for a while before—in these dreams, I mean—and then stopped, then started up again. I'm not addicted. Sometimes I just choose to smoke.

I never have dreams in which I just *happen* to be smoking. When I smoke in my dreams, it's the smoking that's the star. I dream up whole scenarios around it. Sometimes I've started smoking again. Sometimes it turns out I'd never quit. Sometimes I have come up with a system: I smoke only in certain situations, and I have it under my control—just like certain of my friends do, and in real life I watch in amazement.

I don't feel deprived in those dreams. I feel powerful, I feel in charge of my own desires, my own needs. I smoke when I choose to smoke, and otherwise I don't.

And unlike the occasions when Russell or the man I loved two decades after Russell pops up in my dreams—or the two of them combined do—these dreams don't upset me. I don't wake up frightened, breathing hard, angry and sad at the same time. I wake up amused, once the sleepy moment of longing has passed.

In my dreams, smoking isn't a bad habit. It does not seem to be dangerous at all. However much I smoke, in whatever dream scenario I've cooked up, I'm not trying to quit. I smoke with *joy*. I smoke with pleasurable abandon. I'm smoking only for myself.

Gone

My father—a list-maker, a planner, a person who liked to be (and almost always was) in charge—left nothing to chance: he left us instructions—indeed, multiple sets of instructions—for after his death.

He left a document called "special instructions" on the desktop of the PC in his home office, which the rest of us called "the den." He left another, older document (titled "instructions") in the computer's documents folder (it was nearly identical to the more recent one). He left hard copies of both of these—as well as other, older (but also nearly identical) sets of instructions—printed on bright colored paper (orange, lime green, yellow) buried within stacks of papers in the den, which doubled as a guest room (and tripled as storage space: A closet that stretched almost the length of one wall was stuffed with everything my parents had rescued from my grandmother's apartment after *her* death, and there were boxes stacked in every corner of the room, framed pictures they'd replaced with others, photo albums, and scrapbooks and all kinds of memorabilia).

There were a lot of stacks of papers. There were stacks of papers on the bookshelves, papers in stacks stuffed every which way into the drawers of the credenza. There were piles of papers beside the computer and more piles of paper on the folding snack table my father had set up alongside the computer table. There were piles of papers on the desk, a leftover from when he'd had an actual office, from when he'd had his own business—a desk that took up a good third of the room and blocked its only windows (so that they could not be opened), as well as the air conditioner and heating panel below them, which had to be turned on and off by flipping the switch on the circuit breaker in the hall.

It was a completely impractical setup. It was a completely impractical *desk*. He should never have kept it, never have gone to the trouble and expense of moving it into the apartment. But that was how my father was, sometimes: completely impractical, sentimental, impulsive.

The rest of the time, he was thoroughly pragmatic—sensible, practical, knowledgeable about how the world worked, full of good advice I couldn't follow because *I* am not very practical. My father knew how to get things done, how to make things happen, how to *manage*.

And then he was gone, and he left us *instructions*.

He had been sick for five months—since mid-December, when he'd contracted Legionnaires' disease while on a cruise with my mother. The two of them loved cruises. They'd always loved to travel. Up into my father's late seventies, they traveled by air and wandered the streets and museums of farflung cities. When that became difficult for him, they made the shift to cruises, three or four a year—and by the last few cruises of his life, they'd even stopped disembarking at the ports of call. He was eighty-three, and arthritis in his back and hips made it hard for him to walk for more than a few minutes.

On their final cruise, they made a stop in Belize, and as usual they stayed on the ship. That evening, my father felt awful—awful enough to decide that he needed to see the ship's doctor, who promptly checked him into the infirmary. The next morning, he was in the hospital in Belize City.

Eventually, he was cured of the Legionnaires', but his lungs did not recover. And in the course of his first hospitalization in New York, the doctors discovered an aortic stenosis. Over multiple hospitalizations, one long stay on the rehab floor of a nursing home, and a heart attack, he lost fifty pounds and grew weaker, then weaker still.

When he died, it was peaceful. It was easy. He took one breath, and then he did not take the next breath. And then he was gone from his body—and it was as if he'd shed it, as if in that instant it had become of no use to him and so he'd slipped out of it, out of his skin and bones, flesh and blood—and left the room. Left the world.

By noon I had found the first set of instructions. I was not surprised to find them. As Dad would have said—as he always said, when my brother or I called with big career news, or to report that our children had made the dean's list—*I expected no less.*

I was not surprised, either, by the specificity of the instructions, by the numbered list broken down, like the outlines we had to make in school, into lettered sub-lists—and then further broken down into numbered sub-sub-lists. I was a little bit surprised that they were so mundane, that there was nothing of his personality in them—all he'd given us was names (attorney, accountant, stockbroker) and bank accounts and sub-lists of "important documents" and where to find them. There was a short list of small bequests—the coin collection we hadn't known he had was to go to Grace, a star sapphire ring he hadn't worn in decades was to go to one of my brother's sons—but he noted that these were iterated in his will. He was just making sure that everything went exactly as he wanted it to; he wanted to make sure we knew exactly what he wanted. That was how he was, how he'd always been.

He didn't have to say "take care of Mom" or "take care of each other" or even "don't get rid of my desk." He knew we knew all that. There was nothing that was not mundane that needed to be *in* his instructions, it struck me as I finished reading them. He knew we knew what he wanted.

What surprised me, when I started going through the stacks of papers and the hundreds, perhaps thousands, of discrete files on his computer (it seemed that he had not believed in folders), was that there were so many sets of almost-the-same instructions of what needed to be done after his death. This meant that even though he'd never spoken of it—not once, not to any one of us—he'd revisited the prospect many times over the years, making minute revisions to his lists and sub-lists.

I was even more surprised to learn that he had kept junk mail and catalogs, torn-open envelopes with nothing inside them, and all sorts of other useless paper that should have been discarded years ago—and that all of this was mixed in with the papers we needed. There was no system at all to what he'd saved. I found crucial financial documents nearly at the bottom of a tall pile of advertising circulars, political solicitations, and marketing brochures for cruises.

I also found letters I had written to him—letters I had no memory of writing—in the seventies (when I'd lived in Greenwich Village, just five miles away) and eighties, from Iowa, Nebraska, and finally Ohio. I found many drafts of his own writing. Typed lists of all the photographs he'd taken when he'd worked for daily newspapers, half a century ago. Rosters of police contacts from then.

I found typewritten copies of speeches he had made. My birth announcement. Greeting cards from people I had never heard of. Photos of his family—he had so many aunts and uncles, cousins!—I had never seen before.

I found a family tree he'd painstakingly filled in, right up through my brother's first two grandchildren—my father's first great-grandchildren, both born in the last year of his life, after he turned eighty-three.

And amid—beyond—the stacks of paper:

Laminated press cards. License plates. An album of his feature stories that we'd thought had been lost in a flood decades ago in his father's hardware store.

Mementoes of the many trips he and my mother took. The ankle bracelet he gave her in 1947, when they were first dating—a premature gift that my mother says alarmed her: it featured two tiny, connected gold hearts, one inscribed *Morty* and the other *Sheila*. ("We hardly even knew each other!")

Cards—they must have been from the fifties—made from cut-up shirt cardboard onto which he'd glued his own typed recipes for cocktails (and, in a cabinet in the living room that no one had opened in thirty-plus years, the glassware necessary to measure and mix those cocktails, and two silver cigarette lighters meant to be set on a coffee table, which my mother supposes must have been wedding presents she'd forgotten about).

A set of autograph books—both his and my mother's—the kind with colored pages upon which no one except teachers or perhaps a parent would dare to write anything heartfelt. (I have two of these books myself, one from elementary school and one from junior high. Nothing had changed between my parents' generation and my own.) My parents' friends had written—just as my friends had—*When you get old and out of shape/remember a girdle costs $3.98* and *Dated till Niagara Falls* and *Yours till Hungary eats Turkey in Greece on China*.

On the first page of my father's eighth-grade autograph book there's a list of printed questions. His answers are written in blue ink.

Favorite heroes? the book asks, and my father, age fourteen, responds in graceful cursive on the line provided: *Lou Gehrig and Frank Sinatra*. In the blanks for "favorite author" and "favorite book" are names I'd never heard of, and already I've forgotten them. He writes in his "favorite song" and "favorite friend." And then there's this—my favorite of the favorite things:

Favorite motto?

A place for everything and everything in its place, my young father says.

I was not surprised by the discovery that my father was disorganized—anyone looking into the den even glancingly would have known that. Besides, *I'm* disorganized (I am, as they say, my father's daughter). But my father seemed to have printed out and saved every email that he'd ever sent and many that he had received. He'd printed out and saved records for every financial transaction he'd ever made online—then left them unfiled, in stacks, in no discernible order.

I've had to teach myself to stay on top of junk mail, to throw out things I have no need for—but I don't keep drawers full of expired credit cards, every business card anyone has ever given me, old receipts, bank statements going back to the eighties and checkbooks from long-closed accounts, thousands of loose paper clips, empty envelopes with defunct return addresses.

And I don't have a vault for the safekeeping of my Most Important Documents. I don't have a vault at all. Why did I need one, when my father had one? In 1989, when I bought my house, my father said, "Send me the deed. I'll put it in the vault," and I said, "You have a *vault*? How big is it? Where is it?"

"Not like in the movies," he said. "I'm talking about a safe deposit box. In the bank."

I didn't ask him why he didn't call it his "safe deposit box." He always made things sound more important, more dramatic, than they were. (I do this too.) I sent him the deed.

My mother and I went to the safe deposit box at Chase on the corner of York and 79th—confident that we would find the original of my father's will, the deed to my house, the fan letter I received from the novelist James T. Farrell after I published my first short story, my parents' birth certificates and marriage certificate, their parents' death certificates, and all the other important documents listed in his instructions.

As we expected, the box was full.

The coin collection took up most of it. None of the documents was there.

It's possible, I suppose, that my father thought he'd eventually get around to separating out the useful from the useless. Perhaps he thought he had all the time in the world to do that. Perhaps, although he put on a good show of preparedness—that numbered, lettered outline of instructions, repeated over and over again with only the slightest of variations—he didn't really think he was ever going to die. Perhaps he only acted *as if* he knew that death was a certainty, because he knew he was supposed to act as if he knew. But he didn't mean it; he didn't believe it.

That's what my brother thought. Or it was one of the things he thought. We talked about this every day, and every day we changed our minds about what we thought. There was only one thing I never changed my mind about: I felt sure the missing papers were *somewhere*. Like my father was.

I felt him around me all the time. I could hear him in my mind, telling me what he wanted me to do whenever something difficult came up (and everything difficult that came up had to do with him, and in particular the missing documents), and I could see him in my mind shaking his head, looking embarrassed the way he would when he was caught in a mistake of any kind, and egging me on when I scolded someone on the phone or was absurdly, immovably persistent in my demands on behalf of my mother—on behalf of *him*. In his honor.

It felt as if the essence of him, whatever that could mean once he was no longer in the vessel that the essence of him used to be contained by, was in a place I couldn't see or touch. That didn't mean that it was not a place.

I would not have predicted this—I would not have predicted that I would think about him this way, once he was gone. *Gone forever*. Like the papers. Which had to be gone forever (they must be gone forever, I told myself, because I have looked everywhere and haven't found them)—and yet, illogically, I kept on looking for them. I couldn't stop. I didn't know how to stop.

I was waiting for him to tell me to stop. For him to give me some instructions, goddammit.

In early July, seven weeks after his death, I made the trip to Manhattan once again. There was more work to do in the apartment, but also my mother and brother and I were going to host a party in honor of what would have been his eighty-fourth birthday. Grace, home from college for a few weeks before leaving for a summer in Japan, flew to New York with me.

The evening we got there, as we sat with my mother at her dining room table, planning the party, I noticed that a bulb was out in the ceiling fixture. My mother noticed me noticing.

"Daddy always changed the bulbs," she said.

"I know," I told her. "I can do it." I scraped my chair back. "Where do you keep the light bulbs?"

My mother began to cry. "I don't know. I don't know where he kept them."

Grace rose to comfort her, and I said, "Don't worry about it, Mama." I never used to call her Mama. Mama is what Grace calls me. "I'll find them, okay?"

I looked in the kitchen—in all the drawers and all the cabinets and the broom closet. I looked in the famously cluttered den—so recently decluttered—even though I was sure there were no light bulbs anywhere in there, since I'd already opened every drawer and cabinet and both closets and searched every bookshelf. I looked in the closet between the living room and the bedroom, the one where my mother keeps her vacuum cleaner, and, on a shelf, a stack of board games I still hadn't had a chance to work my way through. I looked in the linen closet—I hadn't had a chance to get through it yet, either (I would, though, the very next day). I dragged the stepladder from the kitchen to the closet opposite the door to the apartment—a coat closet, but I remembered that my father used to use the high shelf as a sort of a pantry. At one time, there were boxes of pasta up there, cans of tomatoes, rolls of paper towels. I climbed up and looked there—but it wasn't a pantry anymore, it was another place to store odds and ends. There was a movie projector, seven umbrellas, a lot of baseball caps, two computer keyboards still in their boxes, an external hard drive also still in its box, and a coffee maker (ditto). Two cartons full of my mother's college papers and notes on index cards. Seven telephones—seven! All in boxes—but put *back* into boxes; they were old phones. There were no light bulbs.

I took out everything but the movie projector and umbrellas—I'd figure out what to do about them later. Then I closed up the stepladder and surveyed the bottom of the closet, below the row of coats and jackets hanging there. The coats and jackets could wait till tomorrow. Or the next day. But the floor of the closet was packed tight with stuff. "I might as well finish cleaning out this closet as long as I've already started, okay?" I called out to my mother and daughter.

They were busy talking. They ignored me.

I sat on the floor and started pulling things out. I pulled out a heavy box filled with catalogs from Christie's—from the years when my father was attending auctions, collecting posters. Behind it was a box of catalogs from Phillips—another auction house. A box of my mother's psych textbooks. A shopping bag full of electrical cords. Two more phones. A pile—a great big pile—of galoshes, the old-fashioned kind you put on over your shoes. And behind the galoshes, a shiny gold shopping bag—the sort of bag you put a gift in. I pulled it out of the closet. It was full of manila envelopes.

I considered the manila envelopes.

"Mom?" I called. "I found something."

I opened the first envelope.

I must have shrieked, because Grace came running. My mother was behind her, slower but still as fast as she could.

I'd found my father's will.

I'd found, it turned out, everything that was supposed to have been "in the vault." One envelope held the deed to my house, and the abstract of its title. One was full of birth certificates. Several held documents my father hadn't even listed in his instructions—his honorable discharge papers from both the army and the navy, his grandfather's citizenship papers, his and my mother's social security cards, my grandmother's savings passbook.

My daughter said, "It's Chekhovian, isn't it? Finding what's important behind the galoshes."

And when I called my friend Hula—a musician who practices law part time, who had begun filing the papers one has to file when someone dies without a will—she said, "So *that* was the vault! The gold shopping bag."

I don't know what my father had in mind. Perhaps at one time he actually had all the documents in a different safe deposit box, a bigger one, and then he closed that one and decided to open another.

Perhaps, what with his coin collection, there was no room in the new box and the bank didn't have another one available, so he stashed all the important papers behind the galoshes in a gold shopping bag—a safe place, he must have thought, a place no one would ever look—until such time as the bank had another box available (though why he would have put the coin collection in the box instead of the documents, it's hard to guess; perhaps the coins were so heavy, he was loathe to carry them back up to the apartment after hauling them over to the bank). He put the documents in the shopping bag, and the shopping bag in the closet behind the galoshes, and then forgot about it. That must have been what happened. But who knows? I'll never know for sure. And it doesn't matter, does it? It only matters that I found them—all the documents his instructions promised I would find.

I knew they had to be somewhere. I knew they weren't really gone.

Daily Papers

The scrapbook I found after my father died was wedged into a row of books in the living room, where books were shelved two deep in floor-to-ceiling bookcases. Some of the shelves had books crammed in horizontally too, and it was in one of those stacks that I found it as I went about my business—what I somehow thought was my business—of pulling out the books my mother had no interest in, the ones that had been only Dad's (history, presidential biographies, detective stories, gangster stories) and the ones they should have gotten rid of long ago, like the complete Encyclopedia Britannica from the sixties. When I took hold of the scrapbook, bits of it crumbled in my hands.

I didn't know my father had kept a scrapbook of this kind, although I should have. Long before his death, before I discovered that he had kept *everything*, I knew he was someone who held on to things. The sign that had hung above his grandfather's tailor shop in Keene, New Hampshire, had a place of honor in my parents' living room amidst all the posters and prints he had bought at auctions. The Bulova Excellency watch that had been a gift from his father to his beloved tailor-grandfather—my grandfather's father-in-law—had been solemnly passed down to me (but not until a promise was extracted that I'd keep it "forever").

I even knew he was a scrapbook-maker, having had in my possession for years one commemorating his and my mother's early relationship. (It had fascinated me in childhood, and so when I moved into my own apartment, I'd begged to take it with me.) It was *his* scrapbook, dedicated to them as a couple; he'd left it with her when he joined the army in 1948, and kept sending her photographs of himself in training at Fort Hood and postcards from Texas to add to it, even though my then fifteen-year-old mother had broken up with him before he left (not for the first time, either). On the postcards he had written variations of "Another souvenir for our scrapbook, darling—that is, if you haven't thrown it away by now." She hadn't—she didn't. When he got home, she took him back, and the final items in that scrapbook include the printed menu for their wedding in 1952 and a list handwritten by my father, with cross-outs and edits, of the friends, siblings, and cousins in their wedding party.

It wasn't until after he died that I learned that he'd kept *everything*, not just souvenirs and mementos and things that were meaningful in one way or another. He kept things that had no meaning, sentimental or otherwise. I had to go through all of it to find the things that were important, which were mixed in with the rest.

In those first weeks after his death, I was in constant motion. My mother stood and watched, wringing her hands. Even now I cannot say why I felt I had to put *my* hands on everything—everything he'd ever touched, everything he'd kept. The story I told myself was that I wanted to make my mother's place *her* place. My father's things were everywhere, piled every which way, teetering, collapsing, bursting out of drawers and cabinets, filling the closets. How could she live like this?

But she was already living "like this." She'd been living like this, in this apartment, for nearly forty years.

And even after I was done, the apartment was still full of stuff. Which I should understand. The house I live in is crammed full of stuff too. I too keep things. Not junk mail or printed out emails or old bank statements—*I am not as bad as my father!* I tell myself. Still, every surface in every room in my house is covered. *Re*-covered, I should say, because years before my father died I had a crisis over how much stuff was filling up my house and I got rid of most of it. And then slowly it refilled, and I emptied the house again, when I came home after my father's death and thought about how Grace would have to do what I had just done.

And now, just over a decade later, it is all filled up again.

I am not as bad as my father, but then I am not as good as he was, either, in so many ways.

The scrapbook was—is—filled with newspaper clippings: photographs of fires and crime scenes, apprehended criminals, cops and car crashes and other calamities; news stories and human interest stories and sports stories and editorials and features and reviews—there is a review of the Mona Lisa, on view at the Metropolitan Museum of Art for three weeks in 1963 (Dad thought it was good). All the clippings are from 1962 and 1963. They're from the *Brooklyn Daily* and the *New York and Brooklyn Daily* and the *Brooklyn Eagle* and the *Daily Mirror.* There were so many daily papers then.

Perhaps that's why he was able to get this sort of work—that, and his sheer determination, his chutzpah. How hard he was willing to work for almost no money. He was a high school dropout (too stubborn, my mother says, to take the one course he needed to pass, which would have required a semester of summer school after his friends had graduated). His parents owned a hardware store where he had been working resentfully after school and on weekends for years. The day he met my mother, when he was seventeen and she was fourteen, he was on a lunch break from the store, a block away from where she lived. His parents expected him to work there full time once he was through with school—they expected it to become his life, the way it was their life. This is an old story, an immigrant family's story. Except that my father's parents, unlike my mother's, weren't immigrants. They were first-generation Americans.

My paternal grandmother was born in New Hampshire, the daughter of German Jews who'd settled there; my paternal grandfather's family is a mystery to me—I have only their names to go by, not a single story about them. My father never spoke of them at all, and my relationship with his parents was at best polite (at worst, chilly, angry, bitter). My mother thinks my father's Herman grandparents came from Russia, but she isn't sure; the family name he wrote down on the homemade family tree he created when he was in his seventies and briefly became interested in such things, is one I cannot trace: Herzikov, which was changed to Herman (but by whom, and when?).

There are so many questions I should have asked him.

One always feels this way, I imagine, when someone is gone. I feel this way too about my grandmother—my mother's mother. And I did ask questions of them both, Grandma and Dad, and they both offered up plenty of stories I hadn't thought to ask about. There's still so much I don't know.

During the last weeks of my father's life, and especially during his last days, we tried to cover it all. There was plenty of time: he wasn't sleeping, and when I was at the hospital with him I'd stay all night. We'd talk all night long. During the day, when it was easier for him to rest, to at least close his eyes for a few minutes, I would nap sometimes. But mostly we talked, all day and all night. Mostly *he* talked—that was always how it was with him. And I am a talker! But I cannot hold a candle to my father.

Four days before he died, during the last days of the period when we were telling each other things we'd never told each other before, he told me he had joined the army at eighteen only to get out of working in his father's store, that he couldn't figure out any other way to manage this. But when his stint in the army was done, when he came home and showed up at my mother's door "in his uniform and so slim, looking so handsome," and they started dating again, and soon became engaged, he was back at the store again. What else was he qualified to do?

But it was around this time that he also started taking pictures for which he was paid—not enough to live on, but something. How did this happen? I wish I had asked him that, too. My mother has no memory of when he might first have wanted to be a photographer and newspaper reporter. She remembers that he had a camera, that he was forever taking pictures (I have hundreds of pictures of her, taken by him; there are pictures of his family, too, taken when he was a teenager, perhaps even before he met my mother; and there are many, many professional-looking portraits of me from my first years). Later—but before the newspapers—he took pictures of weddings and portraits of other people's children. He won a contest at Fort Hood for a photograph he'd taken of my mother before she broke up with him, before he enlisted. The prize was a check for a dollar (the check itself is in the dating scrapbook: he never cashed it). In 1953—my parents had been married for a year by then—he took a photo that won honorable mention in a "print of the year" contest judged by the curator of photography at the Brooklyn Museum: a picture of a very small girl reaching up high into the card catalog at the Brighton Beach branch of the public library, a photograph he'd titled "Higher Education."

And somehow, eventually, he started selling pictures to the daily newspapers. He would leave the hardware store in the middle of the workday, chasing firetrucks and police cars with their sirens screaming. My grandparents, my mother remembers, were infuriated. Or we would be out somewhere as a family—or in the car, on the way to somewhere—and we would all go to the fire, to the scene of a fresh murder. "Stay in the car," he'd say, and we would, while he got out and took some pictures.

But he couldn't earn a living at this—or by writing for these newspapers either, which by then he had also begun to do. By the time I am able to remember anything clearly, he had swapped the hardware store for good for a job selling life insurance. That was what supported us from 1957 onwards—his job "in the city." I can't figure out how he kept it and still wrote so many news stories as a "stringer," took so many photographs. I remember how excited he would get, running off to cover a story. I knew the difference even then—age five, six, seven, eight—between this work and his other work, his boring job in the city, the job that paid our rent since I was two years old. The job he'd gotten—so I saw it—to take care of *me*.

Of course I have kept the scrapbook, even though I threw away so much of what he kept. I've kept everything that means something (the ankle bracelet, which with my mother's blessing I made into a necklace I wear every day; the key-chain viewers with their tiny photographic slides—my parents at The Concord and Granit hotels—locked inside them) and I've kept everything my father *made*: the manuscripts of the many books he wrote (novels, a memoir) and never published, in those years after the newspaper years; a screenplay neither my mother nor I had even known he'd written; boxes full of the two- and three-panel comic strips (the strip was called "Person") he made in the seventies with a "partner," a college kid, who drew what he asked him to, after he wrote the "stories" (such as they were). In one, the protagonist—that would be Person—is sitting on a a psychiatrist's couch, declaring that he's had it, he's done, he just wants to die (panel 1); the shrink offers a cup of tea for comfort (2), and Person takes a sip and cries out (3), "It's too hot!"

I kept copies of the digest-sized magazines, *Pageant* and *Coronet*, in which Dad published short comic pieces—both magazines to some extent low-rent versions of *Reader's Digest* (*Pageant*, the prestige item from a publisher of true confessions, tilted toward glamour photos; *Coronet*, owned by *Esquire*, ran poetry and advice along with condensed books—but both also published light, humorous essays, which my father started writing in the late sixties and early seventies). I kept an album—a much nicer album, with a soft leather cover and plastic sleeves for all the pages—filled with all the feature stories he wrote and published later, for *Pictorial Living Magazine* and *Parade* and a German magazine called *Quick*. That was a scrapbook I had known about, one that I remembered him making and that he and I had paged through together when he was in a nostalgic mood. I remembered those stories, too. One was about talent agents who represented child actors—a story I remember particularly well because I wanted to *be* one, and because I tagged along on some of the interviews, and one of the agents offered to hear me out after Dad had bragged about my talents and stage presence (and, in truth, I was a confident, not half-bad singer and actor as a child—the only arenas in which I can remember having any confidence at all) and he declined the offer (that was "no kind of life" for me, he said, and I was furious). Another story was about the wonders of airline food (the article describes Pan Am's fleet as "gourmet restaurants in the sky"). And there was a strange, I guess funny-at-the-time first-person piece about a life-sized inflatable doll dressed in a bikini: Dad brought "her" everywhere with him for a few days and took note of people's reactions. Once he was done with that, he gave the doll to me, and I loved it beyond reason. As far as I was concerned, it was a five-foot-tall Barbie, beautifully made up, with fabulous hair and a polka dot bikini. But my mother was unnerved—unhappy that he'd kept the doll for me. (As I look back, I don't blame her one bit. At the time, though, I was angry. I remember telling her that it was none of her business—I was famously a "fresh kid"; I had a "smart mouth.") I came home from school one day to find that the doll was gone.

When my father was slowly dying, it wasn't as if we had to make up for lost time or trade regrets or make amends. We'd been in harmony for many years by then. We were best friends—a team—again, the way we'd been throughout my childhood.

But as close as we were, I remember being acutely aware, that first night I was with him in the hospital, after I'd arranged for him and my mother to be air-ambulanced back to New York from Belize with what the doctors there thought was pneumonia—and after my exhausted, frightened mother had gone home to get some sleep—that this was more hours in a row alone together than we'd spent in fifty years.

For five months I traveled back and forth between Columbus and Manhattan, where my parents had lived since the late seventies (they fled Brooklyn soon after I did: I to Greenwich Village, Mom and Dad to the far Upper East Side). Some weeks, during those terrible five months, I would spend forty-eight hours in New York, then forty-eight hours in Columbus, then turn around and head right back to New York.

Every time I left the city—every time I left my father—I was anxious, filled with guilt. I couldn't bear the thought that he might die without me there beside him. "But he's not dying," my brother told me when I called one night from Columbus, telling him how sad I was, how scared. He said, "You're being so dramatic. As usual." He told me I was driving him crazy.

It was the only time we argued, the only time we were anything but gentle to each other since our father first got sick. Why was I so sure he wouldn't get better? my brother demanded. What made me think I knew more than the doctors did?

But I didn't think I knew more. What I thought, what I knew, was that the doctors were so focused on doing The Next Thing, whatever that next thing might be (anything they could think of, whether it would make him better or not—and nothing made him better, but they had to do something; they couldn't stand not doing something), they couldn't see the forest for the trees. I could see the forest. I told my brother that. It didn't help. It just made him angrier.

I didn't tell my mother. How could I tell my mother?

My father knew, though. And, some days, I caught myself thinking: *It's the same old story—my father and me together on one side; my mother and my brother on the other.*

Not enemies, by any means. Just separate. Living in two different worlds.

Dad and I talked, holding hands, he in his bed in the ICU, I in the recliner I got someone to drag into the room for me. We talked our way through the eventual diagnosis of Legionnaires' Disease and the treatment for it, and then the discovery that his lungs would not recover from the long assault of Legionnaires. We talked before and after the cardiologist's attempt to put a stent into one of his coronary arteries (not a solution to the multiple problems that had been found since his ordeal began, but something that "might help," the cardiologist told me—and then didn't answer when I said *but might help how? might help with what?*), an attempt that failed because my father's arteries, they learned when they "opened him up," were "entirely calcified—like cement." There was nothing to be done, either for his heart or for his lungs. I had to tell him that. And while I didn't know more than the doctors, I knew that it was possible to live with a good heart and bad lungs, or good lungs and a bad heart. I didn't spell that out for him, but I think he knew that too.

And we just kept talking. Hours and hours and hours of talking. When he couldn't talk—when he was on the BiPap machine that helped him breathe, but silenced him—he wrote me notes. Sometimes he scribbled furiously, filling page after page of one of his yellow legal pads. He had a lot to say. He had always had a lot to say.

We had our last real conversation four days before he died, on the Saturday morning before I made the trip up to the Bronx to look at Calvary Hospital—the only residential hospice in the city for patients with less than six months to live. (There are, I discovered, a number of small programs for people who have two or three weeks left, as testified to by their doctors, which my father's doctors wouldn't do—it had been hard enough to get them to admit at last that he had less than six months.) That morning, early, he had become convinced that this was the day of his death. It frightened my brother, Scott, who still believed he wasn't dying, that he would get better. Hadn't the doctors told us just the day before that "all the numbers" were good? But Dad told him, in a four AM phone call, that it was okay, he was at peace, he was ready to go.

My father had never been at peace, not for a moment of his life. It's possible that his saying this was what frightened my brother more than the possibility that he'd had a true premonition.

He told Scott to tell my mother and me that he loved us and that he was ready to go. He had tried to call me too at four, but—I saw this later—he had accidentally deleted the final two digits of my cell number on his phone. He would have called my mother, I'm sure, but I could see that he'd deleted his and my mother's home phone number too, and all but one digit of my mother's cell number—he'd been fighting with his phone for weeks. Scott's was the only one of us whose number was intact.

I arrived at seven—it was one of the rare nights that I hadn't stayed with him all night when I was in town; I was running out of steam and had hired an aide to sit with him on Friday night so that I could get some sleep—and he was lucid. Not as much at peace as he had claimed to be a few hours before, on the phone with Scott, but not agitated, either. I took his hand and told him that I wasn't going to argue with him or dismiss his intuition, but that my own intuition was different. "I think it's a false premonition," I said. "I don't think it's going to be today."

"Maybe you're right," he said.

Later that morning, in between fitful naps, in and out of lucidity, he pointed at the clock on the wall across from his bed and said, "They're adding a minute to every hour. I wish they wouldn't. I wish they'd take it away. I don't need an extra minute. I'm wasting it."

I promised him I'd arrange to have the minute taken away and he fell asleep again. The next time he woke up, he remembered that I was heading to the Bronx that afternoon, and he asked me the address of the hospital and what it was called. When I told him, he began to cry. "I know that place!" he said. "I lived around the corner from it. I remember it perfectly." He had me take out my notebook and write down his address—both of his addresses—in the Bronx, the apartment building his parents had been living in when he was born and the one they'd moved to when he was four years old. And then he dictated the address of my grandfather's first store. I hadn't even known there'd been another store. "That's why we moved to Brooklyn," he said. "Because he opened the new store there."

He had me write down the address of his elementary school, and then the names of his favorite teachers. There was one who had encouraged him to draw—he had loved drawing as a child. "Why did I give it up?" he wondered aloud. I asked him if he remembered teaching *me* to draw, and the drawings he had made, to demonstrate, then had me copy—a three-dimensional-looking box, a park bench, a road reaching to a vanishing point—and he did. He had me hand him a Sharpie and his yellow legal pad: he drew a box, a bench, a road. Then he drew some other things—a telephone, a table. "I used to draw airplanes all the time," he said. He turned to a fresh page and drew some airplanes now. He filled a whole legal page with airplanes.

After that—all day Sunday and half of Monday—he was fretful, scared, his thoughts confused. He'd forgotten about his premonition and the fact that he'd been wrong. He wasn't always sure where he was. He'd forgotten about hospice. He kept asking me if he was "safe" and if he was "making good progress." He was safe, I told him. He was making excellent progress.

By Monday afternoon he stopped asking me anything. He stopped talking at all.

We were going to move him to hospice on Tuesday afternoon, but by then he was too sick to move.

I'd been with him since six in the morning on Tuesday—I'd once again had an aide come to sit with him for several hours while I went to my mother's apartment and tried to sleep—and my mother had been there too since eleven. At nine PM she went home to sleep. By now she and my brother understood as well as I did—it was almost over.

I sat alone with my father then, talking to him, singing to him. I sang all his favorite songs—songs his all-time favorite singer, Al Jolson, had sung, and songs that had been hits when he and my mother were young, and the lugubrious songs by Leslie Bricusse and Anthony Newley of which he was so inexplicably fond. "Rock-a-Bye Your Baby with a Dixie Melody," "April Showers," "When the Red, Red Robin (Comes Bob, Bob, Bobbin' Along)," and "You Made Me Love You." "Time After Time," "It Had to be You," and "Taking A Chance on Love." "Who Can I Turn To (When Nobody Needs Me)?" and "What Kind of Fool Am I?"

Could he hear me? I don't know. But just in case, I sang. I talked. I retold him the stories he'd been telling me for months. I told him all the same things I'd been telling him for days, for weeks: how much I loved him, how much we all loved him, what a good job he had done raising my brother and me. How much I admired him, how proud I was of him. How generous he'd been, how much help he had been to so many people. It was all true. I told him there was nothing in his life he needed to regret, reminded him how much he'd accomplished, how much good he'd done. And I promised him that my brother and I would take care of our mother—our mother who couldn't remember life before she'd met our father. They'd known each other for sixty-seven years, since she was fourteen. I told him we'd take care of each other, too, told him he'd taught us how to do that.

And then I told him it was all right to go. I held his hand. I watched him take a breath and then not take another—watched him let go.

Through the trees. Into the forest.

I had thought it would be hard to leave him when he died, thought I'd find it terrible to walk away, to abandon him in room 906 at Lenox Hill, where I'd spent so many hours. But it wasn't hard. Even though he looked just as he had a moment before—even though he smelled the same, and his hand in mine was still warm, as was his cheek when I bent to kiss it—I felt no sentimental attachment to the body he had left behind. It was only a body. Now that he wasn't in it, it had no meaning at all. I remember trying to explain this to my mother in the days that followed. I remember thinking that I wasn't explaining it very well at all.

I tore out all the pages he wrote on, the pages he made drawings on. I took his pens, his glasses, his wallet, his phone. I put everything in my shoulder bag and walked home to the apartment, my mother's apartment now, in the dark, in the silence.

At four in the morning, the Upper East Side of Manhattan between Lenox Hill Hospital and Yorkville is deathly silent.

I was lucky, I remember thinking that night as I walked up Lex, then across 80th. There was nothing that I'd left unsaid, nothing left to wish that I could tell him. This wouldn't last forever, but that did not occur to me then—that things would happen, to me or in the world, that I would have thoughts about or that would raise questions I wanted to ask him, or that I would sometimes remember things I had not remembered while he was alive and I would want to talk to him about them.

Still, I *was* lucky. We both were. How many people get to feel this way? I asked myself. I might have asked it angrily—honestly, I'm not sure. It seems an angry thought when I remember it. *Not many*, I said to myself.

I kept repeating it as I went up in the elevator, let myself into the apartment, undressed, climbed into my parents' bed beside my mother, who only half woke up. *How many people get to feel this way? Not many.*

It's over, I told my mother. He's gone.

Gone? He's gone? she said. She wasn't awake, I knew that. I knew she had taken an Ativan when she got home—it was the only way she could sleep at all during those months. Still, she sounded as if she had no idea what I was talking about. Maybe I was angry, after all.

What do you mean gone? *Who's gone? Nobody's gone.*

She didn't say this. It was only what I thought.

All the newspapers my father worked for shut down for good in late 1963, after the Great Newspaper Strike of that year. I remember the strike, how worried he was. I remember when the newspapers shut down, one after another. When *The Mirror* shut down in October and my father cried. I was eight—I'd never seen him cry before. But after that he wrote for other papers—the *New York Journal-American* and the *New York Knickerbocker* and others that remained, on their last rickety legs, or that bravely started up (or that multiple collapsed newspapers merged into). And then, by 1969, when I was fourteen, all of them were gone, too. Every newspaper he'd ever sold a story or a picture to was gone.

And I was gone too, sort of. I had been his best friend, and he mine. I was his sidekick. He took me with him when he went out on assignment: I rode in a police helicopter (it had no doors!); I accompanied him as he covered one of the glamorous Mayor Lindsay's famous neighborhood walks. (I was eleven. The mayor bought me a Charlotte Russe, my favorite pastry—a thin layer of sponge cake topped by a tall mound of whipped cream and a maraschino cherry, packed in a cardboard push-up cup.) At home, I would sit and watch him shave while we talked. He taught me to draw—taught me about shading and perspective. And then overnight I turned into a teenager and had no use for him.

I have always assumed that the period of estrangement between us—which lasted for years, well into my twenties—was the result of my miserable adolescence and his inability to handle it. Certainly he was baffled about how to relate to me once I no longer hung on his every word, once I turned angry and sad. I alternated between disdaining and ignoring him. He disdained and ignored me right back, and he sulked, too, as if he were the child. I know he felt rejected—I knew it even then. But I think now that the loss of his life in newspapers must have been part of his anger and sadness then. That my being lost to him too was more than he could bear. He'd lost—he must have felt he'd lost—the two parts of his life he loved most.

My father was in his early thirties—less than half the age I am now—when he put together that scrapbook of his newspaper clippings. He was just short of his eighty-fourth birthday when he filled those legal pads with the pages of writing and drawings I keep in a file folder in a desk drawer in my study. I take them out sometimes and look at them, and I'm amazed that I was able to make sense of what he wrote at the time. Now I can read only some of the pages—the questions he asked (*Is Scott up to speed on what's happening?* or *What time is Mom coming today?*) and the complaints about one of the nurses, the only one who wasn't kind, and the demands for ice chips or the sudden longing for some particular thing to eat or drink, which he would have lost his taste for by the time I fetched it. On the pages he filled later—with thoughts he wanted to communicate, ideas he'd had while lying in that bed for so long, stories he had just remembered and wanted to be sure he told me before it was too late (oh, and his dreams! On the rare occasions that he slept, he had terrible, complicated dreams, and he'd wake up wanting to tell them to me right away, and if he couldn't speak he'd gesture impatiently for his legal pad and pen and write them down)—I can now read only groups of words, a sentence here and there. And yet at the time I know I understood it all. His handwriting had deteriorated as the months went by, but I suppose because it happened slowly, from one day to the next it didn't seem so different, and I had no trouble deciphering it then.

I didn't read the clippings when I found the scrapbook right after his death. But unlike the fancier album filled with the feature and humor stories he wrote later, the book-length manuscripts, the screenplay, the boxes of "Person" comic strips—all of which I left with my mother in New York—I took the scrapbook home with me when finally I felt I could go home, when I'd wrestled her apartment into shape. I'd hauled out twenty giant-sized trash bags full of recycling; I'd filled a huge cardboard box with papers to be shredded; I'd disposed of broken things, unrecognizable things, thousands of dried-out rubber bands. I had culled the books and given away clothes and office furniture and rearranged the things I deemed worth saving. It had taken weeks.

After that, I came back to the city every few weeks to check on my mother. I did this for years, first at two-week intervals and then at four, and then at eight. For so long, her full-time job had been taking care of my father. I was afraid that being forced into "retirement" would be the death of her—that she would not know what to do with herself. That fear eased as time passed, as it emerged that she was more resilient than I had imagined. I had just decided it was time to stretch the visits out—my mother was doing fine; she had figured out how to live her life without my father, filling it with friends with whom she sat and worked crossword puzzles in front of the Starbucks that had opened right across the street, and yoga-for-seniors classes and books and TV and Broadway plays and concerts—and so in November 2019 I returned to Columbus with a plan to stay put this time until March. It was to be the longest stretch of time I'd stayed away since December 2013, when Dad first got sick.

Days before the flight I'd booked for March, the world shut down. It was over a year and a half before I saw my mother again. And it was not until the seventh anniversary of the day my father died that I took his scrapbook from the shelf in my study where I keep it and sat down to read all that was in it, to look at all the newsprint photographs, to consider fully what my father's working life was like back then. What *he* was like. What he was thinking, what he was doing, in 1962 and 1963.

There's an editorial from the *Brooklyn Daily*, published on December 12, 1962, arguing for the abolition of the death penalty (it ends with the line, "Only then can we look at ourselves in the mirror of life and be pleased"). A news story about the looting of hundreds of thousands of dollars' worth of fluorescent light bulbs belonging to the City of New York—the word "fluorescent" spelled wrong every place that it appears, with the "u" and "o" transposed. (Was my dad, who'd never cared much about spelling, expected to do his own copyediting, his own proofreading? I remember him assuring me, when I was aggrieved because I'd gotten a word wrong on a weekly spelling test*—despite being a good speller myself—"Forget about it, that's what editors are for"). There are lots of news stories about CORE and the NAACP, about sit-ins and other peaceful demonstrations, picketing at schools and restaurants, the Board of Education, City Hall. There are human interest stories about heroic rescues, often by civilians, and many stories about cops who went beyond the call of duty—and, reading these, I remember something I had not thought of in decades: that my father hung around with the policemen he met while on that beat—Irish-Catholic Brooklyn cops with six or seven kids—and that I was sometimes taken to their houses for aboveground swimming pool dates or picnics or barbecues, and that this was a big deal for me because we lived in a third-floor apartment on a busy street, with a chain-link fenced-in concrete "play area." The very concept of a backyard was foreign to me.

---

* I remember the word, too—that it was "cigarette," which I had spelled with two *r*'s as well as two *t*'s. It seems extraordinary now that this was a spelling word in elementary school, even in the early sixties.

And a feature story, from February 1963, about a new phenomenon—hair styling for men—makes me remember something, someone, else. Dominic Zuccaro, a "Paris-trained entrepreneur," had just opened the Look-Well salon for men, in which, my dad reports, he used a straight razor instead of "the expected scissors and clippers" to cut his clients' hair, then wrapped it in a hairnet ("much the way my wife's beautician does hers") before sending them to sit under a hair dryer, after which he spritzed them with hair spray. I remember Mr. Dominic, who after that story cut my father's hair, whenever he needed a haircut, until the late seventies, when my parents left Brooklyn for Manhattan.

The eleven years that have passed since the day my father died amount to nothing, really, in the scheme of things: the seventy years I have been alive, the ninety-five since he was born.

The seventy-eight years since the day he met my mother, on his seventeenth birthday, when he smiled at her in the luncheonette on Brighton 5th Street and she smiled back, assuming that she knew him.

The more than sixty years after the last clipping in the scrapbook appeared in the *Daily Mirror*.

I read all the clippings, holding them carefully with two hands—they are so fragile, pieces of the newsprint still break free, and when I turn the scrapbook's pages yellow crumbs fall from them, littering the floor where I sit, scrapbook on my lap.

At one time all the clippings must have been glued down. Now they've all come unattached—hundreds of them, loose, tucked between the brittle yellow pages. And the pages, tied together with a braid of yarn that loops through the cover—every one of them is empty.

Like an Egg

"Would you slice these?" Grace asks, handing me an onion, a green pepper, a cutting board, a knife. "*Thinly*," she adds. She knows my slicing style (with abandon, in a hurry, resulting in many-sized bits and pieces, none resembling slices, that range from pretty big to very, very big). "And chop the garlic and the ginger finely?"

I don't mind the implicit criticism. Actually, it delights me. It was I who taught her to cook: I had her standing on a stepladder beside me in the kitchen—measuring and pouring, stirring, improvising, tasting, even cutting vegetables with her own special knife—from the time she was a toddler; I encouraged her to cook on her own as soon as she was old enough to be trusted at the stove. And of course she's now a better cook than I am. That's how it's supposed to be.

She's also more precise and patient when it comes to cooking. (All of my precision and my patience are used up in writing and ballet.) And she's more ambitious. Any recipe requiring more than five steps gives me pause; my daughter, on the other hand, doesn't think twice about making her own cashew cream, peeling the skin off chickpeas, crisping, smashing, caramelizing, browning, and deglazing, using every bowl and cutting board and pan and baking dish she owns.

She preps her lunches for the week ahead each Sunday. The work she does now is particularly difficult and draining, and having a nice meal at midday is a small, soothing pleasure that gives her a second wind. So these days when I visit her in her apartment, any Sunday that I'm in New York, I offer myself up as her prep cook. For her, I'll slice an onion carefully, chop a tomato into tiny cubes—I'll do anything she asks.

Watching her measure, pour, stir, whip, blend, layer—shake a pan over a flame, eye the flame as she adjusts it—I think about the way she'd studied for exams throughout her teens, writing everything (math theorems, chemical reactions, Spanish and Latin vocab, names and dates and places) on index cards I bought her by the thousand-pack at her request, then use them to drill herself for hours. Sometimes she'd ask me to help, to hold the stack of index cards and flip through them quickly, reading her what she had written on one side, checking her answer on the other, making new stacks—*down cold, hesitated, wrong*—until the *down cold* stack had all the cards in it.

I was always happy—grateful!—when she asked for my help. Just as I am now. She asks for it so rarely.

My mother did not teach me to cook. She couldn't have, because *she* didn't cook, not really. I grew up on Chef Boyardee ravioli, Swanson TV dinners, instant mashed potatoes mixed with Seabrook Farms creamed spinach. Canned string beans and peas and iceberg lettuce with "homemade Russian dressing" (ketchup mixed with mayo). If we had spaghetti, we had it with ketchup.

There were a couple of dinners my mother kept in rotation that were throwbacks to her own childhood: real food, but only the kind of meals that required very little in the way of cooking (buttered noodles in hot salted milk) or else none at all ("pot" cheese with radishes and scallions mixed in). My grandmother cooked, but she hadn't taught my mother how. She had shooed her out of the kitchen to do her homework or practice the piano—way ahead of her time, I suppose, wanting her youngest child, her only daughter, to "be busy with more important things"—and it never crossed my mother's mind to teach *herself* to cook, not even after she had children.

There wasn't a single cookbook in our apartment. I had to borrow one—*Betty Crocker's Cookbook*—from a friend of my mother's when I was fifteen and the boy I liked mentioned homemade cookies in a way that made me think I might win his heart if I baked some.

To me, that *Betty Crocker* was a book of magic spells.

Not that I cooked anything from it other than chocolate chip cookies. Still, I read it, cover to cover. I read about cakes and pot roast and molded jello salads and omelets and stews. I was no more tempted to try any of the recipes (this was book food, not real-life food, as I saw it) than I was to try out the adventures undertaken by the fictional characters in the novels I was so enamored of. Still, I treasured it. And so I never spoke of it again to my mother's friend, hoping she'd forget she'd ever let me borrow it.

I still have it, too, tucked among the many other cookbooks I've accumulated since.

My grandmother never used a cookbook. Nor did she consult, as I do, a card file box full of scribbled-down recipes and recipes clipped from newspapers or magazines or peeled off cans of mashed cooked pumpkin or evaporated milk. She didn't write things down (she could barely write, either in her first language, Yiddish, or her second); she didn't buy cans of anything.

Grandma roasted chickens and made brisket and tzimmes (sweet potatoes, prunes, carrots) and lokshen kugel (noodle pudding) and stuffed cabbage and helzel (the stuffed skin of a chicken neck) and borscht and chicken soup with kneidlach; she baked challah and sponge cakes and honey cakes and soft, fat, chewy cookies that were nothing like the cookies *Betty Crocker* had taught me to make.

Grandma made her own mustard, her own pickles. I didn't wonder how she knew what to do (I thought she was born knowing). But because I ate so many meals with her, it was not as if I didn't know *about* cooking, not as if I'd never tasted homemade food. I knew that cookbooks existed and I knew that natural cooks existed—I had proof of both by the time I was a teenager—but neither seemed to me a part of ordinary life. Or, anyway, of my ordinary life, in which

Salisbury steak with the little plastic pocket of hot brownie were regular features.

Except for those chocolate chip cookies (which I made frequently; I became known for them among my friends in high school), I never cooked anything—I never even made a salad—until I moved out of my parents' apartment and into one of my own. Grown up now, and walking to the supermarket on Sheridan Square, where I did my own grocery shopping for the first time in my life, I had to start thinking about what I *wanted* to eat. And how I was going to make that happen.

I didn't want to buy frozen dinners (just thinking of them made me feel like a child again). So I bought canned soup—the "fancy" kind, not Campbell's where you had to add a canful of water—and I bought cans of beans. I bought Minute Rice and jars of dried spices. I bought boxes of pasta and jars of sauce. I experimented, tentatively, with fresh vegetables. I remember a friend watching me cut up broccoli to put in a pot with a little water—my plan was to cook it exactly as I would have cooked the frozen variety, which came with directions—and asking me why I was putting the broccoli *leaves* in the pot. "You're supposed to throw those out," Susan told me. "You're not supposed to eat them." And I said, "Yes, you are. The leaves are included when you buy it frozen." She rolled her eyes. "Just because the company that makes frozen broccoli leaves the leaves in doesn't mean you have to."

It was the first piece of information I can remember ever getting about making food for myself.

I visited a high school friend in his apartment and watched, fascinated, as he made dinner for the two of us. He wasn't even concentrating—he was acting the way my grandmother had when she rolled out the dough for kreplach, pinching it closed around a spoonful of meat and onions, talking to me all the while. My friend Marty cut up an eggplant (I'd never seen one whole before and had to ask him what it was), chopped onions and celery, broke bunches of florets off a stalk of broccoli, and tossed them all into a pan in which olive oil and garlic were sizzling. He added a can of whole tomatoes, which he broke roughly into pieces with a wooden spoon, as casually as if he did this every night (he must have done something like this every night). He stirred; we chatted. Then he pronounced the mixture done, and I wanted to ask how he could tell but instead only watched as he spooned it into two plates, tucked a bright green can of ground Parmesan under his arm, and led me to the table, where we ate the meal that I would make myself, in strict imitation, almost every time I made a meal at all for the next year.

And so I began to cook—by imitation and from memory. Each time I cooked, it felt like an occasion: all that chopping and sautéing and attentive stirring. I branched out, little by little (sautéing vegetables in olive oil and *not* adding tomatoes, not using cheese, but mixing the cooked vegetables with Minute Rice—or else making exactly what Marty had made but adding cooked pasta to the mixture and feeling like a genius).

One night, I had the idea that I might try to reproduce something my grandmother had made. Not the helzel or the chicken feet, but maybe chicken soup. Maybe even kneidlach.

I called my grandmother, who was suspicious. "Don't you have things to do?" she asked me. I told her I did. "But I want to do this, too."

What she offered up, once I persuaded her, were "recipes" in which the directions were "add just enough water" or "keep the flame low until it's done"—and when I asked how much water was "just enough" water, she'd think about it for a minute and say, "About like an egg," and when I asked how I'd know it was done, she'd say, "Ach, you'll just know."

I didn't know. I had to guess, and often I guessed wrong. To figure out how much water was "like an egg," I carefully cracked one open, poured it out (into a bowl! I'd learned enough from Grandma to know not to waste it—I made a scrambled egg for myself), and filled both halves with water, then measured the water in my brand-new measuring cup.

I tried this and that. I'd roast a starved-looking little chicken. I'd make a pot of soup, scooping out and discarding "the eyes" of fat that pooled on top, just as my grandmother had told me to, and leaving the carrots whole until they were so soft they broke apart with a wooden spoon. I started inviting one person at a time for dinner. I invited my own brother, who still lived with our parents, and it was over the dinners I made for him that we first became friends.

Becoming a *good* home cook took longer. It's possible I had to be farther away from Brooklyn than a subway ride to fully distance myself from my ignorance about food and how to prepare it, to get over my fear of doing it all wrong, to shake off my timidity about experimenting with it.

In Iowa City in 1984, the restaurant options were minimal and mostly bad. A little group of us had landed there, for grad school, from both coasts and Chicago. If we wanted to eat well, my new friend Marly said, we had no choice but to cook for each other.

We started taking turns during our very first week, even before classes started.

I was very anxious. Everyone was more confident in the kitchen than I was. But there was a lot of recipe-swapping, and a lot of conversation about what we were fixing on *our nights*.

Mostly what we cooked was pasta and one kind of sauce or another, and the sauces Marly, Lynda, Joyce, and Debra made were on the order of "heat a jar of spaghetti sauce and add a quarter cup of heavy cream to it, and drop two handfuls of fresh spinach leaves into the boiling pasta water a minute before the pasta is done." But Debra also had a simple, no-fail recipe for whole wheat bread; if she paired it with an interesting salad, it was a meal too. Marly made what she called deconstructed potstickers: ground pork, garlic, and ginger cooked in sesame oil and spooned over a bowl of noodles doused with soy sauce, chili oil, and rice vinegar. I asked her how she'd learned how to do that and she shrugged. "It's just all the flavors in actual potstickers and their dipping sauce, you know?"

I hadn't known, but now I was emboldened too.

I discovered that people liked each other more and got to know each other faster when they sat together at a table eating a meal one of them had cooked. In my first six months at the Iowa Writers' Workshop, I learned as much, and maybe more, about food and preparing it for others—and eating it with others—as I did about writing.

And then I fell in love with Isaac. He was delighted when I cooked for him, and he enjoyed cooking for me. He taught me how to make the things he knew how to cook best, the Cuban dishes his mother had taught him how to make. Suddenly I had a repertoire. And when he graduated from med school and moved to Omaha to take care of his younger siblings while he was in his residency, I visited on weekends and cooked for them all. I *wanted* to cook for his family—I wanted to cook for him.

After I graduated, I moved to Nebraska too. I bought half a dozen cookbooks and I *studied* them. From Marcella Hazan, I learned how to make much better pasta sauces than I'd made in graduate school, and how to roast a duck so that it wasn't greasy. I found a "Jewish" cookbook and, in long distance consultation with Grandma, adjusted the recipes so that I was able to reproduce almost precisely the meals she'd made in my childhood. From *The Silver Palate Cookbook* I learned how to make pie crust and muffins, the sort of baked goods (goyishe) my grandmother had never made. I learned to make jambalaya, curry, Hungarian goulash, roast duck.

Isaac's youngest sister, thirteen and motherless, began to spend a night or two each week at my little rented house, and I'd cook meals just for the two of us that I thought were appropriate—ideas about "family meals" I'd gleaned from novels and movies: meatloaf with mashed potatoes and green beans, lasagna, homemade (which I'd never even tasted before!) macaroni and cheese, pot roast. For Isaac, on the nights he came to dinner on the way home from the hospital before returning to his house full of teenagers, I made risotto—or duck. Some nights I'd go over to his house and cook for everyone. I made Thanksgiving and Christmas dinners; I cooked for ten, twelve, sixteen people (the children had boyfriends and girlfriends; my own family would sometimes fly out to visit). I made Cuban roast pork; I made the black beans he'd taught me to make, with a few tweaks of my own that I kept to myself (but I dropped in a handful of green olives, just as I'd been told their mother had done, to surprise and delight them when they'd find one hidden in their beans).

By the time I had a family of my own, I was so comfortable in the kitchen and had so many recipes stored away in my mind, it was hard for me to believe that there had ever been a time when I had not known how to cook. When Grace grew up and went away to college, I typed out all her favorite childhood recipes. I had to guess at the amounts: like my grandmother, I had become the sort of cook who never measured anything, but I wanted to spare her the pouring of water into an eggshell. Still: "How will I know when it's done?" she asked me once over the phone, the first time she made my vegetarian chili in the house she shared with her friends, and I couldn't help it, I said, "You'll just know."

The way I cooked for my family was a mixture of what my grandmother fed me, what I made for myself during those early years of cooking, what I learned from all my friends in grad school, what I learned during the Nebraska years, what I learned from cookbooks, and what I figured out myself. When Grace comes home for a visit, I ask her what she misses most and then I make it. She says, "It doesn't taste the same when I make it myself." It's not supposed to, I want to tell her, but I don't.

She cooks for me, too. She cooks on her visits home and when I stay for dinner at her place. She makes things I've never even thought of making—Japanese food, for example—and she's invented plenty of her own recipes. She doesn't write them down. If I asked her for them, she'd have to explain them the way my grandmother did—my grandmother whom she never knew, who died not long after her birth. If I asked how much soy sauce, how much fish sauce, how much mirin, she would say "I don't know. However much seems like enough."

My husband lived on microwaved "baked" potatoes and melted cheese before we met. He used to pause and give thanks after his first bite of whatever I had made for dinner. He liked to say—it was a family joke he started himself, when Grace was small—"Why, this is better than the finest French food in Topeka, Kansas" or "better than you could get at the best Italian restaurant in Gatlinburg, Tennessee."

Once, he gave me a cooking challenge. In those years, he was exclusively painting still lifes inspired by the great Dutch and Spanish still life painters of the seventeenth century, and the late eighteenth- and early nineteenth-century American, Raphaelle Peale, widely considered to be the first American (professional) still life painter. Glen was working on a series of homage paintings, all of which referred to artists he believed had helped to make him who he was. There was an homage to the Spanish still life painter Juan van der Hamen y (Gómez de) León and one to the nineteenth-century American trompe-l'œil painter John Frederick Peto … and one to Jimi Hendrix, one to the Ramones. He made a full solo show's worth of such paintings, and he wanted to make one "for Raphaelle" and had it in his head that he needed a cake precisely like the one in Peale's 1818 "Still Life with Cake" and many of his other still lifes (it was always the same cake, painting to painting). Because Glen painted only from life then, he asked if I could recreate the cake.

It was a fun (and taxing—which is the way I tend to like my fun) project for me. It took four tries. One looked almost right from the outside but, once cut, crumbled to dust; one was much too brown, and one too flat; but then I got it. I baked a cake that looked like Peale's both on the outside and the inside—Peale often painted pieces of the cake—and although I don't know if it tasted anything like the nineteenth-century original (even if I'd tasted it, I mean, because I didn't; it had raisins in it, one of the few foods I will not eat*), it looked perfect. (Glen and Grace tasted a piece of it. They thought it tasted all right.) This felt like the pinnacle of my cooking career.

But it was not the first time I'd created a cake based on a work of art. I had done this for Grace when she was very young. For years, when we read a book together, when any food was described, she would want to eat it. We would pause in our reading and have whatever we'd just read about: some cheese and crackers, porridge (it was easy to persuade her to settle for Cream of Wheat), a plum, a particular kind of sandwich. We'd make mashed potatoes or stew—indeed,

---

* The entire list is made up of what I always refer to as "rendered fruit": dried fruit, jams and jellies and preserves, fruit pies, fruit-flavored ice cream.

my stew recipe derives from a reference, in some now-forgotten book, to "a thin stew," which (oddly enough) sounded appealing to her. But the cake I am thinking of, which I still make from time to time, as it is delicious, was inspired by the first book in the *Betsy-Tacy* series by Maud Hart Lovelace. It was one of Grace's favorite books, as it was one of mine in my own childhood. We had read that first book, *Betsy-Tacy*, many times by then (as we'd read all four of the first books in the series, the ones that take the best friends through the age of twelve), but this time, when the little girls are given pieces of "plain, unfrosted cake" to take to the bench where they like to sit together after dinner and talk, Grace was struck by how exceptionally delicious this sounded. She was five or six; it was the year I had been told by our pediatrician to increase the fiber in her diet—the year I would send her to school with a lunchbox full of hearts of palm, which she loved, and which I figured had to be full of fiber (how could it not if it came from the inner core of trees?); the year I switched to whole grain everything and stirred Metamucil into orange juice. In a stroke of genius, I suggested we invent a plain unfrosted cake recipe—and we put down the book and went to the kitchen. I brought the bag of whole wheat flour to the table. "We'll make a pound cake," I said. "One so amazing tasting it won't need frosting."

And we did: a sweet, rich, whole-wheat pound cake. For years after, we'd make it together and she'd take a giant piece of it to school for lunch. I felt all right about it. It was full of eggs and nonfat milk—plenty of protein, after all—and it was full of fiber.

Unlike what Grace and I named "Healthy Pound Cake" (it wasn't—it isn't; it calls for an unholy amount of butter and sugar), I didn't save a copy of the recipe for Raphaelle Peale's frosted cake with raisins. By the time I managed to make something that looked right, I had made so many changes to my original recipe—one I'd pieced together by incorporating various ideas about early nineteenth century baking that I had found online—I would not begin to know how to recreate it. That's fine with me. It was a cake meant to be gazed at, not to be eaten. Now it can be gazed at forever.

When I leave town, when I leave Glen alone at home, I cook for him before I go. I make a meatloaf or a big pot of jambalaya or black beans; I make chicken soup; I broil steaks and hamburgers and stack them, one for each evening. If I'm going to be gone long, I make several different things, so he won't get bored. I steam vegetables and leave them in containers. I know he won't cook anything for himself. Even if he knew how, he wouldn't bother. He wouldn't even bother to heat up a frozen dinner. He'd wander in from the studio and eat a handful of chips or crackers, peanut butter, cereal, fruit, yogurt. He might not even notice. But I cannot bear the thought of it.

When my father was sick, I was away more than I was at home. For a while it seemed that all I was doing was cooking, flying, sitting at my father's bedside. It wasn't true. I was teaching that semester. Most weeks I spent four days in New York and three days in Columbus. As soon as I was finished with my second three-hour class, every Thursday afternoon, Glen picked me up and drove me to the airport. While I waited for my flight, I read and made comments on my students' manuscripts. Then I got on the plane and read and marked them up some more. At LaGuardia, I'd get a cab and go straight to the hospital.

After the first few months of this, I stopped cooking for Glen during the three days I was at home each week. He didn't mind—he never even mentioned it. *I* minded. I hated leaving him to chips and cereal and peanut butter. But I was too tired and sad to do anything about it.

There was a period, between stays in the ICU at Lenox Hill and so-called rehab at the Mary Manning Walsh nursing home, when my father was at home. He wasn't really well enough to be there, but the rehab stay after his first hospital release had made him worse: it was only hours after he was finally released from Mary Manning Walsh, at home for the first time in months, that he had to be rushed back to the hospital. He'd had a heart attack.

When he was released from Lenox Hill the second time, it was with strict instructions for my mother and me: to put enough weight back on him to strengthen him for the surgery that was supposed to counterbalance the losses to his lungs by strengthening the way his heart worked. My father, who had been overweight his entire life, who had been dieting as long as he could remember, was painfully thin. He weighed forty pounds less than I did. He weighed less than my tiny mother.

My mother called restaurants and ordered in the most tempting foods she could think of (baked ziti, bread pudding, bagels with cream cheese and belly lox). Or my father would suggest something—a pastrami sandwich, soup with noodles *and* dumplings—and she'd order it. Whatever it was, he couldn't eat it. So they'd try something else, and something else again, to no avail.

But he'd eat what *I* cooked. I flew back and forth, just as I had when he was in the hospital and in rehab at the nursing home. In my parents' kitchen, I whipped butter and heavy cream into an egg and two egg yolks and scrambled them in a thick pat of butter, and he ate them. I made junket, which we hadn't had since I was a child (I hadn't even thought of it in fifty years, but I remembered suddenly how much he had loved it; I had too): it was very fattening and also made him nostalgic. I made tapioca pudding—another favorite of both his and mine—and I made smoothies out of whole milk and whole yogurt, protein powder, mangos, and bananas. I tucked portions of whatever I had made for him into the refrigerator and the freezer for when I wasn't there.

It worked: he gained a lot of weight in a short time. But it didn't matter—it didn't help. S'vet gornisht helfen, my grandmother would have said.

Still, how determined I was! Even when he was back in the hospital, even when a feeding tube had been inserted, even when he was subsisting on Ensure, I kept trying to feed him. He had struggled to lose weight his entire life. Now all the foods he had deprived himself of were being urged on him, but he had no appetite. I'd bring morsels—a bite of this, a bite of that—of foods he had once loved, foods that had been forbidden to him for years: beef tongue, helzel, every kind of pudding. I racked my brain for foods he had spoken of with longing in the past and all at once recalled the story of the treat made for him by his mother, who hadn't been much of a cook and had been so disinclined to treats—to kindness of any sort or size—it had made a deep impression on him. The treat, I knew, involved graham crackers and applesauce. He might even have offered to make it for me in my childhood. (I would have refused: I disliked applesauce as much as I disliked raisins. Besides, I was accustomed to my father's love—I didn't need a treat to prove it.)

I remembered what he'd told me about how his mother's treat was made. I couldn't use her method, in which the layers of graham crackers spread with applesauce were slid into the tray beneath the freezer—the tray that was there to collect drips as ice melted. (This resulted in a treat that was less than frozen but more than refrigerated, which he'd insisted was its essence.) Trays like that no longer existed.

I compromised, arranging graham crackers and applesauce on a baking sheet, freezing it for half an hour, then downshifting to the refrigerator. I rushed to the hospital with it once I thought the consistency was right.

My father was glad to see the not-quite-faithful recreation. He ate a bite or two. He pronounced it imperfect but delicious. He explained about the freezer tray.

He did not seem in the least surprised that I had made this for him in the first place.

Everything about this anecdote, I realize, is useful to describe my relationship with my father.

I visit my mother every eight or ten weeks now. At ninety-one, she still lives in the apartment she lived in with my father for thirty-six years—the final thirty-six years of their sixty-two-year marriage. I cook for her before I leave. I make the kasha varnishkes my grandmother used to make or a pot of minestrone soup, or the soup I have invented that tastes so much like my grandmother's stuffed cabbage that the first time I tasted a spoonful of it, it made me cry. Whatever I make for my mother, it's something she can eat for a good week or ten days after I have gone. It's the only thing I can think of to do, to take care of her when I'm not there. I always have the sense that there is—that there must be—something else. But I cannot imagine what that is.

Sea-Change

When she was two and a half, and I was on sabbatical from teaching—and from Ohio, where we lived, where I felt I was in exile—I took my daughter to a children's production of "A Midsummer Night's Dream." We were living in New York City then, just for that year: the place I still thought of as my real home—or, as I taught my child to say, her "ancestral home." It was the sort of phrase we'd pull out to dazzle people with the wit and wisdom of my tiny daughter. (Yes, I know how obnoxious that is. Somehow I did not know it then.) Grace was small for her age, too, so people were especially amazed—shocked—when she said the things she said. It seemed to me that both of us enjoyed this. It is entirely possible that this attention was what started her on a path toward her first career, in theater, even before she saw her first play.

That year of my sabbatical, we were bartering my husband's skills in exchange for a rent-free apartment that needed remodeling in Brooklyn Heights. Mornings, while I wrote, Grace and her father made drawings and paintings together or built complicated block structures in the living room of our construction-zone apartment. In the afternoon, after I'd rejoined the two of them for lunch, sometimes all three of us ventured out together to a museum or one of the many playgrounds of Central Park before Glen headed for the studio that was his for the year in Tribeca; sometimes Grace and I would have our own adventures in the city and he would go straight to work. Either way, eventually she and I would return to the apartment—Glen rarely came home before midnight—and play let's pretend for hours before bedtime. *Let's be orphans,* she would say. Or, *let's be sisters who are teenagers.* Or, *I'm the bunny and you're the girl who finds the bunny in the woods.*

Let's be best friends. Let's be farmers and it's time to pick the vegetables and take them to market. Let's play I'm the mama, you're the baby.

We were characters from her favorite books, the ones I read to her at bedtime—the friends-for-life Betsy and Tacy from the series both of us loved most, or two sisters from *The Five Little Peppers and How They Grew* or *All-of-A-Kind Family*. We were enchanted creatures in a forest. We were lost at sea.

❧

It's been twenty-nine years since my New York sabbatical. I have lived in Ohio for longer than I lived in New York City, even when I take into account that bonus year, years later. I left when I was twenty-nine, intending to return after I had finished grad school. Instead, I moved farther west for two years, to Nebraska, then turned and headed east, but only as far as Ohio, where I found a job and finally gave up subletting my sublet in the city (*the city* was what I called Manhattan growing up, and it's what I can't help calling it still—just *the city,* as if there weren't any other).

I'm in my thirty-seventh year in Ohio. The first three decades of my life seem so much longer in my memory than these last three and a half, in Columbus. The years of my daughter's childhood, for instance, seem to have flashed by. The years of my own childhood took forever.

This is a not uncommon way of processing one's memories, I know. But that doesn't make it any less astonishing to me. Just as the knowledge that everyone is surprised by their own aging doesn't make my own more palatable. My grandmother, with whom I was perhaps closer than anyone until my daughter came along, used to say, "Inside I feel the same. And no one knows! No one can tell I'm just the same." She wanted to make sure *I* knew that she was the same person she'd been in the stories she told me—stories of when she was a little girl, in the shtetl not far from *Białystok*, playing at her great-grandmother Ruchel's feet while she sold bagels in the market, and about the long, hard trip she'd made alone from Poland in 1913, when she was fifteen. Of her life on the Lower East Side of New York, living on Essex Street with her older sister and those of her brothers who had made the trip before her, and about my grandfather, who'd won her heart with the gift of a bracelet engraved with her initials. What it had been like to be the harried young mother of four in the same small one-bedroom apartment we were sitting in as she told me these stories.

I was sixteen, eighteen, twenty, but I thought I understood what she was saying, what she felt. It seemed to me I could project myself into my future. *Yes*, I thought. *I'm going to feel the same way.*

And I do. I look in the mirror and see the sixty-nine-year-old version of me, and, just like my grandmother, inside "I feel the same." I never thought to ask my grandmother how old she felt. My own true self seems to be in her early forties, when Grace was very young. Those miserable teens and twenties, those fraught thirties, are far behind the permanent me, the one who has found herself.

That this self lives in Ohio seemed for a long time like a cosmic joke. But I've made peace with it at last. I have even been enjoying it.

One reason for this, no doubt, is that the time to leave is near, or near-ish. It was my job that kept me in Columbus for the first thirty or so years despite my multiple complaints about it (all of which boiled down to one great overarching complaint: that Columbus had too many of the disadvantages of a real city without the many advantages—a complaint that neatly covered such matters as traffic, bad air, parking, noise, and crime, as well as the absence of good public transportation, theater, galleries, museums, and, I used to claim, interesting people).

But now I am retired from teaching, and at some point in the next few years, I'll leave Columbus. Where I'll go depends entirely on Grace. Which is ironic, I suppose. Free for the first time in my life to choose where I want to live, I cede the choice to my daughter. Because I want to be the sort of grandmother to her children, when she has them, that mine was to me.

It's almost certain that Grace and her family will be in, or near, *the city*. It's where she has lived for years now—the place she set her course for as soon as she was able. That's my doing, I know: I taught her that New York was home, our real home. Now she can't imagine wanting to live anywhere else. She calls Columbus "the place where my parents live."

◆

Five years ago:

It is after midnight when I finally take a break from dancing at my sixty-fourth birthday party to sit for just a minute on the couch beside my husband, who doesn't dance—who has never danced. Glen is a Southern Baptist preacher's son, an introvert, paralyzingly self-conscious in social situations (so I do my best not to put him in them very often—but this is a special occasion: my will-you-still-need-me/will-you-still-feed-me birthday). Me, I'm a Brooklyn-born Jew, an extrovert who craves connection to other people, who hasn't a self-conscious bone in her body. We're an odd couple who get along the way only people who are completely mismatched can. Which is to say: we let each other be, and be who we are, even when we're mystified by the form that being takes. Like now.

Are you having fun? he asks. The answer is obvious. I am surrounded by people I love. We are dancing to a mix of Beyoncé and the Isley Brothers and Prince and Talking Heads and Celia Cruz and I'd asked my friends to please bring food and needs, so there is plenty of wonderful food, sweet rice cakes and crispy tofu and macaroni and cheese and cookies and pâté and bread (they have mostly neglected to bring needs). I shrug and smile. I know what he really means is: Can you explain why is this fun?

I can't answer that—that would be a matter of explaining why I am who I am. We've both tried over the many years of our marriage, lots of times, to explain ourselves to each other. It's possible that we've gotten along as well as we have *because* this question is still interesting to both of us and also because it's unanswerable. And I'd give it another shot right now, but the next song on my party playlist has come on, and it's Celia Cruz's "La Vida Es Un Carnaval," one of my favorites, so I'm up on my feet again even as Glen is saying, *But you didn't even know any of these people a year ago.*

He's exaggerating—it's been more like a year and a half—but I know what he means by this, too. My life has changed completely over the last year and a half. The party is full of people I've met in the ballet classes I take every day.

And this is the other reason I am at peace with—that I have found joy in—my life in Columbus after all these years. I have fallen in with a crowd of other late-to-ballet dancers, lifelong dancers, dancers who take only classes other than ballet. Eighteen of these new friends are the other serious amateur dancers who are going to be onstage with me in a few weeks in an experimental dance and theater piece we've been rehearsing for months.

All of this is puzzling to Glen. I can't blame him. It surprises me too.

Back in Ohio after the sabbatical year, a children's cartoon-style biography of Jackson Pollock became one of Grace's favorite books—we read it every night at bedtime. There was a panel on one page that showed Lee Krasner, Pollock's wife, demanding to know what Jackson had done with her eggbeater—and, in the next panel, there he is bent over a canvas, using an eggbeater to fling paint.

When Grace asked, one morning, for *my* eggbeater, I didn't have to ask her why. Her father and I covered the playroom floor with taped-together vinyl tablecloths, and for many days over many weeks, she splashed and splattered and egg-beat and dripped paint on large sheets of posterboard we taped to the vinyl. *I'm Jackson Pollock*, she told us. *I am not me, okay?*

"A Midsummer Night's Dream" was the first play she ever saw. She had been listening to music—Hendrix, punk, the Grateful Dead, jazz, heavy metal, hiphop, R&B—since she was in utero, and looking at paintings since the day she was born (when Glen held her up to one and said, "Look at this, Grace Jane. This is called a *landscape*"). On hot days, that first summer of her life, I'd strap her into a front-facing pack and walk laps through the chilly galleries of the Columbus Art Museum. And that year we lived in the city, we spent so much time at the Metropolitan Museum that she nicknamed all the abstract paintings in the Lila Acheson Wallace Wing, and if her father and I lingered too long elsewhere—looking at seventeenth-century Dutch still lifes or Quattrocento paintings—Grace would cry, *Get me back to the twentieth century!*

And she was the daughter of a writer, so books were as much a part of her life as breakfast and bathtime.

Now here was theater.

We sat side by side on a hard bench watching simplified complications ensue in an adumbration of a forest. I kept a careful eye on her for signs that we should bolt—at any moment, I feared, she might scream, *Get me back to real life!* But she was silent and attentive. And then Puck cast his spell and Bottom's head was swallowed by a *papier-mâché* ass's head and my daughter gasped and stood up on the bench and grabbed me, one hand on my shoulder, the other grasping my hair—and when Titania began to stir, she shouted, *Oh NO! She's going to fall in love with a DONKEY!*

She was laughing and crying at the same time. *I can't believe it,* she said. *Mama, I just can't believe it.*

This wasn't what she meant, I knew. She meant, *I believe it.* She meant she was amazed because she did.

I remember that I used to make a joke—what I thought was a joke—when Grace was four, then five, taking classes at the ballet school downtown, that they should offer simultaneous ballet classes for the parents who were sitting around waiting for the children to get out of class. We all brought books, or work—or knitting or a crossword puzzle—but what we actually did to pass the time was talk. It was all right—it was nice. I didn't mind chatting with the other mothers (it was always mothers in the mid to late nineties in Columbus).

I spent a lot of time in those years talking to other mothers while our children danced or sang in choir or took a music lesson or auditioned for a play. I spent so much time (we all spent so much time) waiting around. While we waited, we compared notes. Sometimes we told each other things we didn't tell anyone else, about our kids, about our marriages. Because we saw each other only once a week, only while we sat and waited, only in this place—it felt safe to tell each other secrets.

※

By spring of my first year of dancing, I'd signed on for a performance project even though the prospect scared me. I'd asked Grace what she thought, whether I should do it. She said, *You'd be surprised by how much working toward a performance motivates you.*

We were on the phone—she was in *the city*; I was in Columbus—and I said, *That means yes, I should?*

Yes, Mama, she said. *That means you should.*

And so, less than a year after my first ballet class, I was onstage at the Franklinton Playhouse in Columbus, Ohio, where I'd lived so uneasily since 1988. Ten of us, aged twenty-two through seventy-four, danced in a contemporary performance piece that had been made for, made *on*, us.

That was all it took for me to become as hooked on performance as I was on my daily classes. When Russ proposed another, more ambitious project—a full evening of dance and experimental theater—with a longer rehearsal period and twice as many dancers, I was the first to say *yes*, to ask *when do we start?*

※

At Grace's senior thesis show in college, the audience stood, they danced, they shouted. They were laughing and crying at the same time. I was crying too, but not only because of what was happening onstage—a Kabuki dream unfolding, a romance, injustice, villainy and tragedy, the mystery of what was real and what was not—or even only because I was so proud of her. I *missed* her. I missed her already, even though we were, for the moment, in the same room.

I had been missing her for years—she'd just spent four years in college in Connecticut, hundreds of miles from Ohio (and just that past summer she'd been thousands of miles away, in Kyoto)—but soon there would be no pretending anymore that these were sojourns, that she "really" lived with us. Soon, home would be elsewhere—she would be gone for good.

I spend a lot of time—too much time, Grace would say—thinking of her. I don't *worry* about her. Friends ask me that—*is that the trouble, that you're worried?*—but it isn't worry, it's just longing, so sharp it sometimes feels like grief. I miss her company, her conversation. But it isn't only that. I also miss the child she was. I think about that child, too, so long gone now. I think about Jackson Pollock's eggbeater, I think about that afternoon at "A Midsummer Night's Dream"—I can summon up the memory in such particular detail, that small, trembling, excited child, her hand on my shoulder, crying out in joy and dread, that it is just as if the scene were unfolding before me now, three decades on.

I think about *let's make up commercials for pretend products* and *you be Tacy, I'll be Betsy*, and when she "directed" herself and her friend Kristin as they acted out *Black Beauty*—Kristin playing Ginger, Grace playing everyone else, horse and human both—and I think about the time I took her to a stage adaptation of "Charlotte's Web" and afterwards she met the actor who played Charlotte and I saw the wheels turning, saw her *decide*. And about the summer after that, when she was seven, when "Charlotte" became her first acting teacher and introduced her to Kabuki. And two summers after that, when she was reintroduced to Shakespeare, when she memorized and then performed her first-ever monologue—Miranda's from "The Tempest."

One of the first shows she would devise with the theater company she founded after college was called "Revel's End: A Tempest Dance Party." It was, of course, a reinterpretation of "The Tempest."

In those early years of her career in theater, she supported herself as the part-time nanny of a little girl. Every weekday afternoon and evening it was *let's be fairies in the forest, let's be girls at summer camp, let's pretend this is a restaurant, let's put on a dancing show.* The subway stop nearest to where she lived then was the last stop in Manhattan on the B line—which made its first stop in Brighton Beach, where I was born, where my parents met and married. About halfway between the two was my old subway stop from when I was the age that Grace was then, fresh out of Brooklyn College.

I think about that girl—the one I was—and how much she'd have liked my daughter. If I concentrate, I can make time collapse, I can put the two together—*let's be sisters, let's be friends*—and imagine for a moment what that looks like.

The girl I was isn't really gone. She is only invisible. The little girl my daughter was is still here too, deep within her. I thought about this for the first time only after I woke up one morning from a dream that had seemed to be about my daughter and the child she cared for in the city: the child, who in the dream was Grace's and my shared responsibility, had wandered off—I feared she was lost for good. But Grace set out to find her, racing up many flights of stairs and forcing her way past crowds, and in the end she did find her, she was safe, and when at last I made my own way through the crowds, I saw that Grace had the child on her lap on a small bench at the top of the last flight of stairs and they were talking quietly.

I woke up thinking—marveling—*she knew exactly what to do*, and I saw then that the dream was not about Grace and her six-year-old charge, Ruby. I woke up thinking about how the child my daughter was had been entrusted to the woman she'd become—how she was the one who took care of her now.

My sixty-first birthday:

I am visiting Grace in New York, and together we go to the Museum of Modern Art to see a Jackson Pollock show.

We linger in front of every painting—they are like old friends we haven't seen in a long time. As we stand together before one of the first of the drip paintings, Grace bends to read its title. I think—how would it be possible for me not to think?—about the year we lived in New York together, the year between her second and third birthdays, when she didn't know or care what titles artists had given to the paintings they'd made, when she'd name them herself—*Boom!* and *Black Angry Storm* and *Red Green White Fog*.

Now she says, *Mama, look.*

The painting we are in front of, it turns out, is called "Full Fathom Five."

It's from "The Tempest." It is Ariel, invisibly singing:

> *Full fathom five thy father lies;*
> *Of his bones are coral made;*
> *Those are pearls that were his eyes:*
> *Nothing of him that doth fade,*
> *But doth suffer a sea-change*
> *Into something rich and strange.*

We both laugh. She has just begun work on her "Tempest." We both say, *I can't believe it.* But that isn't what we mean. We do believe it. It is both surprising and inevitable, like the end of any good story—Jackson Pollock and Shakespeare, why not? The way everything manages to come together.

3

Old House

I bought my house, the two-story wood-frame house I've lived in since 1989, from a woman named Barb Culp. I liked Barb. I met her only a couple of times, but I liked what I knew of her—what I could see of her, of her life. I liked that when I first saw the house there was stripped and half-refinished as well as fully finished furniture everywhere—all of it cheerfully, inexpertly hand-painted (leaves and flowers, polka dots, abstract geometrical designs). I liked that she hadn't ruined the house by painting over all the woodwork or converting the old fireplace into an electric or a gas one, or removing the two sets of French doors, the way the owners of so many of the other hundred-year-old houses I had looked at had. I liked that she kept a kiln in the small back room that would become, at first, my breakfast room and four years later would become the playroom—until my daughter and her toys outgrew it, and my husband and I swapped it with the dining room (then swapped it back again when she outgrew the need for a playroom, so that the little back room became our family room, with a TV and a futon couch)—and is now a too-small dining room once more, as the actual dining room is full of my husband's band's gear. The band is Glen's hobby, and I am all for hobbies, even when they're loud and take up a lot of space.

I liked even the weirdness of the wall-to-wall shag carpeting in Barb's house—three shades of green in one room, three shades of orange in another—over the hardwood floors I knew would have to be refinished, and the wacky colors she had painted all the walls (orange, lime green, turquoise) that I'd have to repaint. I liked the giant fish tank in her bedroom. Honestly, I liked the whole vibe. It wasn't my vibe, but it felt like the right one for the house I'd buy. Or else it was just that Barb Culp seemed like the right person for me to buy a house from.

My real estate agent, a very nice middle-aged lady with cropped white hair and a wardrobe of pastel pantsuits, stayed quiet as we picked our way around the painted and not-yet-painted rocking chairs and child-sized desks and dressers, paint-soaked brushes, and open cans of paint; I could tell she disapproved. Mary and I had gotten to be something like friends, we'd spent so much time together. She was rarely quiet. All that spring, as we looked at one turn-of-the-century, three- or four-bedroom house after another, she'd say, "You don't need this much house," and, "Why don't you let me show you something smaller?" She also kept saying that I'd probably be happier in the long run in "a somewhat newer build" and reminding me that I was from New York City (as if I could have forgotten), so I might want to look in a neighborhood "with a more urban feel" than the one I'd chosen. I know I puzzled her. But I think I also amused her. She laughed—at me? with me? (but I wasn't laughing)—at my insistence that if I were going to live in the Midwest, I wanted to live *in the Midwest*, with a front porch swing and a backyard meant for cookouts—not in a pale imitation of a real city.

Barb Culp's house was a bridge too far for Mary. When she finally spoke, it was to draw my attention to its many imperfections. The house had no insulation, no storm windows, *ten* windows (Mary counted) that did not open at all because the wood had warped so badly; the kitchen and the bathroom would have to be redone, and so would all the wiring; and it would not be long before I'd have to replace the ancient gravity furnace in the basement—which, by the way, she noted, would flood when it rained (well, I knew this, didn't

I? We had just sloshed through the basement, as it happened to be raining on that very day). I didn't care.

What I did care about were the built-in bookcases on both sides of the green-tiled fireplace, with their leaded glass-and-wrought-iron doors, and the mantelpiece that stretched along that whole wall of the living room; I cared about the homemade, rough-hewn, floor-to-ceiling bookcase opposite it too, alongside the stairway—and about the cunning piano window (Mary had to tell me that this was what it was called) set high up in the wall of the dining room, where the flower-embossed chandelier (said Mary—with a sigh, as if this were a shortcoming and not a virtue) dated back to the house's conversion from gas to electric lighting.

I could picture hosting friends for dinner at a beautifully set table under that tin chandelier. I didn't have the friends yet, or the table (or a set of dishes or wine glasses or any silverware that matched), but all at once I was sure that I would. I would have all of it—I'd have everything I wanted.

The way I felt reminded me, even then, of what happened every time I fell in love with a new boyfriend. Mary's worry and dismay, her disappointment in what she considered shortcomings, were so like my parents' when I introduced them to each new object of my affection. Except that she didn't tiptoe around me, hinting at what troubled her, the way my parents did. She spelled it out. (Then again, all she had to lose was a commission.) She made me promise to sleep on it before I made an offer.

It was June 1989. I'd looked at so many houses since mid-March, when I'd started looking, halfway through my first year in Columbus. Before then, it had never crossed my mind that I might ever buy a house. My parents had never bought a house—they didn't even own their apartment in Manhattan. My second-generation American experience did not include the impulse (or was it the gene?) to own a piece of property.

But in Columbus in the eighties, renting was expensive, and houses for sale (or some houses, the kind of houses I was looking at) were cheap. My mortgage payments on the house Barb Culp was eager to sell to me for $77,900 would be less than half what I'd been paying to rent a much smaller and less interesting house. I was thirty-four years old and for the first time in my life had a full-time job I loved. I was earning what seemed like a fortune—$27,500 a year, more than three times what my last full-time job had paid—and I had a contract in hand for my first book, a novel I'd begun in grad school and finished in Omaha. Isaac and I had broken up. My new boyfriend wasn't someone I could count on to be in the picture long-term—I could see that already.

I was tired of waiting, I decided, for what I had long thought of as my "real life" to begin. This was my real life

So buckle in, I told myself, and bought Barb Culp's old house.

I met Barb herself soon after my first walk-through of her house, after I had made the offer against Mary's better judgment, after Barb accepted it. I had returned, by appointment, with a tape measure and a pen and notebook. We talked as she showed me around, as I measured and took notes and admired, once again, the bookcases, the pocket doors, the dark-stained oak mantelpiece. She was giving up the house regretfully, she said, and only because she was getting married for the second time and thought it would be good for them to start over somewhere else. She'd raised her children in this house—it was the setting for almost the whole of her first marriage.

I didn't meet her kids, not then and not at the closing in a conference room in a law office in the suburbs, the only other time Barb Culp and I met, but I knew there were two of them because I'd seen their bedrooms. I knew the older one was a teenaged boy. His room was particularly terrible. It wasn't really even a room at all, but a hastily converted sleeping porch. Six of the house's stuck-closed windows were in that room. There was no ductwork to it from the old furnace, so it was unheated but for a scary baseboard heater I was advised to disconnect immediately. Plus, despite the bother somebody had gone to to install the sketchy baseboard heater, there were no electrical outlets—and no overhead light—so the room had been lit with a floor lamp plugged into an extension cord that wound out the door and into the slightly larger, actual bedroom next door, which would become my guestroom and, four years later, my daughter's room. (Eventually—when she was fourteen—my husband would break down the wall between her room and the former sleeping porch, which we'd used until then as a catchall storage room, and build a sort of two-room suite for her, adding electricity and insulation and ductwork from our new forced-air furnace, and for good measure a bathroom of her own where there had once been nothing but thin air. The bathroom was the second-story part of a bump-out addition he built for us that year. On the first floor, there was now a smaller extra bathroom, a pantry, a coffee bar, and a tiny office area/workbench he made for himself.)

The room that had been the Culp family's TV room became my study as soon as I moved in. The door to it was plastered with stickers featuring characters from comic book versions of *Star Wars*. I scraped off as many of them as I could, but some bits of them were stubbornly unscrapeable, and all these years later they are still there (I'm looking at them now). I remember how this bothered me at the beginning, when I was doing everything I could to fix things up, to make the house my own. But soon enough I ceased to notice them, the way all the things one doesn't deal with right away in a just-bought house fade into the background. I have to make an effort, as I'm doing right now, to see them.

The truth is that now, over three and a half decades after I moved in, these traces of the house's former life do not displease me. It's not just the half-scraped *Star Wars* stickers either. In the living room, there's that floor-to-ceiling homemade bookcase, which Barb Culp told me her first husband had built from reclaimed wood—what was left of a collapsed barn the Culps and some of their friends came upon one day out in the country. In the kitchen there's a floor-to-ceiling set of shelves, just a few inches deep, made of that wood too. I keep jars of spices and boxes of tea on them.

I never replaced or repainted Barb's old metal mailbox, or the three white tiles that make up my street address, which I think may predate Barb, above it. Both are affixed to the wood siding, right beside the house's front door. The mailbox is pale pink and splattered with green and gray and yellow dots and dashes—Barb's own handiwork, which to this day makes me think of my first visit to the house, and all the furniture that she had painted or was in the midst of painting that I had to navigate my way around.

From the start, I guess, I didn't want to erase all evidence of the old house's old life. Not that I could have, even if I'd tried. The house itself stands as evidence: it's been standing almost twice as long as I have. Or, to put that another way: when I was born, in 1955 in Brooklyn, this house, 557 miles away from the one-bedroom apartment my parents brought me home to from the hospital, was already middle-aged. It was owned then by a family named Logue. When I was born, they'd already been living in it for as long as I have now.

I have been thinking a lot lately about this, about the long existence of "my" house, about the others who have lived here. It fills me with something like pleasure (but not pleasure, not really; it is more like the absence of sorrow—a sort of easing, a sort of calm) to think about it. That the house I think of as mine was once other people's—that someday, again, it won't be mine (or won't only be mine)—makes me feel a part of something. Something long, that lasts through time. I like thinking about time. About continuity.

At the closing, back in 1989, Barb gave me the Abstract of Title she'd been given by the woman *she* had bought the house from, fifteen or so years before—Isadore Logue, a widow, who had lived in the house for over fifty years and raised a son in it; she'd stayed on alone after her husband's death in 1970, her son long since grown and gone. The last page of the Abstract notes the house's valuation at the end of 1974, when she turned it over to Barb Culp: $1680 for its land and $5620 for its "buildings"—the house itself, and the detached garage that Barb used as a tool and garden shed, that Glen remodeled as a studio in 1992, when he moved in with me.

All these years, the Abstract of Title—a sheaf of documents held together with two old-fashioned metal paper fasteners—has been in the fireproof box I keep in my study (the Culps' TV room—and what did the Logues use it for, I wonder?). I knew it was there, along with the deed to the house, the title to our car, our passports and birth and marriage certificates, a journal I kept for the nine months of my pregnancy, an external hard drive that holds the digitized copies of my father's 8mm home movies of my childhood. I never open that box unless I have to, most often to put something in it—ten years ago, copies of my father's death certificate; two years ago, copies of Glen's and my new wills, finally replacing the ones we had drawn up when Grace was a child and we needed to name a guardian. Still, it surprises me that I gave the Abstract no more than a cursory glance when Barb handed it to me, and that I seemed not to have thought of it again until I began to write this essay.

I have no memory at all of attending to the fact that the last three sole owners of the house have all been women—or that Isadore Logue's husband's name was Glenn (which in any case would have meant nothing to me when I bought the house from Barb, two years before I so much as laid eyes on my own Glen). I have no memory of knowing anything about the house, of ever thinking about anyone who lived in it, before the Culps.

I can't tell whether to be angry with myself for not offering myself the comfort of this knowledge sooner—or to wonder at the change in me: perhaps, before now, it would have left me cold. That is, I might not have cared, I might have found the details in the Abstract boring. Perhaps it's only my own age—old age, I mean (that hard pill to swallow)—that has got me interested in Glenn and Isadore, who moved into the house in 1922, when their son was two years old. Before the Logues, there were the Ickeses, Fred and Minnie, who lived in the house for just a year—Fred Ickes sold the house immediately upon Minnie's death. Before Fred and Minnie, there was Dudley Stewart, widower—who also owned the house for no more than a year—and, before Dudley, Elmer and Izora Wilson. Were the Wilsons first? The Abstract doesn't make this clear. The Lanes—Clara and John—bought the land (worth $170) where the house was to be built, and in 1917 they sold it to the Wilsons. (But did they live in it first, or did the brand new house stand empty while they found a buyer for it?)

I keep thinking about all these people, imagining them moving through the rooms, the porch, the backyard of my house. *My house*—the phrase seems wrong now that I've spent so much time examining the Abstract. If the house is anybody's, it's the Logues's, who lived in it longest (and not just longer than I have, but longer than I will).

Or it's the Lanes's house, since it was theirs first. Even if they never lived in it, even if they only built it. The house was their idea, which might make it theirs more than any of the rest of ours. Except that many houses in the neighborhood were built at the same time in nearly the same way. So it wasn't an original idea. They just happened to have the money to do something with the parcel of land they'd bought. Maybe that means it's less theirs than it is any of ours, all of us who made a home of it.

And yet here I am, spending my days reading and writing on the front porch in good weather, and in my upstairs study when it's too hot or too damp or too mosquito-y outside. When I'm on the porch, neighbors pass by and say hello, compliment my garden (the whole front yard is a garden, mostly of native plants), and I like the reminder of the world beyond my house.

And then there's the world inside it, where it's just Glen and me and all the things we have accumulated over three-plus decades—I like that world too.

The plan is that we'll stay here until Grace is pregnant with her first child. This is something she and I have been talking about for a long time—casually, just for fun, when she was much younger (and always in the context of what my childhood was like, with my grandparents close by and part of my everyday life), and more seriously, if still theoretically, as she grew up. Now that she is married and I have retired—a bit of unplanned synchronicity—the theoretical will soon give way to the real future.

It used to be that when I talked to Glen about this plan, daydreaming aloud, forgetting for a moment about his anxiety about time's passage, he would shudder and say *please, please will you stop*. For a while, when Grace was in her early twenties, I thought it was a schtick—that he was playing the part of a sitcom dad: *Don't you dare make me feel old* [cue laugh track]. But that wasn't it at all. It was only a part of his antipathy to all things other than the present. *What will happen will happen when it happens. What use is it to think about it now?*

And about the past, he says—genuinely mystified when I reminisce about Grace's childhood, or about our own earliest days together, or about something that happened long before I met him—*What possible good can it do to think about that?*

To be honest, it's hard for me to picture what it will be like to live anywhere other than in this house. I've lived in it for so long (so much longer—more than four times longer—than I have lived anywhere else), it feels like an extension of me, less a place by now than a part of my body.

Glen's attachment to it is not so visceral. If you were to ask him, he'd insist he's not attached to this old house at all. He says the idea of "home" means nothing to him.

And to me it means everything. To this day, my first apartment—third-floor rear, in the squat brick building that housed only five apartments on Christopher Street where it intersects with Gay Street—plays a role in all my fiction. And I often think about my family's apartments in Brighton Beach and Sheepshead Bay and Kings Highway and a nameless-neighborhood stretch of Gravesend Neck Road—I can see all of them clearly in my mind. I visit them, too, in real life, whenever I can. By which I mean that I stand outside the buildings, wishing I could get inside my old apartment. And once I did go inside—into the building, not the apartment—on Brighton 5th. I took a long hard look around at the lobby (it had changed completely since my childhood), rode up in the elevator, and walked down the fourth-floor hallway to pass by both my grandparents' one-bedroom apartment, in which they raised all four of their children, and our own, a few doors down, where I lived for the first three years of my life. Even after we moved to Sheepshead Bay, I still thought of Brighton Beach as home. My grandparents *were* my home.

I once made the same kind of visit to the building in Sheepshead Bay, after years of stopping by every few years and standing on Avenue Z, gazing up at the fourth-floor fire escape where I used to sit reading all day long every summer. Glen and Grace were with me the one time I went inside, rode up, stood outside the door. Considered knocking and decided against it.

Glen was surprisingly patient with me. Grace, who was seven or eight at the time, was surprisingly interested.

Grace moved to New York as soon as she graduated from college. She started out in Brooklyn—what I think of as "new Brooklyn," not my Brooklyn—then moved to West Harlem with her roommates, then to Washington Heights with her then-boyfriend, Nathan, and three years ago she and Nathan moved into an apartment north of the city, a way station while she was in grad school nearby, training for a new career. It remained convenient even after she had finished school and started full-time work.

We all may have to move farther north (Grace and Nathan will need room for their future children; Glen will need a studio) to find housing we can afford. I'm open to anything as long as we're near a Metro North train station. (If I'm going home, I want to be able to go *home* as often as I feel like it.)

Glen is ready for the move, he says. Unlike me, he never got over how much he disliked Columbus when he first arrived in 1990 for grad school. (Then again, unlike me, he doesn't get out much, so he hasn't noticed the improvements in Columbus over all these years and has to take my word for it.) It's also true that for years he's longed for a bigger studio. The converted garage where I'd once kept the rotary lawn mower I used for the backyard, a wheelbarrow and bags of topsoil and my gardening tools, and charcoal for my Weber grill—not to mention everything Barb Culp had left behind, which I'd never cleared out, and perhaps whatever the Logues and anyone before them had left in there too, if the Culps were as uninterested as I was in what was a "garage" in name only—is very small. (I can only assume that it had never been used to shelter a car. Not only because of its size, but because of its idiosyncratic placement in the backyard and its double open-out barn doors.)

So lately Glen's been dipping his toe gingerly into what's ahead. It's premature, but he's begun to look at properties for sale in possibly, potentially affordable places in Westchester County. He shows me pictures online of fixer-uppers with large outbuildings or properties far enough from the city that there's space in the yard to build a studio from scratch.

But none of this happens until Grace has children. And she's in no hurry, and although I'm looking forward to grandchildren, I'm in no hurry either. As it turns out, I'm going to be sad to leave Columbus (how shocked my thirty-three-year-old self would be!). Not only sad to leave my house—house, backyard, front porch, garden—but sad to leave the dance studio, sad to leave my friends. My friends! It took me close to thirty years to find my people here, and now that I have found them, it is painful, it is actually shocking, to think of leaving them behind.

And even if Glen won't or can't admit it, moving will be hard for him too. He's used to our life here. He knows what to expect from it from day to day, so that he doesn't have to think about it and can concentrate on his work. This matters to him more than anything. And when he's not making paintings (or fixing things around the house, which always needs fixing) or making other things for pleasure (bass guitars, distortion boxes) or as gifts (lamps, jewelry, diddley bows), he's making music with his band. In the ten years since he started it with one of my then-MFA students and the boyfriend of another, there have been four drummers and three rhythm guitarists; the band's only constants over the last decade have been Glen and his bass (his growing collection of basses), his songs, the band's name (bottleflies) and the logo he drew for it (a blue bottle fly), and the place where they practice (as noted: the room in our house that was meant to be a dining room). When we leave Columbus, I know he'll miss the band. He'll miss the room, too.

I don't tell him this. I know he doesn't want to hear it.

I was on my front porch, laptop on my lap, in the hammock chair I bought years ago at the Ohio State fair, when a man's voice called out, "Ma'am? Excuse me, ma'am—I'm so sorry to disturb you."

I sat up straight, which isn't easy in my hammock chair, since to make it viable for working in, recumbent, for many hours at a time, I use a complicated setup of lumbar and neck and underneath-the-knees support—lots of sturdy pillows and tightly rolled blankets—all of which I must extract myself from if I'm to sit up. I was prepared to brusquely cut short a sales spiel for new siding or windows. But the man (fiftyish, large, boyish the way certain middle-aged men are) was already bounding up the porch steps, saying, "Sorry, ma'am, so sorry! I didn't mean to startle you! My name's Tommy Culp. I grew up in this house."

"Barb Culp's *son*?" I said. Then, inanely: "Barb Culp's teenaged son?"

Now I was trying to get out of the chair altogether (a bigger ordeal even than sitting up, impossible to manage gracefully). "But this is amazing," I said.

He was as amazed as I was. "You're the woman who bought the house from my mom? You still live here? I can't believe it."

I had to pause to consider this. I had indeed lived in the house—his house, my house—more than twice as long as he had, and his time there represented his entire childhood. So, yes, that would be something of a shock. It was also true that, until a few years before, there was only one house on the whole block in which the people who were living in it when I bought this one still lived in theirs (one of Grace's childhood best friends, Anna, had lived there); since then, since Anna's parents sold their house and bought an apartment, it's just me. Tim and Lorraine, across the street and two houses east, bought their house—one of the few that's older than mine—in 1997, when Grace was four. Their younger daughter, Hannah, was soon part of a triumvirate with Anna and Grace. Back then, these three were the only small children on the block, which was otherwise all old people whose children were grown and gone.

Today there are small children in almost every house. But until this moment, in the face of former teenaged Tommy Culp's astonishment to find me still living there, I hadn't thought of myself as an old timer (one of those old people, like the neighbors who surrounded me when I moved in) in this now mostly young people's hip neighborhood. (There's one couple who moved in across the street when they were in their twenties, twenty years ago—when Grace was young enough to be entranced by them and their two dogs, one small, one large; she used to cross the street to visit them as often as they let her, just to pet their dogs, before I gave in and we rescued a puppy of our own—and somehow I still think of them, Nate and Colleen, as among "the new neighbors.")

"Yes, it's me," I told Tommy Culp. I told him I was glad to meet him and asked him how his mother was.

Barb Culp was fine.

Was she still throwing pots and turning old furniture into art projects?

No, she was making lamps these days.

I laughed. A coincidence, I told him. My husband had just started making lamps last Christmas.

I don't know how long it took me, as we stood making awkward small talk on the porch, before I realized there was someone with Tommy—a woman, hanging back politely near the bottom step, and smiling. Tommy saw me see her and he introduced us. She was Jennifer, a friend from high school, who unlike Tommy no longer lived in Columbus. She happened to be visiting for a few days from Chicago, so they were taking a tour of their youth together. The house was a stop on their itinerary.

"Honestly, I can't believe my luck," he told me. He'd been driving by the house for years, he said, hoping to find somebody outside. "I figured it would have been too weird to knock, you know?" I did know. I told him he could have knocked, though—I would not have minded. I would have been glad to show him around. I asked him if he wanted to see the inside of the house now.

Tommy said oh no, he didn't want to impose, he had only wanted to see the house up close, talk to the person who was living in it now, tell someone who might care (would they care? he'd wondered) that he'd lived there for all of his childhood—but I'd opened the front door by then and waved him and his friend in.

As soon as he set foot in the house—the door opens right into the living room—Tommy gasped. "My dad made that bookcase. That's my dad's bookcase."

I told him his dad's spice rack was still standing, also still in use, too. I led him to the kitchen so he could see for himself. I'd redone the kitchen years ago—before Glen, when I had to pay someone to do it (and the work was shoddier than anything Glen had done in the years since; when he first moved in, Glen had shaken his head over it)—but I'd left the rough wood floor-to-ceiling spice rack. I told Tommy I'd always wondered how his mother managed in the old kitchen, which had no countertops and just the one tall cabinet that was original to the house. There'd been a too-small freestanding sink, with nowhere to set down the dishes that had just been washed and dried by hand. Nowhere to put a cutting board or a mixing bowl. "We had a butcher block," he said, "right here in the middle of the room." I told him I remembered that from when I'd first seen the house. "She did everything on that butcher block," he said.

Tommy pointed then: "So that's where you built the addition." The doorway to it had once led to a mudroom and then out to the backyard. Tommy said he'd been looking at the addition from outside—from the alley—for years, every time he passed through the neighborhood, and he'd been curious about it. I was still trying to figure out how it was that he'd never happened to come by when I was on the porch, since I'm out there for a good part of each day three seasons a year. Propped up and surrounded by my constellation of support pillows, I've read and marked up thousands of my students' manuscripts, planned classes, and reread whatever I had given them to read for class—I had even taught my classes over Zoom from the front porch through the worst months of the pandemic (I'd spent most of lockdown, even when it was too cold to reasonably spend time there, on the porch, bundled up and drinking from a thermos of hot tea). I'd read my students' theses and prepared for their defenses. I'd written years' worth of advice columns, short stories, and essays. I'd written whole books sitting on that porch.

I was about to tell him that, but all of his attention now was on the addition. Tommy, it emerged, was a contractor. He was impressed with the work a hobbyist builder like Glen had done on his old house.

I told him that when Glen knocked down the back wall, we discovered that the mudroom had been hanging in midair, jutting out from the back of the house with no connection to the foundation and no beams. It was a miracle that it had held out as long as it had, that no one had ever fallen through the floor.

We agreed that we had all been lucky, that we supposed that none of us had ever lingered on it long enough.

Back in the living room, Jennifer and Tommy told me that they hadn't just been friends in high school: they had dated sophomore year—only a few years before his house became my house. They hadn't even been in touch for at least the last fifteen years. He'd called her "out of the blue," she said, just a few weeks before; by pure chance she would soon be in Columbus for a few days, so they made plans to meet and make the rounds of the landmarks of their teens.

"We spent a lot of time in my family's TV room the year we were fifteen," Tommy said.

"A *lot* of time," Jennifer agreed.

"Well, let's go look at it then," I said.

Upstairs, with Glen asleep behind our closed bedroom door (have I mentioned that he often works all night, then sleeps during the day?), I told Tommy I was sorry that he couldn't see his mom's old room. I told him there was nothing much to see—that there were two dressers side by side where his mother's giant fish tank used to be, that Glen had enlarged the closet years ago. Tommy was more interested in the two other bedrooms anyway—the ones Glen had made over fifteen years ago as a single room for teenaged Grace. He peeked into the bathroom Glen had built—the second-story part of the bump-out—just beyond what had been Tommy's room's north-facing wall with its three windows that didn't open. The other three windows, on the west wall, still don't open—I showed Tommy that, too. Then I led him and Jennifer into my study, the Culps' old TV room, where suddenly Tommy, who had been near tears since his first glimpse of the barnwood bookcase his father had built, began to cry.

He was staring at the door, most of which is covered with taped-on photographs and postcards—and a heartfelt handwritten letter, with illustrations in the margins, from Grace when she was ten, begging me to let her "go on TV and become a popstar"—and at first I thought he was looking at an eight-by-ten print of me when I was nine months pregnant, one of my favorite pictures of myself, but why would that move him to tears? And then I saw it. Just below that photograph were all the remnants of the Star Wars stickers I had not been able to scrape off the door.

After the tour, after he had thanked me for the dozenth time for showing him around, and his friend had thanked me too, telling me how touched she'd been to see the room in which she'd passed so many hours as a fifteen-year-old, I asked Jennifer what had brought her to Columbus and what she did in Chicago. I was just making conversation—it's what I do.

She told me she was a film professor, that she was in Columbus to give a talk about a film of hers that was being screened this week. I asked her about the film and about her teaching job; she told me she'd just been promoted, that she was now a full professor. I congratulated her. I told them both—I hadn't mentioned it till then—that I'd just retired from Ohio State. "It was my teaching job that brought me to Columbus," I told Tommy. "I'd just finished my first year of teaching when I bought your mother's house." I was about to say something more, to Jennifer, about what my own promotion to full at Ohio State had meant to me, when Jennifer, looking flustered, stopped me. "Wait," she said. "What department?"

"English," I said.

"Creative writing!" Jennifer said. Now *she* seemed to be near tears. "Oh, I can't believe it! You're Michelle Herman. I thought you looked familiar, but it was so long ago. I took your class. You changed my life."

It had been a very long time ago, and just that one class—she was an art major, taking a brief dip into creative writing, which she had not believed she had any talent for (or any interest in). Apparently I'd told her otherwise. I had no memory of her, but then in those days I'd taught five sections a year of intro to fiction writing. Hardly any of the names and faces of those early students have stayed with me (though I have learned, since they began to send me friend requests on Facebook in 2008, that if they told me what they'd written about when I taught them—if *they* remembered—I could often summon up a memory of who they were). Jennifer declared that I'd said things in that one class she took with me that she still thought about—that it was that class that had led her toward making films. "Until then, I didn't know that I could tell a story, or even that I wanted to."

I'd never seen any of her films. (I still haven't, because she makes psychological art-horror films, and I can't bear watching anything that's scary, creepy, violent, or just plain dark, no matter how artfully made—not even when it's feminist art-horror, like hers.) But I'd heard of one of them, and since (re)meeting her I've read about them all.

I have no business being proud of Jennifer, whom I taught so briefly and so long ago. I can't even find my teaching notebook from the year she took my class, so that I can look up what I wrote about her in it and remind myself of what she'd written, the way I did when a long ago former student turned up one day in my house as a short-lived bottleflies drummer. Or when a handsome local TV personality reintroduced himself to me when my choir was featured on his morning show, and explained that he had changed his name to something snappier (but I remembered him as soon as he told me his old name, even before I looked him up, because he was such a wiseguy—which was exactly what I'd written in my notebook). Or when my department's new development officer visited my office on campus to tell me she had been my student in the early nineties (*she has real potential but seems to be too lazy to make use of it*, I'd written—and when I emailed her to tell her that, she said, "That was exactly true. Still is").

Nevertheless, I was—am—proud of Jennifer. I'm proud of all of them for their accomplishments, just as if they were my children (even the wiseguys, even the ones who didn't/wouldn't/couldn't live up to their obvious potential).

I loved teaching so much. I came to it fairly late, after I had tried and disliked so many other ways to earn a living. Before I discovered teaching, I was sure I'd never find a job I didn't hate, that I would have to bite the bullet and just try to live with the least objectionable job I could find, whatever that might be. And so I never took teaching for granted. I never took being good at it for granted, either—I worked hard at it. Teaching came naturally to me *and* I worked hard at it (this is how I think about writing, too). After a while, *teacher* was as much a part of my identity as *writer*—and as *mother*, and as *New York City native, Brooklyn-born granddaughter of immigrants.*

And yet I retired from it. I retired because I wanted to have more than just my summers to spend writing, and because I have interests other than writing that take up a lot of time too—I wanted to divide my time between *them* and writing, instead of slicing up the pie so thin. I retired, too, because so much of my job had nothing to do with teaching—because I didn't think I could sit through one more department or committee meeting or write one more annual review letter or graduate fellowship justification. And because—I'll just say it—I am old. Not as old as my house, but old by human standards. Old enough to retire from my day job; not so old—never so old, I think—that I want to retire from my *work*. And while some humans do retire from the latter (think of Philip Roth), they tend to be those who did not have day jobs to retire from.

Old houses, to be sure, retire neither from their artmaking (making the humans who live in them feel at home) nor from their day jobs (protecting human beings from the elements). Old houses just keep growing older until someone knocks them down or they crumble on their own. I like to think of my old house as continuing to age, continuing to exist in the world, long after I am gone from it. I mean gone from the house, and also from the world.

There was a time before the house—before it existed in the world. When the land that it was built on—when only two other houses stood nearby (or nearish by: the houses seem to have been planted in the land like scattered teeth in an otherwise empty mouth)—was only land. And before that, too—not only before John and Clara Lane bought this patch of land worth $170 and built my house on it in 1916, then sold it the next year, but before this land was subdivided in this way, when it was part of one half acre "beginning at a stone in the south line of Andrew Wilson's Home Farm" in 1874—it was land without any edifices built on it. And before it was Wilson's farmland it was part of fifty acres on the "easterly side of Whetstone River" (1806) and before that it was part of "between 1460 and 1600 acres, and lying on both sides of the Whetstone River" (1805) … and in 1800 it was part of 4000 acres spread across many states, "granted in pursuance of the Act of Congress passed July 1, 1796, entitled 'An Act regulating the Grants of Lands Appropriated for Military Services and for the Society of the United Brethren for Propogating [sic] the Gospel among the Heathen.'"

Those grants of land were awarded to soldiers in the continental army in lieu of pensions for their service. But the land was not the U.S. government's to dispense. It was taken from the Shawnee, Potawatomi, Delaware, Miami, Peoria, Seneca, Wyandotte, Ojibwe, or Cherokee peoples, ceded in the 1795 Treaty of Greeneville and the forced removal of tribal nations through the Indian Removal Act of 1830, then given away.

The Abstract of Title does not take note of this: it begins, on its first page, where the United States in the eighteenth century decided it began, with an outline map of the United States Military Lands. Quarter Township No. 3, Township No. 1, Range No. 18.

The Whetstone River is now the Olentangy River—that much was easy for me to figure out. "The Heathen" must have been the Ohio Wyandot, who are mentioned nowhere by their name in the Abstract of Title that Isadore Logue passed along to Barbara Culp, who passed it along to me. As I shall pass it along to whoever comes next. But first, I am going to add notes. About the Wyandot, before what the Abstract presents as the beginning. And, at the end, a note about the Culps, and about us. So that the history of this old house is complete.

Or perhaps I will simply punch two holes into a copy of this essay and attach it, using the same paper fasteners that hold the Abstract together now.

But the history will still not be complete, will never be complete. Even if I could somehow assure that those who live here after I am gone continue adding to the record—continue adding pages, unbending and rebending the ancient paper fasteners, thickening the document until it is the size of a fat novel. Even after this old house is gone—because I know it cannot stand forever—and the land it's on has been reclaimed by what grows only in my garden now, or has been repurposed once again, and something else stands in its place.

When I first sat down to write this, I was thinking only about Tommy Culp and his surprise visit, and about the interesting coincidence of Jennifer, which led me to thinking about the relationship between my life as a teacher and my life in this house. But by now I've found a photograph online that I think is of Isadore and Glenn Logue's son, Robert. I believe he had a son of his own, named after him—Robert Logue Jr.—who must have visited his grandparents' house (*my* house) when he was a child. I've found a census report from 1940, when Robert Sr. was twenty, still living with his parents in the house. I've learned that his father, Glenn, was appointed the Deputy Director of the Bureau of Location and Right-of-Way for the Ohio Department of Highways in 1939—seventeen years after he and Isadore bought the house—and that Isadore died only a year after she sold the house to Barb and her first husband.

I've found obituaries, and through obituaries I've found the names of relatives, and that has led me to descendants—but I hasten to say that I have not reached out to any of them, and also that this did not require restraint on my part, for the living descendants of anyone who lived in the house before the Culps did are too young to have ever set foot in it, and this, after all, is my only—and tenuous— connection to them, which means that we have no connection at all.

The Culps are another matter, though. When I began writing about the house, I looked online to see if I could find the date Barb Culp's first marriage ended; I could not. (I didn't want to contact Tommy Culp to ask him. It seemed wrong—cold, inappropriate, intrusive.) But in the process of my search, I found a list of "possible relatives" of Barb's, and one of them was David Culp—a name that seemed familiar. Surely I did not know Barb's ex-husband or one of his relatives?

I was curious enough to send Jennifer a message. Did she happen to know if Tommy's father's name was David?

It was not. But David was his uncle, his father's older brother.

I typed the name into the Facebook search bar—the easiest, laziest way to find out if you really do know someone whose name rings a bell.

I did know David Culp. He'd sung with me in choir, I realized. We had eighteen Facebook friends, all choir members, in common. In the small round profile picture, he looked exactly as he had the last time I'd seen him. I remembered then that he had died, although I wasn't certain when. I might have stopped to think about him then—David Culp, whom I recalled as kind, a joker, politically active, and so enthusiastic about singing with the choir that he was back onstage with us not long after he'd had a lung removed. I might have shaken my head thinking too about the strange coincidence that for four years I'd known Barb Culp's ex-husband's brother without ever making the connection in my mind. But I was too distracted by the Facebook cover photo—the big horizontal background photo at the top of the profile—to think clearly about anything else.

It was a black-and-white photograph of a young David Culp, whom I'd known only as an old man, taken in what seemed to be the seventies. Handsome, in a flannel shirt, acoustic guitar in his hands.

And standing in front of my bookcase, in my living room, in my house.

Animal Behavior

1

I see dogs every time I open Facebook—which I do too often, using Facebook just the way I once used cigarettes: to take a quick break from writing and thinking, from living so much in my own mind. In the old days I would take my time removing one Marlboro from the pack and lighting it, I'd take a long drag or two, and then I would balance it on the edge of my ashtray, using the moment to collect myself; now I scroll aimlessly down through my "newsfeed"—I can't remember what I did to grant myself this time, this grace, in the two decades between quitting smoking and beginning to use Facebook— and there are the dogs, one after another. As if Facebook, god of the internet, had a vested interest in my relationship with dogs—as if it were intent on sending me a message from the universe.

As if it were aware, as gods are aware of all things, that there is no dog in my house right now, that I might be in need of one.

I am not interested in bringing a dog into my life right now. No—*interested* isn't the right word. I am *interested*. I am full of complicated interest; I am full of longing. I am not *going* to bring a dog into my life right now.

It is entirely my fault that Facebook fills my newsfeed with dog images and narratives. With heartbreaking stories—dismaying and distressing and disturbing stories, stories that bring tears to my eyes (which is easy; I am so often on the verge of tears these days). But also—although fewer—stories with a happy ending (elderly, blind, deaf, abandoned ancient dog has found a home; deathly ill dog has recovered and been placed in foster care). It is my fault because I follow Stop the Suffering Animal Rescue of Ohio and the Franklin County Dog Shelter and Columbus Dog Connection and a great champion of rescue dogs in central Ohio, where I live, the former U.S. Representative for the fifteenth congressional district (mine), Mary Jo Kilroy—she uses Facebook mainly to tell people about dogs in need. I am also a member of a Facebook group that has thirty-two thousand (and counting) members internationally, all of us grieving in a particular way. New members post their stories along with photos of their dogs. Old members, still grieving after weeks or months or years, are still posting pictures of their dogs.

And as if this all weren't enough, Facebook's algorithm, the same one that shows me photographs of flowy linen tunics, wide-legged trousers, and dancewear—ads, that is—also populates my newsfeed with happy-looking dogs who advertise raw food and pet health insurance.

And then there are the dogs I know in real life, dogs I am fond of, whose human companions post their pictures. And the dogs I haven't met but who belong to people I know: former students, colleagues, friends I haven't seen in years, cousins I have found through Facebook, writers I don't in fact know but whose work I know and/or who know mine. Everybody seems to have a dog.

Not me. I don't have a dog. Not now.

My daughter, whose dog's name is Sergeant Pepper, no longer posts pictures of him. But she does not post anything anymore—not on Facebook, which has been taken over by my generation and Gen X, and no longer on Instagram, to which she had migrated years ago along with the rest of the millennials. Her presence on these sites is ghostly. She hasn't removed herself: she's just frozen in time.

But losing interest in social media doesn't mean she doesn't take a lot of pictures of her dog (or her bearded dragon, Rubber Soul). If I ask her to, she's always glad to send me a photo of him—my grand-puppy, we call him, but only out of earshot of Nathan, who objects to this sort of thing (I can't blame him; in principle, I don't like it either). Sergeant Pepper is a gentle, sweet, and very nervous dog, a pit bull whose history is unknown—he was full grown when Grace and Nathan adopted him from a shelter in Harlem—but we can guess that it was bad. He is terrified of cars, crowds, noise, most other dogs, and random people. The only outdoor surfaces he's unafraid of walking on are grass or dirt. Grace and I have speculated that before he landed at the shelter he had either spent his life outdoors, perhaps as the pet of a person who had no indoor home, or else had never *been* outdoors. Either way, he's happiest when curled up on a couch with his favorite humans. His temperament is good. He is afraid, but he expresses his fearfulness by being fearful—not aggressive, like many fearful dogs. He's not very smart, but he is very loving and will climb onto my lap when I visit, even though he is too big for a lapdog.

He is not the only dog I love who lives with someone else. There are all the dogs I got to know during lockdown, some of whom became deeply attached to me and I to them. The people they lived with—the people they still live with—became my friends. They were the only people I ever saw in person during that long period of isolation. It was as if I'd entered a separate world, one in which only dogs and people who had dogs existed. I still have one foot in that world. But I don't belong there anymore.

2

Molly, a ten-week-old, nine-pound brindle mutt of indeterminate origin, was never supposed to be my dog. But like every other dog, as far as I can tell, that's ever been adopted by an eight-year-old who's begged for one (who's competently tended to two guinea pigs for a whole year to prove she could attend to one), she soon became the mother's, not the child's.

But Grace had picked her out and named her—picked her, out of all the rescue puppies, because she was the one who climbed into her lap, then jumped up and bit her nose, while all the others either rolled around sleepily where they'd been dumped out on the lawn by the man who had been fostering them, or else shyly backed away from her when she cooed to them and tried to pet them; and named her Molly because there had been a dog named Molly in the last two books she'd read and eight-year-old Grace believed in signs from the universe. But it was only a matter of days after we rescued the rescue puppy from what had seemed to me a shamefully grim foster situation (except that I was grateful to the man who'd fostered her, because even though he'd kept her in a cage in a garage crammed full of cages occupied by other dogs and puppies, he had rescued her from the shelter she had been in for the two weeks after she'd been found, all by herself, alongside a highway; she was scheduled to be put down because the shelter hadn't found a home for her) before she was mine.

And then a decade later Grace grew up and left home for college, and Molly, who had long since grown up too (into a still-excitable, ever-exuberant, and very barky seventy-five-pound dog) became *super*mine. From the start I'd been the one to walk and feed her, to fuss and fret over her when she wasn't feeling well, but when my only child packed up and moved to Connecticut for college, I hung on to Molly for dear life. I talked to her all day long; she lay beside me as I wrote or read, or while I read and marked up my students' writing. When I left the house to teach, I kissed her goodbye, and when I returned, she greeted me—as dogs do—as if I had been gone for years, just the way my daughter had when she was very young. I hadn't realized how much I missed that (I hadn't realized I *had* missed it, all those years). My husband would sometimes say, "I think you like that dog better than you like me," and I'd tell him sweetly that if *he* were ever that happy to see me, I would reconsider.

I'd long been silently scornful of people who believed their pets were their children. But I became one of them. I didn't call the dog my "child" or my "fur baby," the way people do, but I adored her; I paid constant attention to her. She slept in the bed with me, starting out each night at my feet and slowly making her way to the spot beside me, where my husband slept if he had come to bed (but he rarely had; he more often painted in his studio all night and slept in the daytime). For years she'd leap onto the bed in one beautiful, big, arcing bound. Then, as she aged, I'd have to help her up, boosting her from behind.

She developed all the usual big dog problems as she aged. I coaxed supplements and painkillers into her and mixed turmeric into her food. When she stopped being able to get up onto the bed even with my help, I had Glen build her a set of broad, shallow wooden steps. When those steps began to worry her, I put sandpaper stick-ons on them to make her more surefooted. And when, after a while, the sandpaper wasn't enough, I put carpet on them.

And when she could no longer use the steps at all, either because of her arthritis or her growing fear of falling or the fact that she was slowly losing her vision, she and I both resigned ourselves to her sleeping on the landing halfway between the first and second floors of our house, on the soft carpet there. When I woke up in the middle of the night, she'd lift her head to look up at me as I passed by, on my way to the bathroom down the hall. I'd say, "It's okay, go back to sleep, sweet girl," and she would, with a sigh, laying her head back down on the dark green carpet I had put in years before to make it easier for her to get up and down the stairs.

A vivid childhood memory: I have just woken up, just walked into the living room of the apartment we have recently moved into, where my little brother and I for the first time have separate bedrooms. It's early. I've come to the living room to look again in wonder at the tropical aquarium my father had set up the day before. I am eleven years old; my brother Scott is seven. Our father is prone to enthusiasms—big enthusiasms, most of which tend to pass quickly. Some of these phases of his aren't interesting to us, but this one is. We'd watched enrapt as he had filled the tank with corys, guppies, neon tetras, swordtails, angelfish, kissing gouramis, zebrafish, black mollies, catfish—I've already memorized their names because that's one of *my* enthusiasms: I like knowing the names of things; I like collecting words.

I am barefoot on the carpet, which is tweedy looking, black and white. I feel the fish before I see them—but then I look down and see them, too.

The carpet is littered with dead fish. They had jumped out during the night because my father hadn't put a lid on the tank. No one had told him to, he explains later. How was he to know the fish would leap to their death?

In the afternoon my father will restock the tank. He will buy a lid for it and make sure it's secure before we go to bed that night. But I am still thinking about the fish scattered on the carpet. I won't look at the tank again—won't join my father in admiring the different kinds of fish, their shapes and colors, the way they dart across the water—for a long time. But eventually I'll give in. I always do, where my father is concerned. He likes to talk about the fish, to point out what he considers the most interesting facts about them. The silvery and coral-colored kissing gouramis aren't really kissing: that's just the way a male gourami fights with other male gouramis. See how many babies the black mollies keep having? That's what mollies do. And they are social fish, as are neon tetras—see how they congregate in schools?—while angelfish keep to themselves.

I am his best audience, always. I'm his best friend, his cheerleader, his sidekick.

But the dead fish, and my father's failure, his negligence—more than that, his ignorance, his failure to have known something he was supposed to know—haunt me. I forgive him—I will always forgive him—but I don't forget.

3

The truth is that I hadn't thought about the fish in many years. It shocks me, really, how clearly I remember them—how clearly I remember everything about those first days and weeks after my father brought the fish tank home, set it up and stocked it, then restocked it. I remember little else about that time, that apartment we lived in for just a little while before we moved again. I remember that there was a swimming pool inside a fenced courtyard, that the building's super had two skinny, very blond sons I played with in that pool even though they were much younger than I was, and that there were three girls near my age—Mavis, Ann, and Joni—who would become my friends in the most glancing, short-term way, because of proximity alone, and who would vanish from my life completely once we moved again.

I'm thinking about all of this now because I'm in a fragile, tearful state of mind. I'm probing all the delicate and painful places—I can't help myself. I'm thinking of the fish tank in particular because I am thinking about all the animals that have passed through my life. And because I'm thinking a great deal these days about failure and about forgiveness.

It's 1968 and we have moved again, leaving Mavis, Ann, and Joni and the super's skinny blond sons and the pool and the fish tank behind. We've moved this time to the top floor of a small, square, brick, three-story house—the first *house* I have ever lived in, although we're still renting, it's still an apartment. I'm thirteen, halfway through junior high. I have two friends at school, Amy and Maria, and I feel lucky to have them. Everyone from my old elementary school went to one junior high, and I to another. I'm lucky, I think, to have any friends at all.

My father has decided that we need a dog, a German Shepherd. It is another of his enthusiasms. He'd written a feature story for a newspaper about a man who called himself Mr. Lucky, who bred and trained German Shepherds as guard dogs, and he's gotten it into his head that we should have one and that Mr. Lucky should teach him how to train it. My mother is skeptical; my brother and I are nervous and excited. We've never had a dog—no one in our extended family has had a dog. We are going to be trailblazers.

I am given the task of naming the dog, an eight-week-old black German Shepherd puppy who starts out living in the bathroom, the floor of which is covered with layers of newspapers (it's Mr. Lucky's method for housebreaking). I am still embarrassed, over five decades later, to report that the name I chose for him, with the help of my friend Amy (who had a dog herself—the only dog I was personally acquainted with—named Marc Antony), was Sir Lancelot Von Herman. (In my defense, I'll note that he was a pedigreed dog; my father *wanted* a fancy name for him.)

From the start, though, he is called Lance, and he is my father's dog—there is no pretense otherwise. The job of naming him was only mine because it's the kind of thing I'm good at, everyone agrees.

And we all love that dog, Lance, even though he is unmanageable. Either because Mr. Lucky's techniques don't work, or because my father's enthusiasm about the project of training the dog wanes before he can get it done properly, or because he does it no more than half-heartedly, as well as sporadically, all along. Or all three—probably all three.

My father is restless during those years, the first few years of Lance's life. He'd opened his own insurance office after working for other people since he'd first started selling life insurance in 1957 to supplement his unreliable income writing and taking photos for newspapers. By 1969, though, all the papers he had worked for have shut down. He still covers news from time to time for the Associated Press, as a stringer; he still writes the occasional feature story for a second- or third-tier magazine. But this sort of work has long since taken a backseat to his day job, and opening an office of his own is a big deal: he's rented the first floor of the house we live in to use for his business. (The landlord lives sandwiched by us: on the second floor, between the business and our home.) Next door to our square brick house there is a grocery, where we're allowed to run a tab—a novelty (Amy and I use it to buy cans of Spam and bags of shredded coconut and frozen melon balls—foods that seemed exotic to us, that we had never tasted). There's a tiny fenced backyard that Lance can play in, if one of us is willing to go out and play with him there. That doesn't happen very often.

Lance never learns even the simplest commands, and when he is left alone he destroys the pillows in all of our bedrooms—there are feathers everywhere when we return, as if he's murdered a flock of birds. He unrolls the toilet paper. He knocks over all the wastebaskets. But at night he sneaks into my bed, which pleases me, and sleeps beside me. And he is remarkably indulgent with me: I have photos of him draped in a fringed, flowered shawl, wearing my glasses. My father disapproves of this sort of thing—I remember that. My father wants Lance to be tough; he likes it when he walks him and people seem afraid.

Why wouldn't they be afraid? Lance wears a choke collar and he strains against it, gasping. Later, when I am in college—still living at home, commuting—Lance will bite someone, a boy I know, because he doesn't like the way the boy is acting toward me (I don't either), and while it isn't a bad bite, it is enough to send us into court: the boy's family sues us, and I suppose they win (that part, I don't remember). All I know is, after that, Lance is muzzled for his walks—poor Lance. He will live to be twelve years old, but in all of that time it would never be made clear to him *what* was expected of him. Still, he did his best, the way dogs do.

4

I am working up to telling the most recent story, the hard one. The one that's left me heartbroken and scarred, both metaphorically and non-metaphorically. The deep scar on my forehead, my friend Judith says, looks ceremonial. At the hospital, in the ER, and then again a few days later in my doctor's office for a recheck of my wounds, there was talk of plastic surgery: "Even if you don't think you want it"— because I had already said, not once but many times, that I wasn't interested, that scarring was the least of my concerns—"just a consult, just to think about for later." Finally, in the doctor's office, I said what I had been afraid to say in the ER (would they call for a psych consult if I did?) and unwilling to confess to the young resident who saw me first at my recheck appointment, or to her not much older supervisor—who could not make up her mind if the worst of my wounds was infected. She called in a senior attending doctor to take a look at it, and while he did, she told him that I was "refusing a plastic surgery consult." The older doctor—older even than I—said, "Is that so?" He pronounced the wound as healing nicely and asked me to tell him "the whole story," so I did, in great detail, and at the end of it I told the truth: "I *want* the scar."

Both of the young doctors looked uncomfortable. The older doctor said, "Of course. I get it. I would too, if it were me."

Molly was not the first pet I brought home for Grace who soon became mine. Before the puppy, it had been a bird, a cockatiel.

This was not even my first effort to solve the problem of her longing for a pet. There had been goldfish and a turtle, none of which had lived for very long, and they hadn't satisfied her, really, during their short lives—not when she wanted a pet who would express affection and receive it. The cockatiel, then, was the first successful effort that I made. She *was* affectionate and also stuck around for years, loved by the whole family. But cockatiels can be one-person birds, and this one picked me.

In between the cockatiel, whom Grace named Cody, and the puppy, Molly, came the guinea pigs, Squeeky and Missy. The guinea pigs were Grace's idea. My own would have been a cat (I'd had cats before I had Grace—I still had one when Grace was born; she died three months later, of old age plus a broken heart) but she was horribly allergic to cats.

What happened, two years before Molly, a year before Squeeky and Missy, was that a child at her school, whose house Grace had visited exactly once, had a cockatiel. "It's so cute," Grace reported. "And smart, too. And friendly. It sits on Chloe's mother's shoulder and you can put out your finger and call its name and it'll jump right onto it." So I called Chloe's mother, who told me about the breeder who raised birds by hand, and I visited the breeder—I visited the breeder many times, over many months—and tried to decide if a bird was a good idea. Eventually, I too fell for the charms of cockatiels, and that Christmas I surprised Grace with a twelve-week-old one of her own.

For the first few months, Grace and Cody were inseparable. Grace would build a Tinker Toy perch for her on the floor of the playroom and Cody would hang out on it and watch her as she went about her Playmobil or Barbie business. But a child has other things to do besides keeping a bird company, such as school and homework, practicing the piano, piano lessons, play practice, *clarinet* practice, guitar lessons (but somehow never practice), dance classes, playing outside in the snow, playing in the house with friends—games a small bird wasn't welcome to partake in—and so, more and more, Cody was with me. Except when I was teaching, or driving Grace somewhere, my activities were all bird-friendly. Cody would sit on my shoulder napping on and off all day long while I worked, and when she was awake, she'd nibble on or coo into my ear. She sat on my shoulder while I cooked, too, and while I folded laundry, paid bills, did the dishes, or talked on the phone. Sometimes, when I was in the kitchen, instead of perching on my shoulder, she'd be on a wooden dowel we'd put up for her across the kitchen window. She liked to watch the outdoor birds. If she heard a noise that frightened her, she'd fly into the dining room, where we kept her cage, and perch on top of it. She was never *in* her cage except at night, when we would cover it so that she would sleep, or when no one was at home (if I went out and anybody else was home, they would sometimes keep her on one of *their* shoulders, at least for a little while; sometimes my husband would wear a baseball cap he kept just for this purpose and Cody would sit on top of it).

And, of course, I was the one tending to her (I nagged Grace to do it until I got tired of nagging her). It was I who replenished her seed bowl and scrubbed out and refilled her water bowl, I who chopped up vegetables and fruit to supplement the birdseed, I who used the kitchen faucet sprayer to give her a bath, I who cleaned her cage and then repapered it with discarded, marked-up drafts of my own manuscripts. She soiled every page of every draft of *Dog* and *Stories We Tell Ourselves*.

When I left the house and no one was around to entertain her I would put her in her cage; when I returned, when she heard my key in the lock, she would shriek with pleasure, hopping from perch to perch in her cage and trilling at me until I set down my school bag or the bags of groceries and came to let her out and put her on my shoulder where she felt she belonged. (If she heard my key in the lock and she was out of her cage, on top of Glen's head or on Grace's shoulder as she sat at the table doing homework, she would fly to me. As I say: my bird.)

And thus, because she didn't turn out to be Grace's after all and Grace still wanted a pet of her own, the next year first one guinea pig and then the other (to keep the first one company) was adopted. This time I elicited a solemn promise from her to take full responsibility; otherwise, I swore (and I meant it—my aversion to rodents made this easy), we would give the guinea pigs away. In turn, Grace secured from me a promise that if she proved that she was responsible enough to take care of her two guinea pigs with no help whatsoever, a dog would be next.

Meanwhile, there was Cody.

Cockatiels are long-lived. I'd expected twenty years (and when we first got her, we talked about what would happen when Grace grew up, whether she'd be able to take the bird with her to college—but that was before she became mine). Cody was just thirteen when we lost her.

Glen and I were off on a rare outing together, so she was at home alone with Molly (Squeeky and Missy long gone by then; Grace away at college). When we returned—only a few hours had passed since we had left the house—Molly rushed to greet us at the door as if we had been gone for years, but Cody was silent in her cage. I knew right away. I was in tears even before I reached the cage and saw her.

What we pieced together was that we had left the dishwasher, full of dirty dishes, open (a mistake, since Molly loved to lick the dirty dishes; we didn't ever let her) and that Molly must have gotten into it—we found both of her tags on the kitchen floor, as if they had been flung there, into separate corners: her rabies tag in one spot, her heart-shaped ID tag in another; the wire ring from which the tags had hung from her collar was on the floor, too, far from where both tags had landed, stretched out almost into a straight line. We surveyed all of this as if it were a crime scene and worked out that in Molly's excitement over so much access to the dishwasher, she'd put her head all the way in and the thin metal ring had somehow caught on one of the dishwasher's spokes; that in her thrashing to get free—which broke the flimsy ring and sent the tags flying—she had made a lot of unfamiliar, terrifying noise. That Cody had been scared to death—had died of a heart attack, or else had slammed into the cage's bars as she frantically tried to get away. It was gruesome, it was awful. And it was my fault, or possibly both Glen's and my fault. But I was the one who loaded the dishwasher; his job was to unload it. My fault, then.

I did not think that day, or in the days or months or years that followed, of my father and the fish tank—I've thought of it only now. My fault, my negligence, my failure. Like my father, I should have known better.

5

Two months later, my father got sick.

Glen stepped into the breach to care for Molly, to feed and walk her and coax medicine into her, during the days every week that I was gone. I cried when I left her and I cried when I returned.

When I returned, she would cry too. She would cry and moan and climb into my lap the second I sat down, on the floor or on the couch, which I did as soon as I got in. I cried and she cried. She'd put her head on my shoulder; I could feel her trembling. After a few minutes, she was calm. I could *see* her taking it in: I hadn't, after all, left her for good. All was right in her world once again.

And I would calm down too—she calmed and soothed me as much as my presence calmed her. Whenever I was in Columbus during those last months of my father's illness, I spent every minute that I wasn't teaching with her. As I caught up on my schoolwork, Molly lay beside me, her head on my knee. Whatever I was doing, there she was—next to me on the couch, at my feet if I was in a chair or standing. She followed me from to room. If she hadn't, I would have followed her.

It had broken my heart, losing Cody. Now I felt like all of me was in a million broken pieces. For part of every day, I held on to Molly, I cried into her fur. She let me, for as long as I needed to.

※

She loved me, but she was the kind of dog who loved everyone (and at first sight, too). Walking her was thus a special kind of pleasure. She greeted every human being that we passed as if they were her long-lost dearest friend. Sometimes people were unnerved by this—by the way she pulled me toward them, her tail wagging so hard that her whole back end wagged along with it, but she was a big dog, she *looked* scary if you weren't someone who could easily read dog language, if dogs made you nervous. I would hold her back, apologize, tell them, "Don't mind her—she just thinks you're her best friend. Everyone she meets is her best friend she's never seen before. It's just how she is. She doesn't mean any harm." Some people liked it, though. Then I would say, "You're her new best friend. Congratulations."

But as much as she liked people, she liked hardly any dogs. Two or three in the neighborhood—the rest, known and unknown both, were her sworn enemies. So walking her could also be a challenge, since we'd have to cross the street to avoid people who were walking their own dogs. Molly would look longingly at the human at one end of the leash and bark warningly at the dog at its other end, then for good measure bark in frustration at the human too, as if she were saying, "What's wrong with you? Why are you ruining any possibility of friendship between us?"

Glen said that she'd be a good watchdog if someone broke into our house and had a dog with them: "She would show no mercy." But he liked to say, too, that "if the burglar was all by himself, she'd welcome him, she would be thrilled. She'd gladly show him where we keep the valuables. She'd say, 'Help yourself.'"

※

My most recent dog, Ella, would have attacked anyone who broke into our house by the time she was a year old, but not because she was a good watchdog. She was a playful, gentle, loving, sweet dog—still a puppy, although she no longer looked like one. She was gigantic, a surprise to me (I had her DNA done when she was eleven weeks old and learned that she was fully half Great Pyrenees), but she was afraid of almost everyone, and as she shed her earliest puppyhood, her fearfulness—which had before then shown itself only as shyness and as jumpiness—became the kind that was expressed in rage. Her fury didn't last more than a few seconds, but that was long enough: for those few seconds, when something triggered her worst fears, she was a different dog. She was ferocious—she was terrifying.

And then she was herself again. She would look at me in wonder. It was a look that said, "What? What just happened?"

Most people never saw it. They saw only her sweetness and her timidity. What they saw made them say, "Aw, poor thing"—or even laugh—because it *was* sad or else utterly absurd, this enormous dog backing away from them, trembling and crying, trying hard to hide behind five-foot-two me.

If they had dogs of their own, though, they'd see the best of her, because unlike Molly she loved *all* dogs, loved them from the start and was undaunted if they didn't love her back. She had half a dozen best-friend dogs she played with every day.

As she approached the one-year mark, however, sometimes her anxiety would show up even with her best friends. If I gave one of them too much attention. If I gave one of them a treat. She'd snarl; she might snap at them. It passed so quickly that their people weren't worried about it. I was. I was watching her so closely by then.

6

It isn't true that the only people I saw throughout lockdown were the people I met because we had dogs. These were the only people I saw *socially*. We became a human pack, meeting up each day, huddled together with our dogs. Sweating together, fogging up our sunglasses, in our masks all summer; shivering together all through that pandemic winter. Watching the dogs play, trading our life stories, becoming close friends quickly the way people do when they are isolated together.

The other people I saw, at least for a period of several weeks, August through early October 2020, were some of my graduate students. While I taught my undergraduates on Zoom each week, I had proposed before the start of the semester that my graduate workshop in fiction writing meet in my backyard until it became too cold, at which point we would shift to Zoom. The class was small and my yard was just large enough for us to each sit six feet away from anyone else. I had a set of masks custom-made—identical masks with the alphabet in an old-fashioned typewriter font printed all over them—and each Friday we met in the yard and talked about the stories that were "up" that week.

The puppy I'd adopted in July was part of the proceedings—she was too attached to me to be put in the house (and honestly, I would not have wanted to). But she was a complicated puppy, and because she made up her mind on the first day that just two of the assembled student writers were to her liking, the others vied for her attention (she was afraid of them; she'd run away when any of them tried to pet her or even speak to her)—while sometimes the ones she liked were overwhelmed by the force of her attention. And I was constantly distracted by the need to distract *her*, offering her treats and chew toys or holding her in my lap while I taught. She was still small enough for that then. But it never seemed to me that I was able to pay *enough* attention to the students, especially the new ones, the first-year MFAs who'd moved across the country to be here, who were feeling dislocated and adrift, who themselves never saw anyone in person except one another, once a week. And me. And my puppy.

After my father died, on May 14, 2021, I stayed on with my mother for two weeks, helping her adjust to her new life. I stayed on to help myself adjust, too. Mostly I did this by keeping myself busy—going through his papers, sorting things and cleaning up, hauling away trash, making a thousand phone calls. I was in motion every day from early morning until late at night. It's the way I've always coped with grief. It's the way I cope with anything.

Back in Columbus, I was still dealing with banks and credit card companies, Verizon, Medicare, the hospital. I argued with everyone I talked to. When I wasn't on the phone, wasn't doing something that had to do with my father's death, I worked on sorting and discarding things in my own study. I'd come home thinking about how if I did not, I was leaving it for Grace to do someday. But even as I filled trash bags with manuscripts and cards and letters and old AAA TripTiks and maps of cities I'd once visited and never would again, I thought about how much there still would be for her to do once I was gone. About how all the things that mattered to me—everything I was sure I still needed, that could not be thrown away—wouldn't matter anymore once I was not around to need them.

On May 30, 2014, in the middle of the night—or, really, early morning of May 31—I was in bed, awake as usual. Molly was sleeping on the carpet on the stairway's landing, as she had been doing every night for many months by then. I remember wishing she were with me in the bed, the way she used to be, the way she'd been for so many years. And then I heard a terrible sound and I jumped out of bed and went running. She was at the foot of the stairs, unconscious.

She'd had a stroke, it turned out, but I didn't know that yet. She was still unconscious when they sent me home after I'd sat in the waiting room at the veterinary hospital for hours. They said it could be days before she was awake, that she might not wake up at all. They promised to call me the second she woke up, no matter what time it was. I made everyone—the vet, vet techs, and vet students—repeat that promise: "Even in the middle of the night, yes."

I was sure I'd lost her. I could not stop crying. I cried all day, I cried as I climbed into bed that night and lay awake. I was still awake when my phone rang at five AM. She had just come to, the voice on the phone said. She'd had a stroke—that had been confirmed. "But she's conscious now?" I said. "How does she seem?" The person on the phone laughed. "Fastest recovery from a stroke I've ever seen. She's not only conscious, she's wagging her tail and giving kisses. You should come and get her as soon as you can. She's fine."

She was. But she was a changed dog after the stroke. Overnight—over two nights—she had become elderly. She was frail and cautious. She turned inward. She wasn't interested in meeting new people; she didn't bark at other dogs. All her life, she had been the barkiest dog anyone had ever met. She would go out through the pet door to the backyard and look up at the sky and bark. She'd bark when she was frightened, when she was excited, when she heard or saw or smelled something surprising. She barked when she was happy. She barked just to hear herself bark. Sometimes she barked so much she got laryngitis, and then her "barks" came out as croaks, or with no sound at all.

Now she hardly ever barked. She was quiet and slow-moving. I put a freestanding baby gate up on the front porch—an obstacle she would have knocked down easily before the stroke, which now might have been a solid wall—and a thick blanket on the floor, and she would slowly follow me out to the front porch and groan as she settled herself down there. I would sit or lie beside her, reading.

She couldn't make it up the stairs at all, not even to the landing halfway up. She had lost enough weight so that I could carry her upstairs, but it wasn't long before I saw how selfish this was: she was so afraid of going *down* the stairs—even with my help, one carpeted step at a time, sitting and sliding alongside her—that as soon as I set her on the landing to catch my breath before I picked her up again and carried her into the bedroom, she'd cry and gaze yearningly, anxiously, downstairs.

I let her stay put. She never went upstairs again.

I was a changed woman too, that summer. I was a woman whose father had died, a woman whose only child had a new permanent address. My daughter and I had been thick as thieves from the day she was born, but in the natural order of things, she had moved on. She was supposed to move on—I understood that. I was happy for her. And I had my own life, my own interests, my work. And I still had Molly.

I was older than Grace was when I left home; my life was at a different stage. I'd lived with my family throughout college, biking the two miles up Bedford Avenue to the Brooklyn College campus, not moving out until I'd graduated. Even then it was just to Manhattan—to the Village, a half hour's subway ride away (although it might have been the distance of a transatlantic flight in all the ways that mattered most to me). My father and I had hardly been on speaking terms for years at that point. Still, it must have been hard for him. He must have missed me terribly. He must have been missing me terribly for a long time—since I'd started high school and withdrawn from him. But once I left home, the cold war between us became tangible.

Before that, we had been so close—not just close, but intertwined—it would have been unfathomable to me that I'd ever want to grow up and move away. (I'm pretty sure it was unfathomable to him, too. I think this is probably what is meant by the term "enmeshment.") I was a lot like him. I *wanted* to be like him. He was so effortlessly outgoing, such a good storyteller, a performer. A natural-born leader. What I didn't notice then was that he was someone people either gravitated to, admired, and liked very much, or actively avoided and disliked: there was nothing in between. I became such a person too. (I was so "outgoing" that my report cards every year recorded my schoolwork as "excellent" in every category but *personal and social development and behavior*, in which I was graded "fair" in most subcategories—*follows directions, obeys rules*, etc.—and "unsatisfactory" in the subcategory *self-control*. Every teacher, every year of elementary school, noted in the space for comments that I was a "chatterbox.")

Later on, we would be close again, but when I first left home, at twenty-one, that reconnection was more than ten years away. Even after my parents left Brooklyn too, two years after I did (following me to Manhattan, as I thought of it—renting an apartment in Yorkville, on the far Upper East Side), I kept myself apart. And in truth the distance between Yorkville and the Village was as metaphorically vast as the distance my parents traveled when they moved from Brooklyn to Manhattan. My younger brother, painfully aware of this, moved only reluctantly into *the city* and returned to Brooklyn as soon as he could.

My father had already had his own cataclysmic life upset, though it was one he had encouraged and supported. My mother, who'd left college at nineteen to marry him, had gone back to school (back to Brooklyn College, where she overlapped with me during my senior year, then with Scott, for his freshman year, before she graduated). This was followed, not long after my parents' move from Brooklyn to Manhattan, by my mother's heading off to Mexico for medical school. She was forty-seven years old. Universidad del Noreste was the only one that would accept her.

Left to fend for themselves in the new apartment were Scott and my father—but Scott was hardly ever there, what with school and work and a girlfriend back in Brooklyn—and the dog. In practice, then, it was just Dad and Lance. Lance slept in my mother's place, his head on her pillow, in the queen-sized bed.

And that was where he died. Dad called me when he found him in the morning, still and cold beside him. Lance was twelve years old and even after two years had not really recovered from the move. There were too many people on the street, too much concrete and too little grass, too few trees. So much noise, so many cars and cabs and buses. He skidded around on the uncarpeted parquet floors of the new apartment; he had to take an elevator, which frightened him, just to get outside. His body gave out that night in his sleep, but I think he'd lost heart when he left Brooklyn.

Scott wasn't home that morning—he might have been on his way to class, a long trip from Yorkville—and my mother was 2000 miles away in Tampico, where it was even earlier than it was in New York. So my father called me. I don't remember what I said. I only remember the sound of my father, who'd barely talked to me except to scold me since I was fourteen years old, sobbing into the phone.

I had pets of my own by then, in my first apartment. I had cats, two of them. I'd adopted Lizzy six months into my new life post-college with my own new "permanent address." She was only a few weeks old, so small she could be held in one hand, when my longtime friend Amy found her in a snowdrift in the backyard of her parents' house that winter. Amy was home visiting, on a break from *her* first year of med school (med school seemed to be an epidemic). She bottle-fed the kitten, weaned her, fed her canned food from her finger, and then, once the kitten would eat from a bowl and use the litterbox, started begging me to take her before she went back to school.

I'd never had a cat and wasn't sure I wanted one, but how could I say no to this—a tiny, scared, abandoned kitten? I took the subway back to Brooklyn; Amy handed me the kitten—whom I named Elizabeth, the name I'd secretly been saving for a daughter all my life (but who knew how long it would be before I'd have one of those? or if I ever would?); and I put her in my pocket and got back on the D train.

Before Lizzy, I hadn't been lonely exactly in my studio apartment—or anyway I didn't call what I was feeling loneliness—but I'd heard myself tell anyone who'd listen (friends, first dates, people at work at the job I hated), "I could just not come home for days on end—I could be dead—and nobody would know." (And sometimes people would say, kindly, "Yeah, I get it. Living alone can be weird." But more often they rolled their eyes at me.) And yet except for that—the weirdness (if that's the right word for it, for the recurring thought that if I disappeared for days, no one would care, no one would even know)—I liked living alone.

And then suddenly I had a kitten. She would know, I thought, and the thought made me feel better. At first it didn't even matter that I almost never saw her, that she had set up housekeeping under my dresser, coming out to eat and drink and use the litter box only when I was asleep or out of the apartment (which wasn't often, since I'd quit the job I'd hated and was freelancing instead, and I had no money to spend on outings). But after a few months, I noticed that while I felt better, I did not feel *good*. And so I adopted a plump, full grown cat, rescued from a hoarding situation after the death of the woman she had lived with, along with dozens (so I was told) of other cats and kittens and a mountain of stuff.

Cadence was sociable and affectionate (needy, in fact, but in a way I liked). She slept on my head, snoring into one ear and flicking her tail against the other. When I sat down to work, she climbed into my lap. I believed that either she would teach Elizabeth a nicer way to interact with me (i.e., *to* interact with me), leading by example, or that her need to be close to me at all hours of the day and night would make up for Lizzy's aloofness (as if the two extremes might average out to one something-like-normal cat).

And Cady did seem to teach Lizzy how to live with me, demonstrating that I wasn't to be feared. Lizzy took to *her*, too, and within a year I had two cats who stayed close while I worked, Cady in my lap and Lizzy on my desk beside the typewriter, and two cats in my narrow bed at night (Lizzy at my feet, Cady on my head). If I were up and moving about—getting dressed, making rice and beans for dinner, or pacing and smoking cigarettes as I talked on the phone, winding the long cord around my wrist—they curled up together in the boxy yellow armchair that I liked to read in.

When my father called, in tears, to tell me about Lance, I cried too. I cried for my father and I cried for Lance and I cried for myself, because I felt the loss too—I had also loved him. He had spent years sleeping in *my* bed, the very twin bed that my cats and I now slept in. I'd taken the bed with me, with my parents' blessing, when I moved—they planned to turn my room into a den; they didn't need it—along with the dresser Lizzy had lived under until Cady coaxed her out. I'd also been allowed to take the armchair in which I had spent whole days (and whole summers) reading, and a table that cunningly folded into a convenient semicircle, which my parents had had since the first days of their marriage.

I saw what lay ahead. I hadn't thought about what it would be like for me when the cats were gone—hadn't thought about the obvious, how they would be with me for ten or twelve or fifteen years and then they wouldn't.

I was twenty-five, and Lance's was the first death that came close to me. I had been lucky.

Two years later, in 1982, my grandfather would be gone. By the time Cady died, in 1989, I was more experienced at grief. It didn't make it any easier. Nothing makes grief easier. Keeping busy, the only weapon I have ever found to arm myself against it, doesn't make it easier. It just makes a lot of noise, a lot of clatter and commotion—it helps to drown it out.

As soon as I stop, grief roars right back at me.

7

When my graduate class moved indoors that pandemic autumn to our separate homes and screens, I was relieved. There had been too much tension during those in-person meetings. It wasn't just the dog and the way she played favorites, or the increasingly anxious efforts of my students to engage her—or my anxious puppy's increasing discomfort with their efforts—or my having to jump up and rescue someone's shoe or notebook, or pull her off a student whose lap she was trying to climb onto. It was a tension in the class around the work itself—a level of tension, of pushback from some of the first-year students, that I'd never experienced before. One insisted that every one of us was wrong about her story, that we were misreading it. One said, in response to my remark that even if the reader didn't understand the characters' motivations, the writer had to, "I don't agree. I don't *have* to know anything." And so it went, for weeks.

But indoors, at home, each of us alone in front of a screen, it wasn't any better. Instead, it was worse, the way most things are worse online. Mics off except when people had something particular to say, there was no laughter. The conversation became increasingly stilted, polite at best, sometimes unkind, always chilly. And then one Friday one of the first-years said something no student had ever said to me in over thirty years of teaching. Said it brusquely, harshly, so there was no mistaking it for an attempted joke.

"Nobody agrees with you. You should just stop talking."

Everyone stopped talking then. It seemed like a long silence, but I'm sure it couldn't have been. Silences on Zoom are shatteringly long, even when they last just for a minute.

I wanted to end class right then, but we still had another story to discuss. We moved on, dispiritedly. All the joy, the sense of camaraderie and shared impassioned purpose, the warmth, the good humor that I'd been so proud of fostering in class, was gone. The whole rest of the semester was like that, in that class—everyone glum and exhausted, with abrupt flashes of bitterness, hostility, ugliness. And I kept having to turn off my mic and beg the puppy to please settle down, to just let me get through this three-hour class. I muttered this as if it were a prayer.

⁂

My surviving cat, Lizzy, changed after Cady's death. She mourned for months, sitting and staring at the front door all day long, waiting for her to come home. And then, out of the blue, she seemed to set her grief aside. Perhaps she had at last resigned herself to it; perhaps she'd only tired of it. Who knows what a cat thinks? I don't think she forgot. Perhaps she squared her shoulders, told herself it was time to get on with it.

She turned into a cat a lot like Cady.

She was at my heels as soon as I stood up and left the room. When I sat down again, she climbed into my lap. At night, she slept on my pillow, just above my head (unlike Cadence, though, she didn't snore). When people visited, she greeted them as if she had been waiting for them all her life.

By the time of Cady's death, we three were living in Ohio; we'd just moved from the little rental house we had been living in during my first year of teaching, into the three-bedroom, hundred-year-old wood-frame house I'd bought when I began my second year, when I decided it was time to start my grownup life. The house had a fenced-in yard the two old, city-bred cats could lie in the sun and roam in. Neither one of them could climb a fence by then, and as I sat on the back steps and watched them enjoy the yard, I thought about the first time they had ever been outdoors—when we'd first left New York and moved to Iowa, five years before. I'd opened the front door, and Cadence didn't hesitate: she dashed out, leapt off the porch, and climbed halfway up the tree next to our tiny house. (Lizzy, as usual, sat perfectly still and stared at her, amazed.) I remembered the first time they saw snow, that first Iowa winter—how Cady jumped from the front porch "onto" the mountain of it and dropped down a good four feet into the hole her body made. I remembered Lizzy peering down into the hole and meowing at her, and how strangely calm Cadence was as I dug her out.

My parents had never owned a house. My grandparents hadn't either. My younger brother and his wife had just bought one, though, a year after the birth of their first child. It felt right to me that I, thirty-four years old and single, with no plans to ever live with anyone except my cats, should have a house of my own too.

Six months before I bought the house, I had ended a four-year relationship that had been marching steadily toward marriage. I had only recently begun a volatile, unstable new relationship, and the volatile man to whom I'd attached myself was so outraged by my having moved ahead with my plan—hatched in the immediate wake of that painful breakup—to buy a house of my own ("It's clear that you have no faith in *our* future," he said), he broke up with me. (I'll note that this worked out for the best. He was not even divorced yet from the wife he had left suddenly right before we started dating, whom he'd been with since their sophomore year of college. Besides, it soon emerged that he already had his eye on an undergraduate at the university where we both taught.)

Cady died two days after the breakup with my volatile colleague. She was fifteen or sixteen years old, perhaps even older. I suppose I should not have been surprised—shocked—by her death. But I was. I was shocked and heartbroken, alone with Lizzy, still surrounded by unpacked boxes in what felt like a too-big old house I had been foolish to have bought.

Four years later, nearly to the day, and weeks after the birth of my daughter, I lost Lizzy. At seventeen, she was an ancient cat. She had been with me for all but the first weeks of her life—she'd been with me through *my* entire adulthood, something I could not stop thinking about. I nursed and rocked my baby and sang lullabies and nonsense songs to her, and wept.

And then, when my daughter was just six months old, I lost my grandmother.

A whole half year, late spring through early winter, of birth and death.

There'd been no one I had ever been as close to for so long—for my whole life—as my grandmother. There was no one I trusted more. She was the first person in my family I told I was pregnant, when the news was only days old, when I was not even halfway through my first trimester. I'd talked to her every day for years (and in my middle twenties, which corresponded to her early eighties—a rough stretch for both of us—sometimes we'd talked more than once a day). I took the subway out to Brooklyn every weekend or hitched a ride with my mother to spend half a day with her until I moved away for grad school—and then, less than two months after I did, days before she turned eighty-six, and for the first time in her life, she got on a plane and came to see me.

I don't know how I would have borne the loss of her *and* Lizzy—with whom I had lived for so long and through so many surprising changes in my life—if not for having a new baby to take care of, to devote myself to. I could not shake the idea that both Grandma and Lizzy, both of whom had been failing for some time, had held on until my child was born, to make sure I would be okay without them. And I was, mostly. I was busy with the baby, day and night, day after day, week after week.

And by the next autumn, when my friend Amy died of cancer, I was juggling my teaching job, my writing, and a toddler. I kept my head down. I just kept going.

※

In the final months of Molly's life, I stayed home with her all day long every day. The semester had ended; I didn't have to go anywhere. I wrote or read on the front porch with her beside me, or on the living room couch with her draped across my outstretched legs—or with my legs resting on her back, as if she were an ottoman—once I'd picked her up and set her there.

For two years, ever since the stroke, I'd put off going to bed until late each night because I so hated leaving her alone downstairs. Now I stopped going upstairs altogether. I dragged my old twin-sized futon out from where I'd stored it in my study for two decades and unrolled it in the living room, where we slept together for the three months it turned out that she had left. I put the futon on the floor next to the couch, where she had decided she preferred to sleep. Every night I helped her get up on the couch and then I lay down on the futon, just below her. I would hold her paw in my left hand and watch her as she fell asleep. I watched her all the time, then. I wanted to make sure I'd know exactly when the time came that I'd have to let her go.

And each morning I'd get up and cook for her because she could not, or would not, eat dog food anymore. She'd never had much interest in it, really—she was not that kind of dog; she'd never been "food-motivated." (I used to pour her food into her bowl first thing in the morning and she'd nibble daintily at it all day—she almost never finished it before it was time for bed.) But after the stroke, she would barely touch her food, no matter how I doctored it with cheese or flakes of tuna fish, so I cooked ground beef or boiled chicken and white rice for her, and when she couldn't eat that anymore, I made scrambled eggs with heavy cream and lots of butter—the same way I'd made them for my father during his brief stay at home during the months before he died, as he'd lost so much weight his skin hung on his bones. I thought about how I had coaxed him to eat ("Please, just one more bite, I know you can do it"—my father! who'd been on a diet his whole life!) as I fed Molly scrambled eggs out of my hand. She had given up the bowl, given up sitting, standing—she spent all day lying down. I lay on the floor beside her, my hand full of eggs, as she looked out through the glass storm door to the street beyond. She'd take a lick or two, and then five minutes later she would take another.

She still enjoyed her walks, though, and so I walked her many times a day—every hour or two. I'd offer her a walk, and if she lifted her head and her ears perked up, if she wagged her tail, I'd put her leash on her and take her out. She needed my help getting up, and she needed to rest often as we made our way around the block—and she needed help with the porch steps when we returned—but the walks themselves, so short and slow now, gave her so much pleasure it was worth it.

Her life and mine had narrowed to a point—the living room, the front porch, the single block we walked around so many times a day—and I knew that it would not be long before I would have to let her go. *You'll never find the right moment*, everybody told me. *Either you'll do it still wondering if it's too soon, or, more likely, you'll wait too long. You'll know you should have done it sooner.*

I didn't answer them. What was the point? I would know, I was sure. I was watching her that closely.

One morning in early July, she woke up at five AM, as usual, and I put her leash on for her first walk of the day, the walk I took her on in my pajamas, before I even washed my face, before I made her scrambled eggs and drank a cup of coffee. But this time, as soon as we stepped off the porch, her legs failed her. She collapsed on the sidewalk without a sound. I sat down next to her, stroking her with one hand as I called the university's vet hospital with the other, then called and woke my husband, who had come in from his studio and gone to sleep only an hour or two before. I told them both, vet hospital and husband, that it was time. The woman who answered the phone said they'd be ready with a gurney when we pulled up at the hospital. Glen said he'd be right out.

I remember the veterinarian who sat with Molly and me on the cushioned floor at the university vet hospital when the time did come. It was not even five-thirty AM on a Friday; everything was quiet. And the kind and very young vet asked me to tell her about the day we'd brought Molly the puppy home. I told her the story. I kept telling her the story until Molly wasn't with us anymore.

I didn't realize until later that it was July 8, my father's birthday. The day he would have turned eighty-six.

8

I wasn't sure I'd ever get another dog. Everybody told me that I needed to. But when people said this, I felt as if, after my father's death, they'd said, "Why don't you get another father? You'll feel better."

There was so much that was strange about not having Molly with me after so long, especially after I'd curled my life around her toward the end. I didn't know what to do with myself. I'd wake up in the morning, in the bed I hadn't slept in since late March, and go downstairs and stand in my kitchen, unsure what to do next. I couldn't figure out how to arrange the day, with no one to take care of. It was the first time in my adult life that I hadn't had someone to take care of.

I did what I could to take advantage of that. A month at an artists' colony. Six weeks in London. I'd go to New York for a month, six weeks, at a time. By sheer luck, it was the year following her death that I took my long-deferred sabbatical from teaching, which I'd had to apply for many months ahead of time.

And after my sabbatical, once I was tethered again to Columbus, I started taking dance classes. I also signed up for emails from Petfinder—just in case I changed my mind, I told myself. I checked almost all the boxes: puppies, young dogs, adult dogs, small, medium, and large. I never opened any of the emails.

Until four years after Molly's death—four years to the day, on July 8, 2020: nearly four months into the pandemic's lockdown. The day that would have been my father's ninetieth birthday. I woke up at five that morning, just as if Molly were still with me in her final days, wanting her first walk before the sun came up, and reached for my phone. For the first and only time, I opened up my daily email from PetFinder.

9

Ella was ten weeks old—a small, floppy puppy, white with brown spots, like a cow. She was very shy. At first she wouldn't meet my gaze, and when I held her up high from where I sat on the ground, on the sidewalk in front of the pet store where the woman who had been fostering her had told me to meet her, the puppy turned her head away.

"Is she afraid of me?" I asked the foster mother.

"Well, she's a fearful little thing. But she attaches easily." the woman said. "She's already attached to me."

I could see that. The puppy was straining in my arms, trying to get back to the woman who'd been looking after her.

On the way to Grove City, to the strip mall where the pet store was located, I'd told Fili (who'd offered not only to go with me but to do the driving, because I was so anxious about meeting the puppy) that I felt like a contestant on a reality TV show, "the kind where you meet someone and have to decide instantly whether to marry them or not."

"Are there shows like that?" Fili asked me. I didn't know. It seemed like it was possible.

We were both anxious, masked, side by side in Fili's van. We'd cranked all the windows down. Hot air blew in at us. It felt like a long drive.

Now I considered the puppy squirming in my grasp. I spoke quietly to her. "What do *you* think?" I asked her. "Are we meant for each other? Are we going to be together for the next thirteen, fourteen years?" All she wanted was for me to put her down.

I turned to Fili, who was standing a few feet away. "How am I supposed to know?" I said. "She's cute all right. But all puppies are cute."

I'd been worried about how I'd feel, meeting the puppy. Would my guilt about replacing Molly make it impossible for me to take her home? It had not occurred to me that I would be this unsure of myself, that I might not fall instantly in love. "She's so different from the way Molly was right at the beginning. It was so clear to Grace and me both that she was ours."

Fili said, "Don't compare her to Molly. She is someone else entirely."

I nodded—yes, of course. Fili was right. And wasn't I determined *not* to try to replace Molly? I cradled the puppy in my arms. I could feel her heart beating hard and fast.

"Why don't you take her to the other end of the parking lot?" Fili said. "Get to know her away from us."

The foster mother—I'd use her name here but I have forgotten it—thought this was a good idea. "She's too attached to me," she said. "But that's a good sign. It means she'll easily attach to you, it means she's capable of it."

I walked to the far end of the parking lot with the puppy. It did help, I could tell, for her not to have the foster mother in her sight. She definitely seemed more interested in me (or at least less interested in escaping from me), the farther away we got. When Fili and the woman were so far away I couldn't see them clearly anymore, I lay down on the ground and held the puppy to my chest. I can't imagine what people thought as they walked by on the sidewalk—and a surprising number of people were out and about at the strip mall in Grove City. I hadn't seen this many people at once in four months. But I didn't care what any of these strangers thought.

I brought my face to the puppy's. This time she didn't try to wriggle away. I pulled my mask down to my chin and kissed the top of her head. She did not object. But she still wouldn't look me in the eye. She's shy, I thought. Shy is not a bad thing.

When I walked back, the puppy draped over my shoulder like a human baby, the foster mother said, "You see?" I nodded. But I still wasn't sure. Did we belong together?

I stalled. I asked the woman questions about her life, her house. She seemed to live on a sort of farm, someplace "out in the country," she said vaguely. She had many other animals besides dogs—and she had many dogs, both her own and a steady stream of fosters—and several small children (at the time, this all struck me as idyllic for a newly rescued puppy). She mentioned that this puppy was the most submissive of her litter, or anyway of the four she'd been fostering—whom she'd named Ella, Stella, Bella, and Fella—since the seven-week-old litter had arrived from Oklahoma, where they had been found. There was a fifth puppy in the litter, one more male, but he'd been placed with a different foster, who had named him Milo. It had been Milo's photograph I'd seen in the email from PetFinder, the one I'd contacted the rescue to inquire about. But he'd already been adopted by the time anybody read my email, and when the rescue offered me the chance to meet his sister Ella, whose photo had not yet been uploaded, I told my husband and Fili that it must be kismet, since Ella was the name I'd had in mind for my next dog. I was joking—or half joking. Or possibly pretending to be joking. Because while Ella *was* on my short list of names, I did not—unlike my daughter at age eight—believe in "signs from the universe." Or so I would have sworn.

The foster mother said she had to go, she had a lot to do that day. Did I want the puppy or not? If not, there was already a long list of people interested in her. Surely I had heard that everyone in quarantine was trying to adopt a puppy.

Ella had been in my arms for so long by then, it felt like she belonged there. I said yes, I wanted her.

By the time Fili and I got back to my house, she was sound asleep in my lap and I was sure about her. I already loved her. By the next morning, after she'd slept in my arms all night, I could tell she loved me too. She couldn't bear to have me out of her sight. And from then on, we were inseparable.

As she and I settled into a blissful daily routine, I came to believe that the reason I had waited for so long to adopt a dog after the loss of Molly was that I had been waiting for *her*. It was a thought that was so unlike me that it made me wonder if the months of isolation at home had changed me. Unhinged me.

Or maybe, I thought, the truth was that I'd always secretly believed in fate—so secretly I'd kept it from myself until this lonely time. Maybe that little joke I'd made about the puppy's name hadn't been a joke at all.

It didn't matter. All that mattered was that Ella was the perfect dog for me, the dog I would have requested if an order could have been put in. At twelve weeks—sixteen weeks, eighteen weeks, five months, six months—old, she was wholeheartedly devoted to me. She never left my side. She draped herself across me as I wrote or read, reclining on the couch, and Glen as he passed through the living room would say, "That's an awfully big baby you have there"— because by six months she weighed fifty pounds; at ten months, eighty-five.

She slept in my arms, the first few weeks. When she got too big for that, she curled herself around *me*. If Glen came to bed, she would move down to the foot of the bed, on my side, and sleep on top of my legs. On the mornings after he'd spent the whole night in his studio, I'd wake up and Ella's head would be on his pillow. She'd press her nose to mine. When I opened my eyes and said good morning to her, she would lick my face.

She was so affectionate, and she so appreciated my affection: she not only let me hug her, she seemed to hug me back, putting her front legs around my shoulders, setting her big head against my neck.

She was also smart, eager to please, and easy for me *to* please. Did she want a walk? Oh yes she did! Did she want to share the couch with me for hours? Absolutely. She also enjoyed performing (just like me). And unlike Molly (but also just like me), she was extremely food-motivated. This made it easy to train her. Unlike Molly, she always came when called, so I was able to unleash her in the park as I had never been able to unleash Molly. We even played in the ballfield that was fenced in only on three sides, where Ella's favorite game was "wait." I'd tell her to sit and wait while I went to the farthest end of the field, so far away that she was a white speck in the distance—a speck that remained perfectly, alertly still—until I called "Come!" and she'd run toward me like a colt, a great loping run that filled me with delight.

And she was social. She loved other dogs, all other dogs—she never met a dog she didn't like. Even when a dog was mean to her, she would be glad to see him the next day. Fili and Russ's dog, Sole, growled at her every single time he saw her, and she was unfazed by it; every time she saw him, she would pull out all her tricks—bowing to him, lying down and making herself flat from head to tail, rolling over to expose her spotted belly; she would slither toward him like a snake and try to kiss him. Being snarled at—even snapped at—didn't worry her. She was the most forgiving creature in the world.

Because of Ella, even mid-Covid, I had a social life again. The first new friend I made was Turvi*, who lived on my block but whom I'd never even seen before. We met the day after I adopted Ella; she had just adopted a dog, too. We were both trying to wrangle our new puppies—hers, Yuri, was a little older than Ella, a lot stronger, a little harder to manage. The puppies liked each other right away, and Turvi and I fell into an easy conversation. It turned out that she taught at the university too, but in a discipline so far removed from mine we never would have met on campus. Soon we were meeting every morning, early, to walk our dogs together, trading information and laments (Ella destroyed a pair of sandals; Yuri, Turvi's favorite sneakers). We began to take them to the schoolyard nearby, a vast grassy space that was fenced in and that was not in use even as summer ended, since schools didn't open in the fall. Others joined us there and soon we were a little band of dog people: Zack, Eric, Aleks, Kelley, Hannah, Sarah. Some of us became close, talking about the dogs at first and then also about work, our families, our histories.

A whole group of us began to text each other when we were on our way out. Eventually Turvi had to stop bringing Yuri, who wouldn't come when called and somehow managed to escape the schoolyard several times—forcing the back gate open, or sliding under the fence in a place where it wasn't tight—running across the busy street, Turvi running frantically after her. So instead of meeting with the rest of us, Turvi and Yuri, and sometimes Turvi's shy, artistic teenaged daughter, started coming to my backyard every evening so the dogs could play. But at eight most mornings, all that fall and winter and the next spring, Aleks and Kelley and Zack and I met up, masked, in the schoolyard; while Ella played with Arlie, the blue heeler puppy she adored, and Arlie's "older brother" Jackson, a

---

* The only name besides Issac's that I have changed in this book.

foxhound, and Zack's small, energetic mixed-breed puppy, Roxy, and whoever else turned up—Q, Maisy, Remy, Scout, Leo, Bernice—we humans talked.

Over time, Ella grew accustomed to, and even came to love, some of the people at the other end of her dog-friends' leashes. She especially loved Aleks, Zack, Zack's son Oak, and Turvi. And there were a few other people she decided (randomly, it seemed to me) she loved: two women on my block, for instance—one who lived next door and whom I hardly knew, as we had never talked till then except to say hello, and who had two dogs of her own with whom Ella was acquainted only through the slats of our shared backyard fence; one a dance friend, halfway down the block. When these women were outside, she would run toward them, just as she ran to Russ and Fili, dragging me behind her. As these few beloveds bent to pet and murmur to her, she would hug them the way she hugged me, then lie down and roll over for a belly rub.

Other people with dogs envied me. She was so gentle and obedient. She never barked—not at other dogs, not at strangers of whom she was clearly petrified. Her fear of people was so quiet that sometimes (too often) people would protest, saying, "Oh, your dog can't be afraid of *me*" as Ella crouched behind me, shivering. "All dogs love me!" They'd reach toward her, or walk around me to get to her (or go so far as to cross the street after I'd crossed it to avoid them), and she would freak out, pulling me so hard I'd start to fall backwards—all without making a sound.

Sometimes I would confess that she was not as "easy" as she seemed to be. No one believed me. But I could not get through a virtual dance class anymore because she needed my attention every minute. She would climb on top of me when I folded forward; she would grab my leg when I extended it (or she would just lie down on the floor under the barre Glen had built for me, so that I couldn't make use of it). Or she would destroy things—shoes, books, a wooden foot massager—in a bid for me to chase her and stop dancing.

The two extremes of I love you/I am mortally afraid of you were becoming increasingly worrisome, especially since Glen, as time passed, was falling into the second camp. She began to hide behind me from him, frantically trying to wedge herself between my back and the couch cushions I was leaning on if he came into the room where I was reading.

She jumped out of her skin when a text notification pinged, when the microwave beeped, when the kitchen timer went off ... or when a chair was scraped back loudly in another room. A cabinet door banged shut. A taped-up box peeled open.

And while she still never barked outside the house, she began to explode into frenzied, panicked barking and leaping at the window—so that I was afraid she would crash right through it one day—not just when the mail was delivered, or groceries or packages were dropped off on the porch, but also when anyone walked by on the sidewalk in front of our house ... or even across the street. Eventually I had to put up frosted glass stick-ons on the windows to keep her from seeing out, which helped but not enough. If she heard footfalls, even distant ones, she'd still go wild with fear. Once, as I sat reading on the couch and she lay in my lap, she reared back so suddenly she gave me a black eye.

She was an odd duck, I knew. But she was *my* odd duck. Neurotic, yes, but so adorable, so charming, so much fun, so cuddly. She was perfect company for me. The universe had been kind to us, bringing us together.

10

The real trouble started one night in December, in the middle of the night. She was seven months old. I'd woken up because I'd felt or heard her jump off the bed. I sat up. She wasn't in the bedroom. So I got up too and followed her. She was on the landing, vomiting. "Poor girl," I said. It was not the first time she had vomited (she was a dog who would eat anything; thus vomiting often ensued), and I did what I always did. I went to fetch a roll of paper towels—we had one in the bathroom—and then, still speaking softly to her (*oh, poor baby, it's okay, I'm here, oh, my poor girl*), moved toward the landing to clean up the pool of vomit. But this time, unlike any of the other times, she turned her head toward me and snarled—a deep, low, threatening sound—and crouched, about to spring at me. I backed off—ran, in fact, back to the bedroom.

Shaken, I lay in the dark listening. She was *eating* it—I could hear her. Gross. But okay, I thought, dogs can be gross. The aggression toward me, though—that was something else. An anomaly for sure. She wasn't feeling well; she wasn't quite in her right mind because of that.

Before too long, she jumped back onto the bed. We both went back to sleep. In the morning all the vomit was gone; there wasn't even a stain. It was as if it hadn't happened.

But it had. And after that, an episode I learned to call "resource-guarding" (the trainer I had worked with when Ella was very young, whom I called first thing the next morning, offered me the phrase and told me it can happen when a dog gets hold of an especially rare and desirable resource—in this case, disgustingly, her own vomit; she suggested that from now on, when Ella vomited, I should just stay away from her, since "eating it won't hurt her, and being grossed out won't hurt you"), this sort of thing happened again. And again. And again.

She began "resource-guarding" not just her own vomit but trash she picked up on the street on our walks and anything she picked up in the house that wasn't hers. She'd growl and threaten to bite me if she had a glove or shoe, a spatula, a sock, a sweater she'd pulled out of the laundry basket. If she stood up at the sink—by now she was easily big enough to get into the kitchen sink—and I told her to get down (which I had done a hundred times before, which she had listened to before), she growled at me. If she snatched a knife out of the sink and ran away with it and I forgot myself and moved toward her, afraid she'd hurt herself, she'd turn on me, snarling, teeth bared.

Once, she gnawed off a piece of hard plastic from a laundry basket, and I made the "don't do that" sound the trainer had taught me in her younger puppyhood (I was afraid she'd swallow it—I felt I had to do something) and she did drop it. My relief was as profound as if I had just pulled her back from falling off a cliff. *Thank goodness*, I remember thinking. *She is not beyond reach*. But she returned at once to gnawing on the basket, and I told myself that since she was distracted, I could grab the piece she'd dropped to make sure she wouldn't pick it up and swallow it. And so I reached down for it and instantly she turned on me. I say "turned on me" because in such moments she became another dog, a dog who didn't know me. She forgot herself, forgot everything she knew.

The laundry basket incident resulted in what I refused to call a "bite" (the way I described it to myself, and on the form I filled out when I made an appointment with an animal behaviorist at the university's veterinary hospital, was that "my arm got in the way of her snarling and snapping at the air to warn me") but which drew blood and left my arm bruised and swollen. And a few days later came another "incident": she managed to get hold of a roll of Scotch tape in its small plastic dispenser—I heard her crunching on it—and while I did remember to stop and think before reaching for it, instead saying quietly, "Drop it," when she did obediently drop it, for some reason I once more thought it would be okay to pick up what was left of it (I was so slow to learn!) and the same thing happened.

My appointment with the animal behaviorist was still weeks away, but living with ten-month-old Ella had become a minefield. I talked on the phone with the behaviorist's assistant, who gave me advice about how to handle it when Ella got hold of something valuable or dangerous ("Anything else, just let it go") and I got better at that. I would stay calm, pretend not to care about the knife or pair of eyeglasses she had in her mouth (if I didn't care, she'd drop it, daring me to intercede) and stay far away from her as she watched me to see what I would do next, and then I would discreetly get a handful of treats and drop them casually in a room that could be closed off with a door. I was always afraid she would pick up what she'd just dropped before she headed off to get the treats, but she did not—she went for them, and I could shut her in the room while I removed the dangerous/valuable "resource." When I let her out, she had forgotten all about it.

I waited, anxiously, for our appointment with the animal behaviorist. I took notes. Although she hadn't started resource-guarding her own food or toys (not yet—that would come later), there came a day when I moved to readjust the blanket I kept on the back of the couch where we spent so much time, and she growled warningly at me. Then she didn't want me to touch her dog bed, even when she wasn't lying on it. And while by eight months she'd already started growling at Glen when he touched her—so he had stopped touching her—now she was growling when he walked by. Or, sometimes, just because he'd looked at her from the doorway.

But all the rest of the time—most of the time—she was the same dog she'd always been. She still slept with me, still licked my face when we woke up, still played "wait" with me and played nicely (almost always) with her dog-friends. Still liked meeting new dogs. Still lay beside me while I worked. Still was the perfect dog for me, my best friend, my always-companion. I made jokes—they seemed like jokes—about how she was ninety-five percent angel and five percent furious wild beast from hell. I worried out loud to the closest of my dog-people friends—Aleks and Kelley, Turvi, Zack—and to Russ and Fili and my daughter and my mother and my husband. It became hard to think about anything else. To talk about anything else. To *do* anything else. I kept watch over Ella. "That's my job now"—another joke I made that was not a joke.

When at last we saw the animal behaviorist, Dr. Lilly—Ella's therapist, I called her—Ella was nearly a year old. It was late April by then. I reiterated everything I'd written on the intake form and then read from my notes—all the things that had happened since I'd called for the appointment. I made the joke I'd prepared, about how I felt like I was my dog's "emotional support human." Nobody laughed. Dr. Lilly said, "Yes, that's it. That is exactly what you are." She said this so gently and so seriously, I felt my eyes fill.

That was how she talked the whole time—seriously, softly, kindly—as she asked questions and made observations, both about what I reported and what Ella was doing at any given instant (explaining my own dog to me; in effect, translating for her), and spoke of the research that had been done on "highly fearful, anxious dogs like yours." All the while, she and her assistant did things with their hands that I could not make sense of—but which Ella seemed to understand—and made noises in their throats and dispensed a lot of treats as Ella paced relentlessly around the treatment room. (Until I saw it typed out in the visit summary that was emailed to me later, though, I didn't know—I hadn't noticed—that for the first hour, her tail was tightly tucked between her legs.)

Ella was pronounced by Dr. Lilly "on the far end of severely anxious and fearful." She added, "What you must understand is that these are the filters through which she experiences the world."

I was bewildered by this diagnosis, which seemed too expansive. "But most of the time she seems so happy. Are you saying that she's anxious *all* the time, even when she seems okay? That I'm just not seeing it?"

"I am," Dr. Lilly said. "I'm sorry."

She told me, too, that the sort of fear-based aggression I was seeing in Ella typically started to show up in "dogs like her" when they were seven or eight months old, so Ella was "right on track." Dr. Lilly described it as a time bomb waiting to go off. She told me that the aggressiveness generally leveled off at about age four, but until then it tended to increase. And there was often a dramatic increase right around twelve months.

"You mean, like right now."

Yes, that was what she meant.

It was at this point, I think, that I asked the question that had been on my mind all along. Not just today, but for months. I had spoken of it, sometimes as if I were joking, sometimes in a hush, with tears in my eyes, to some of my dog-people friends. Could this be my fault? Had I done this—had I ruined her? And to my horror, as soon as I spoke these words now, I began to sob.

I hadn't broken down once in the months since she'd first growled at me. I hadn't let anyone in on how anxious I had been since then—not even Grace. But now, as I wept, I confessed to Dr. Lilly—it felt like a confession—that for the first two weeks I'd had Ella, I had kept her in my arms at all times except when I took her for a walk, or when I set her down in the backyard after I carried her there in the middle of the night to pee, then swept her back up in my arms again. She was so small and so afraid of everything! I treated her as if she were a human infant—I treated her the way I'd treated my own human infant in the first weeks of her life. I slept with her in my arms, just as I'd slept with my newborn baby. I'd just wanted her to feel safe, to know she was loved.

Had I mishandled Ella's fearfulness? Should I have let her toughen up right from the start? Had I done this to her?

Dr. Lilly said, "Oh, no—no, no, no, no. Ella was born this way. You saw that for yourself the first time you met her. She was full of fear. Fearfulness at this level, anxiety as profound and constant as this, is genetic. It's inborn."

I was still crying, but I managed to say, "I can't believe that that's all there is to it. You're talking about, what, a gene for anxiety and fear?"

"It's more complex than that, as I'm sure you know. And the genetic predisposition is often exacerbated by maternal stress in utero. And then by early experience." Before I could protest that this was just what I was talking about—before I could say that Ella's early experience was with *me*, and that instead of giving her a chance to learn to cope with everything she was afraid of, I overprotected her, I coddled her, I acted as if I agreed with her—that the world *was* a scary place—Dr. Lilly said, "Let me be clear. When I say 'early experience,' I'm not talking about those first weeks or months with you. Don't make the mistake of confusing dogs with humans. When we talk about early formative experience in humans, we're talking about something on the order of the first five years. But in dogs, all we've got is twelve weeks. A dog born with the genetic makeup Ella has might have stood a chance if for the first ten weeks of her life she had the sense of safety you gave her for those last two weeks before that window closed. Two weeks wasn't enough. It was too late."

I looked at my puppy, who at this point in the ninety-minute session had at last settled down (albeit tensely, in a posture that demonstrated high alertness, according to the visit summary, and this hadn't happened until eighty minutes in), and I thought about the litter she had been a part of, about which I had been told only that it came from Oklahoma and that fostering began at seven weeks. When had they been parted from their mother, the full-bred Great Pyrenees the DNA test I had sent away for had told me about? What had happened to her? Had she died? Abandoned them? Had they been taken from her? And was seven weeks (just barely old enough to be away from her) the age the litter had been found (surrendered?)—or had the puppies languished somewhere else before they were taken to Ohio by the rescue group? Why had they been taken to Ohio, anyway? What had that long trip been like for them? Nobody had told me and I'd never thought to ask. I'd never thought to ask any of the questions I had now.

Or no, not "never thought to." Didn't want to. Couldn't bear to.

What *had* I asked the rescue that had let me adopt her? Nothing, really. We'd communicated by email and then they'd given me the foster mother's phone number.

And then there was the foster situation. I remembered what the woman had told me about the many other dogs "and other animals," the houseful of children. How idyllic it had sounded. Was it? Or was it chaotic, overwhelming? Particularly for a dog like Ella.

A dog like Ella. I could not imagine any other dog like Ella.

"For what it's worth," Dr. Lilly said, "if you hadn't shown her so much tenderness—what you're now calling 'overprotectiveness'—those first weeks she was with you, things would likely be worse than they are now."

We talked then about medication—the various options she wanted to try, one at a time: trazodone, gabapentin, sertraline—and some aspects of training that I hadn't worked on yet—learning how to redirect her quickly and efficiently, teaching her to quickly go to a spot I picked out (her assistant, Rebecca, would be helping me with this), teaching her to remain in one room while I was in another—and how careful I would have to be to avoid her triggers, both those I'd already discovered and the news ones that arose. "Because there will be new ones." I'd have to be attentive, Dr. Lilly told me. I told her that attentive was my middle name. This time, at least, I got a laugh. A small one.

"The training will help," she said, "but it won't fix the problem. I want to be clear on this." She talked about the notion, reinforced by YouTube videos about reactive dogs and reality TV shows about dog trainers, that aggression could be "trained out of" a dog—any dog—if the right training methods were employed.

"And try to remember that she can't help it when she lashes out at you. Her brain is mis-wired. She acts as if she doesn't know you at those moments because she is—I mean this literally—scared out of her mind. That doesn't make it any less dangerous to you, to others, even to herself. But this is what we're dealing with."

And then she wished us luck, told me she'd send the prescriptions to the pharmacy and that I should call to set up our first session with Rebecca, and sent us on our way.

Ella and I took a two-hour nap together as soon as we got home. I don't think either one of us had ever been so tired.

I was optimistic—even confident—for the next eighteen hours. We had a plan. And I'd worked miracles with Ella before. Back in October I had started working toward getting her used to being left at home (otherwise, what would happen when I had to go back to work in person next fall?), either by herself or with Glen if he wasn't in the studio. And at first, she wouldn't move a muscle the whole time I was gone: I'd come home and she would be in the same spot she'd been in when I'd left, right by the front door (if Glen had been home, he'd report that she'd sat staring at it for the hour or ninety minutes of my absence). She would greet me frantically when I came home.

But by now she was calm when I left her to take an in-person, masked ballet class, to get vaccinated, to go shopping for the first time since March 2020. She'd lie on the couch while I was gone; sometimes she'd even fall asleep. And when I returned, she didn't always jump on me—she showed some restraint. I'd *fixed* this. I was proud of myself. I'd reported all of this to Dr. Lilly, who congratulated me on all the progress I had made when it came to separation.

We still had a ways to go, though. When I left her, she still wouldn't eat or drink, play with a toy, chew on even a favorite chew stick, or use the pet door she had access to all day to go into the backyard to relieve herself. And she still wouldn't have anything to do with Glen if he was there while I was gone (she growled warningly at him if he made any effort to engage her). It was also clear that she could not be left with anybody else, not even for five minutes. If one of her best dog friends and the human who had brought her over—even if this were someone she loved and trusted, like Turvi—were visiting in our backyard and I had to go inside to grab something or to use the bathroom, she would follow me, close at my heels, and she could not be coaxed to go back out until I went out with her. But mostly I'd succeeded, hadn't I? And I had done that on my own, before I'd had the help of Dr. Lilly and Rebecca. Now I had help. I could do this.

I tried not to think about one of the things that Dr. Lilly had said during our appointment, when I'd asked about when I might be able to travel, to leave Ella overnight. I hadn't seen my mother, who was eighty-eight, since before lockdown; I hadn't seen my daughter in eight months—not since she'd rented a car and driven to Columbus from New York after quarantining for three weeks, just so she could meet the puppy, in early September. I wasn't quite ready to get on a plane yet, I told Dr. Lilly, but I'd like to do it soon, now that all of us were fully vaccinated. How should I begin to build on what I'd done thus far? What might I do to help Ella be all right without me for a few days?

Dr. Lilly said that it would be a long time before I'd be able to leave her overnight. The way she said this—gravely, ominously—it sounded like she didn't mean just *a long time*. It sounded like she'd purposely not added *maybe never*.

I told her I'd wait, it was okay. I'd sort of known I wasn't going anywhere anytime soon. But then I said, half jokingly, "I won't miss my daughter's wedding, though, right? It's fourteen months away, a year from June. By then I'll be able to leave her with somebody."

"Maybe," Dr. Lilly said. "Let's hope so."

It's an indication, isn't it, of how much I loved my dog that I accepted this without a word of protest? That I soldiered on, even though I'd just been told that I might have to skip the wedding of my only child?

I think I also accepted this because I did not believe it. I would do everything that I was told to help Ella get better. If I did, then I felt sure it would turn out okay. Because it had to. Because I would make it so.

But the next morning, just a few minutes after Ella's second dose of trazodone, all my confidence, my can-do optimism, drained from me. I was standing at the foot of the stairs in my house and thinking, for the first time, *I'm not going to be able to keep her.*

Since Ella was five months old, I'd fed her in the morning with a treat ball stuffed with kibble—we'd go downstairs as soon as we woke up, I'd let her out into the backyard to pee, than I would fill the treat ball and we'd head upstairs again, where she worked on getting her breakfast from the treat ball while I showered and dressed. On this morning, though, for the first time in her life, she stared morosely at the ball. She didn't touch it. I thought the trouble might be that the medication had made her too sluggish to dig her food out of the treat ball. I said, "Okay, sweetpea, let's go try your bowl instead." I picked up the treat ball and she followed me back to the stairs and down them—and then, when we reached the bottom, she turned back toward me and lunged. And this time she bit me for real, hard, on my right hand. Then she trapped me there, at the foot of the stairs, snarling and snapping at me. I stood as still as I could, blood dripping on the carpet, speaking to her in a whisper—"It's me," I kept saying. "Ella, sweetie, it's just *me*." It seemed like this went on for a long time. I cannot remember how I got free, how I made it to the kitchen sink to run water on the bite, to wrap a towel tightly around it, to sink into a chair and call Dr. Lilly.

I do remember that as I sat talking on the phone—it was Rebecca I reached then, in that first of many phone calls that day—Ella came and lay her head on my knee.

She knew I was upset about something. She had come to comfort me.

11

Later, after everything that happened, most people I knew rallied around me, knowing how much pain I was in, how fragile I was. But one friend—Turvi, whom I'd thought of not just as the best friend I had made through Ella but also as one of my closest friends, dog people or not—refused to see or speak to me. Turvi and I had talked about traveling abroad together once the pandemic was behind us; we had celebrated all our milestones in my back yard—toasting to our birthdays, hers in February, mine in March, and to every piece of good news either one of us received. But now she ghosted me. My texts to her, I see as I reread them now, were increasingly frantic sounding, even as I speculated on her silence (she was nearly as grief stricken as I was, or she was trying to give me space—"but honestly," I wrote, "I don't want space. Our friendship has been one of the greatest gifts Ella has given me. I miss you"—or was it that she simply couldn't think of what to say?). Finally, after a month, she texted me to say that she was shocked and disappointed, that she couldn't be my friend, that she and her daughter and Yuri would be moving away from the neighborhood and she expected never to have to see me again.

I've been proved wrong before about my certainty that someone would be a part of my life forever, that someone understood me perfectly and that I understood them too. I am not that good a judge of character, it turns out. Or at least not a good judge of who won't let me down or cause me pain. Is anyone?

I suppose if it were possible to know ahead of time who'd hurt us, we'd never be hurt.

Dr. Lilly's theory about what had happened at the bottom of the stairs was that the medication she'd put Ella on had caused her to lose her appetite, "but without taking away her extreme concern about food." She asked me if I was sure I was okay—I was not sure, but I said yes, I was—and suggested that we try a different medication.

The next one restored her appetite, but made her alternately sleepy and agitated. (About the agitation I was able to make a weak, desperate joke—my fallback when in despair—since Grace and I both have had paradoxical reactions to drugs. "It runs in the family," I told Dr. Lilly.)

The third medication neither agitated Ella nor sedated her, nor made her lose her appetite. But was it making her less anxious? I could not be sure. I thought she did seem somewhat more at ease some of the time (or maybe *I* was somewhat more at ease, so that she only seemed to be—or maybe she'd picked up on my semi-relief that we seemed to have found something that might work, and she was reacting to it). Still, it would take up to six weeks, Dr. Lilly warned me, before a real difference might be seen.

In the meantime—just as Dr. Lilly had predicted—Ella, as she passed the one-year mark, got worse. While most hours of the day and all night long, she continued to be the sweetest, gentlest, most affectionate of dogs, her resource-guarding now extended to her toys, to her food at all times, to treats, to anything she spotted and was interested in (a stick, a paper wrapper on the ground), and even to my attention. I could no longer show affection to another dog; I couldn't give a treat to any of the dogs we played with, as I'd always done before (a semicircle of dogs gathering around me in the schoolyard when they took a quick break from their wrestling and chasing one another, all of them sitting nicely as I handed each one something from my treat bag). Now if I looked like I might even be thinking of giving anything to anyone but her, she snapped at both the other dog and me.

So I stopped carrying treats. I became measured in my greetings to her dog friends. I started putting all her toys away when her friends came to our yard to play with her. And then one evening, when a dance-friend, Christine, was visiting with her own extremely anxious dog, Daisy—with whom Ella had played sweetly twice before—Daisy went to the water bowl I kept on the back deck, and Ella growled and lunged at her. Poor Daisy ran to the farthest corner of the yard and huddled trembling there, and although Ella apologized, as usual—trying to kiss her and inviting her to play by bowing down to her—it was no use. Daisy was so frightened, Christine had to take her home. After that, I stopped leaving water out, too, when any dogs came over, just in case.

And Ella became more and more unpredictable. The couch we spent so many hours on? Sometimes, out of the blue, she would come at me, snapping her jaws and snarling, if I moved to join her there when she was already sitting on it. (Sometimes all it took was my rearranging the blankets and pillows on it while she was elsewhere in the living room, occupied—I'd thought—with something else.) Sometimes my moving a chair that was askew, or straightening the rug—sometimes just my walking across the room— would trigger her aggression.

I worked on her training, both in sessions with Rebecca at the hospital and daily—many times a day—at home. She loved her training—she still enjoyed performing for me, pleasing me. But she was a nervous wreck, I could see that. More nervous than ever. I'd recovered from the incident over the treat ball (the bite on my hand had healed; the scar was already faint—and besides, it was the trazodone that was to blame, I told myself). But as the weeks passed and I kept a running list of all the things I couldn't do, or had to do very carefully and slowly; as I walked on eggshells with her and nevertheless managed to provoke her at least once a day—and more often many times a day—I found myself thinking that I should consider looking into possibly rehoming her. I put it to myself this way, with this much hesitation, this much doubt. *Consider. Look into. Possibly.* It made me cry each time I thought it.

I loved her so much. But I might not be the right person for her. There might be someone else who would do better with—who would be better *for*—her. But how would that work, I wondered, when she was as attached to me as I was to her? More attached to me. After all, I could go the bathroom without wanting her to come with me, I could go into the kitchen for a glass of water without her—I could go upstairs to get something I needed—but she couldn't bear to be without me: she'd come with me to the bathroom, to the kitchen, up the stairs. My shadow. Both of us would be heartbroken if we had to part.

Still. If it were the only answer? If there were someone who knew how to "be" with her, some way I couldn't seem to figure out?

I was still mulling this over on a Tuesday night in June—still crying every time I let myself think of considering it—when I did something I'd done thousands of times before, something I had done perhaps a dozen times that very day. I reached over to pet her and to murmur some sweet words to her—*my good girl, you darling girl, my puppy*—and without even a warning growl, she attacked me. This time she went for my face.

I remember screaming, "Ella, no, no, no, Ella, please, no." I remember that there was a great deal of blood, that I ran not just from her—she let me run; she didn't chase me—but so that Glen wouldn't know yet what had happened. I was afraid he'd kill her.

I remember the sight of my face in the mirror in the downstairs bathroom, running water over my face for a long time so that I could see where the wounds were, so that I could try to figure out what to do. I remember Ella coming in and sitting on the bathroom floor beside me, that she seemed to be trembling, that she was looking up at me mournfully. I remember closing my eyes tightly, pouring first peroxide and then rubbing alcohol all over my face (nothing burned; I was in shock, I realized later—I wouldn't be in pain until the next day), deciding not to go to the ER until I could talk to someone who'd assure me that nothing would happen to my dog if I did that. (It was not until early the next morning that I reached someone at the vet hospital who told me that only a bite from someone *else's* dog would generate an automatic bite report—something I could have learned by googling, I'm sure, but I didn't think of it that night.) I remember packing towels with ice and holding them against my face as I went to tell Glen that she had bitten me—downplaying it, speaking very calmly, acknowledging the blood that was now seeping through the towel on my forehead and reminding him that even the most minor head wounds bled profusely because of the many blood vessels close to the surface there. "Are you sure you don't need me to take you to the hospital?" he asked me and I said yes, I was sure, but maybe tomorrow.

I put fresh ice in fresh towels and went upstairs to bed, clutching the towels to my face. Ella followed me. She climbed onto the bed, and as I lay awake—all night, I think—she fell asleep beside me, her head resting on my legs.

12

In the days that followed, after the ER visit the next morning, which lasted nearly a whole day, I told myself—I told everyone I talked to—that I wouldn't, couldn't, make any decisions, not yet, not while I was still in shock, in bandages, in so much pain. I needed to exhaust my every option, I said. Was there still another medication to be tried? Could Ella be *taught* not to be afraid—or not to respond to her fear in this dreadful way? Or could I teach myself to keep from doing anything that might startle her? I'd already altered my behavior in so many ways. Surely a few more adjustments wouldn't kill me. I could even teach myself not to reach over and pet her, couldn't I?

I had so many conversations with so many people, I'm not sure I can keep them all straight and separate from each other now. I know I talked several times with Dr. Lilly and Rebecca. I talked to my daughter, to my mother, to a number of friends—the most trusted of the dog people I'd met since I'd adopted Ella, and also the most trusted of my old friends. I talked more than once, at length, to a veterinary social worker. But it's one long conversation with a trainer (yet another trainer, this one recommended by Aleks and Kelley) that I remember word for word. Aleks and Kelley had worked with him with their (untroubled, rambunctious) puppy—the blue heeler, Arlie, whom Ella so loved—and they knew that he had worked successfully with deeply troubled dogs. He had rehabilitated his own fearful, aggressive cattle dog, Kelley told me.

I suppose my conversation with him made such a strong impression on me because training was his livelihood and he was so bluntly honest with me about what he couldn't promise. He told me all the same things Dr. Lilly had, and although he said he'd be willing to set up an appointment, "just so that you'll be able to tell yourself you've tried everything that can be tried," he didn't offer me much hope. Once he'd heard Ella's whole story, he told me that, with dogs like her, his success rate was "at best, maybe twenty-five percent"—and by "success," he said, he didn't mean that he could train her to be less anxious, fearful, and reactive; he meant that the fear response might be redirected, that he might be able to train her to do something else when she felt panicked. He also said that even if he was successful at that, he could not (and that no one could or should) guarantee that Ella would not bite again. It was what Dr. Lilly had told me, not once but many times that day, but somehow I only fully took it in when the trainer said it: "There will always be a chance that an attack as bad as, or worse than, what happened on Tuesday night will happen again." He also told me that rehoming her at this point was not a realistic possibility. This too was something Dr. Lilly had told me. Now it sunk in.

I made an appointment with the trainer. The earliest appointment he had was a week away, but that was okay, I thought, since I'd promised myself not to make any decisions until I'd calmed down, until I didn't feel and look like I had been run over by a bus—or beaten badly in a boxing match, or pistol-whipped. A week was nothing in that context.

Except it wasn't nothing. Except that I could not even begin to calm down, and neither could Ella.

Something had snapped in her when she had attacked me.

Although she slept peacefully with me at night, at all other times she was a wreck. All day long, all evening until we got into bed, she was jumpier, more worried, more reactive than she'd been before. She growled at me when I was sitting still; she flinched when she heard any sound at all, even the turning of a page, or when she saw anything move even slightly in her peripheral vision. Her anxiety made me more anxious. And when I saw her slowly approaching Glen as he napped after an all-nighter in the studio—her whole body tense, a growl rumbling deep in her throat—I grabbed her by her collar and pulled her away, certain she was going to attack him. I grabbed her even though I feared that she would turn on me again, that I was in real danger. I was lucky that she let me redirect her. I knew it was only luck.

I thought about—why had I never, before now?—how much *she* must be suffering. How terrified she would have to be to have attacked the person she loved most. I thought about the demons that had her on such high alert that even I had been perceived, just for an instant, as a threat. How hard life must be for her. How much pain she was in.

※

The trainer had spoken to me about "behavioral euthanasia," as had Dr. Lilly. I had believed that I would not consider it. I remember telling the trainer, when he mentioned it, that we don't euthanize *people* who are deeply troubled. We *help* them. I remember that I said this sharply.

"Yes, we do—we try to," he agreed. "And because we know that medication alone is often not enough for people, we use other treatment interventions. Psychotherapy, for example. But dogs aren't people."

"Obviously not. But even so—"

"Besides, as you know, we're not talking about *troubled*. We're talking about dangerously violent. I don't have to tell you what we as a society do to dangerously violent people."

"We lock them up."

"That's right. And I'm not going to get into the ethics of this, but I know this is not what you would want for Ella."

It wasn't. But still I dismissed this part of our conversation even as we were still having it. There was no way—there was no world in which—I would euthanize this dog, this year-old *puppy*, I so loved. And who so loved me.

So I thought, until I let myself, at last, think of her pain. And of how if I did manage to find someone who would take her despite her bite history, despite the advice about rehoming her that I'd been given, her pain would be greater. And the end of her story would be grimmer, because the person she loved would not be there to hold her in her arms and reassure her when it came.

And so I took her back to Dr. Lilly. Glen waited outside. For hours, it turned out, because it took a long time and multiple doses of sedatives before Ella was calm. I spoke to her as she paced around the room, as she lifted herself on her hind legs and knocked things from the counters, as she lay down for a few seconds and then bounded up again, as she got up on the couch where I was sitting and then jumped down. Toward the end, as she finally grew sleepy, before the injection that would end her life, I was left alone with her so that I could put my hands on her and tell her just how much I loved her, what a good girl she was, that I knew she hadn't meant to hurt me, that I would never forget her. The room had been darkened for us. My voice was the last she heard. My touch was the last she felt.

13

I have hundreds, maybe thousands, of photos and videos of Ella on my phone, my iPad, my laptop. It hurts to look at them, but I do. I don't want to stop thinking about her. I don't want to forget the way she ran across the field, or how joyful she could be when she greeted her best friend, Yuri, or the way she looked at me while I was working and she lay beside me. The way it felt to sleep with her next to me, the warmth of her body and her steady breathing, the way she'd nestle closer until it wasn't possible to get any closer, body to body. The way she'd wake me, nose to nose, each morning.

I think a lot these days about what we are entrusted with when we take on the care of animals. I remember how, when Ella was first mine, I loved her so much I became convinced that I had waited for so long to bring another dog into my life after I lost Molly because I'd been waiting all that time for *her*, the puppy who was destined for me. I remember how surprised I was—surprised, embarrassed, skeptical, even a little worried (was I losing my grip?)—when I caught myself thinking this way, because I was not that sort of person.

I was, though. I am.

But what I think now is that what was destined wasn't about me. I think I waited for so long because *she* needed me to wait for her. Because for the short time Ella was in the world, I was the one who could give her the best life she could have had. I was the one who'd know when it was time to let her go.

If You Say So

À Chacun son Goût

"You've fallen in love," Judith said.

We were beside each other at the barre—it was my second ballet class. I had surprised myself two days before by committing to an all-class pass that would renew itself every month, then surprised myself again by coming back to take another class so soon. I confessed this as we stretched our calves, waiting for class to begin.

It's my M.O. to talk to people I've just met as if I've known them all my life.

"I felt *compelled* to come," I told her. "I felt as if I had no choice about it. That's weird, isn't it?"

She laughed and said what she said, then added, gravely, "I completely understand." She and ballet were already in a long-term relationship, she said. She'd been dancing at one studio or another for over thirty years. "Longer than most of these children"—one hand on the barre, she waved the other, simultaneously acknowledging and dismissing everyone around us—"have even been alive."

Judith was an epidemiologist. Like me, she taught at the university. Neither one of us found it remarkable that we'd never crossed paths on campus: the College of Public Health and the creative writing program might as well have been in different galaxies even though the buildings housing them were no more than a ten-minute walk apart.

She was from Los Angeles, so we exchanged the customary "I can't believe I ended up here" pleasantries required when Los Angelinos and New Yorkers meet for the first time in central Ohio.

She was also a full decade older than I ("Do you know how old I am?" she asked—the first of the thousands of rhetorical questions she'd ask in the course of our friendship—before telling me the answer). I would not have guessed that she was over seventy. Was it ballet that was responsible for her well-muscled arms and back, for how slender and compact she was? I wondered but I didn't ask, which didn't matter because Judith read my mind (this too the first of many times): "I take a daily ballet class," she said, "but I also lift weights. I work with a trainer—he's very good." She looked me up and down. "Shall I give you his number?"

Was I insulted? I decided not. I *was* soft and weak-looking, and (especially as compared to Judith) fat. She was only saying out loud what was obvious. And perhaps she too had a tendency to talk to perfect strangers as if she already knew them. (This, I would discover, was exactly right, even if her way of doing so was markedly unlike my own.)

I told her I had tried weightlifting, that I had tried just about every form of exercise there was and had found them all not to my liking. Running had been my least favorite. Lifting weights was a close second.

"Really?" Judith said. "How odd. I enjoy it. I like feeling strong." She flexed her right bicep and glanced at it admiringly before she let it go and shrugged. "À chacun son goût, n'est-ce pas?" Then: "Oh, well. Never mind." She sang those four words—not pleasantly, I thought. As if she had concluded she could not be bothered with me.

Then I was insulted. So much for my first ballet friend, I remember thinking.

But Judith grew on me. We saw each other nearly every day, and every day we talked, both before and after class. I felt that I began to understand her. Her tone, I came to see, could not be interpreted the way anybody else's would—that is, when she sounded condescending or dismissive, it didn't mean she felt that way. Her disapproving tone was something like a reflex, or a habit that she wasn't quite aware of. Or she'd say something that sounded critical or even ominous but was only her way—her odd, very special Judith way—of being friendly.

She always arrived before anybody else—a good fifteen or twenty minutes early—and took the same spot, dead center at the barre mounted across the studio's eastern wall. I was next, most days, and I'd take the space beside her—at first because it seemed rude not to (if I picked a spot farther away, when there were just two of us, wouldn't it look like I was avoiding her?) but then, soon enough, because that was my spot: in front of her when we did the combinations for the first time, behind her when we turned to do them on the left.

"Greetings," she would say when I arrived. "I was wondering when you'd finally get here."

But I was always early too. Not as early as Judith, of course. But still well before the class's start time. I learned not to protest. If I did, she'd sniff and say, "Well, if you say so" in a way that suggested she was going easy on me.

She did not in fact go easy on anyone. But—as she herself would have said—this was one of her charms.

And I *was* charmed. Until I met Judith, I had always been the most forthright and outspoken person in any room I was ever in. I enjoyed ceding the crown.

One day, no more than a few weeks into our acquaintance, Judith said—it sounded like an accusation—"You're Jewish, aren't you."

I told her I was.

"I am too," she said. "*Supposedly.*" There was a dramatic pause before she lowered her voice. "So they tell me."

I was accustomed to Judith's theatricality by then. I laughed. I said, "Who's 'they'?"

"Oh, the *royal* they," she said, with that little wave to which I'd also become well accustomed. "But, you see, my father was Jewish. So was my mother, actually. But she died when I was very young. I don't remember her. My father married a gentile, and she was the one who raised me. So I was raised Christian—not that I believed any of that garbage, even as a child—I mean, who would?—and therefore I suppose I'm not really very Jewish, after all, am I?"

It was hard to know how to answer this, or if an answer was required, so I didn't try. This would turn out to be a long-term feature—not even a bug—of our relationship. As would Judith soldiering on, unfazed. "But people tell me I seem Jewish. What do you think? Do I seem Jewish to you?"

"I'm not sure I understand the question," I said carefully. I was pretty sure I did.

"Oh yes you do," she said. "When I'm in Sweden—I am frequently in Sweden—people ask if I'm Italian. I imagine this is because I'm not blond and blue-eyed, as they all are. But here, the assumption is that I'm Jewish. Do I look Jewish to you? Or do you think it's that I exhibit certain personality traits that Americans, particularly in the Midwest, associate with Jewishness? I talk a lot. I ask a lot of questions, and I'm argumentative—I have opinions. Something I can only assume I learned from my father. *He* was argumentative. He had something to say about everything. And he used to have all these people—men, obviously—over, and all of them would be talking loudly, yelling, debating whatever position one of them had staked out, all of them talking at the same time, and I'd be there listening and sometimes I'd have a thought about what they were talking about and so I'd try to get a word in, and the men would talk over me or shush me, and my father would roar at them, 'Let the child talk! She has something to say.' Whereas my mother—my stepmother, but as she was the only mother I ever knew, I called her my mother—preferred that I stay quiet. She wanted me to 'behave.' I suppose she was more of a 'children should be seen and not heard' kind of parent. Which is not the way the Jews do things, is it?"

Before I could decide if this was another rhetorical question—or if she really wondered and thought I would know the answer (and thought I would willingly provide it, in a roomful of people I was 99 percent sure did not include a single other person who was Jewish)—our teacher, Fili, called out, "Today let's start face à la barre, feet parallèle, and walk it out," and the conversation ended.

That particular bit of it ended, anyway. The conversation about Jewishness and about her father—they were intertwined for her—stopped and started many times.

We had other subjects too. We talked about Russ and Fili, about how encouraging and warm they were, how patient and kind ("and so charming," Judith always added—*charming* was one of her pet words). She told me how lucky I was, starting out with them as my teachers. By this time she had given up taking class at the other studios in town. (She sometimes badmouthed them, and Russ or Fili would ask her to stop. "Please, Judith," Russ would say, "it's bad form," and Judith would tell him, "Well, I don't see why. I'm just saying what's true.") We talked about how beautifully the two of them managed the high-wire act of all good teaching: balancing rigor and nurturing—challenging *and* sweetly supporting us; being both exacting and forgiving, serious and lighthearted. Oh, and such beautiful dancers! we said.

We'd both fallen a little bit in love with both of them, we acknowledged to each other sheepishly—or, I should say: I was sheepish; Judith was defiant.

We also talked about the classes we'd be teaching, come the fall, in our worlds-apart departments, and about our students (almost all of whom we loved) and our colleagues (we did not love very many of them). We talked about my writing, her research. She was studying the relationship between the immune system and glioblastoma, a rare and particularly deadly form of brain cancer; I'd just finished writing a novel about a young magician and his father, the magician's aspiring poet wife, her mother, and her poet mentor. "Sounds complicated," Judith said. This did not sound like a compliment.

"Not as complicated as your research," I said.

This made Judith smile—a smile that disarmed me, always.

Making her smile made me feel triumphant, always.

And I often made her smile. I'm proud of that.

She was not an easy room to work.

If You Say So

A ritual developed. I would take my place beside her at the barre on the eastern wall and we would exchange greetings. Then she would tell me about something she'd read in that day's *New York Times*. I'd tell her I'd read that story too (I always had—we both read the paper cover to cover every morning over breakfast), but Judith was undaunted. She just kept talking, telling me about it in agonizing detail until it was time for class to start.

This was both annoying and oddly familiar, although it took some time before I realized why that was. My father used to read me stories from *The Times* as I sat across from him at breakfast when I visited from wherever I was living. He'd done this for thirty years, since I'd first left New York for Iowa, for grad school. He too wouldn't stop even if I told him I'd already read the article myself. Once he got started, it seemed he couldn't stop. He had no brakes—that's how I see it now. No brakes, and no reverse gear either. Judith was like that too.

This made me feel tender toward her, protective of her. Just as I had always felt about my father, whom I'd loved and been infuriated by, who had loved me whole-heartedly and who, for my entire childhood, had made me his captive audience.

My father had been gone just over three years when I first met Judith.

Let the child talk. She has something to say.

Judith spoke so often of her father—his left-wing political leanings, his loudness, his argumentative nature—I sometimes felt as if I'd known him too. I thought I could imagine him as he held court. "Nobody had stronger opinions than my father," she would tell me, as if she'd never told me this before. "Oh, and that booming voice!"

Likewise. Was this because he was from New York? she wanted to know. Weren't all New Yorkers like this? Or was it because he was Jewish?" After a while, I knew better than to try to answer her. Judith liked to ask and answer her own questions. "Who knows?" she'd say, or, "Oh, well, what difference does it make?" And then: "It's very Jewish of me, isn't it, to answer a question with a question?"

I would smile. Or, if I was feeling mischievous, I might say, "Really? Is it?" and, after a beat, she'd smile too. "Very funny," she would say.

When she talked about her father, there would always come a point when she would sigh and say, "It's him I take after."

Looking back, it seems to me inevitable that we would be friends. It wasn't that we had so much in common—we did not, other than a shared devotion to ballet, to our own work, and to our teaching. The way we lived was as different as our disciplines: my house filled to the brim with mementos, tchotchkes, and framed photographs, in rooms crammed with too much antique furniture; Judith's—which she had been renting for close to thirty years—almost wholly unadorned, and unfurnished but for a threadbare Goodwill sofa and two battered canvas director's chairs, a tile-top dining table ringed by a set of black plastic chairs, a bed for her and a futon for her dog, and an office that was fully outfitted for working while standing up. She disdained television, stand-up comedy, most musicals (movie *or* theatrical) and pop music, excluding Motown and Bob Dylan—neither of which she would allow to be called "pop" in her presence—and a couple of the songs Russ used in his dance karaoke class (in which Judith was a faithful weekly participant): Gayle's "abcdefu" and Cardi B's "Bodak Yellow," though mostly for their lyrics.*

---

* Sample lyric (these are the opening lines of "abcdefu"):

Fuck you and your mom and your sister and your job
And your broke-ass car and that shit you call art
Fuck you and your friends that I'll never see again
Everybody but your dog, you can all fuck off

All her movie references were from the 1950s and 1960s (and were usually Bergman). She did not read novels or literary nonfiction—except, eventually, all of mine—and I rarely read *non*literary nonfiction, as she did almost exclusively, for pleasure. And she lived alone, had never married, had no children. I hadn't lived alone since 1992.

But I *had* lived alone, for sixteen years, and there were times I still missed it—longed for it. And when I told Judith this, as I told almost no one else, she understood. She also seemed to understand, better than most, why soft-spoken, reclusive Glen was the right match for me, why I had been willing to give up my solitude for him. And she was interested in Grace—more interested than anybody else I knew who was not a member of my family—and when they met for the first time, four months after Judith and I had, they adored each other.

At the studio, we came to be thought of as a pair. We were so much older than most of the others (though even the others who were older, like Pat and Brad and Cynthia and Nancy, saw Judith and me as a unit) and we were both Jewish ("whatever that means," as Judith would have said). We were both talkative and cracked a lot of jokes in class (But then so did Pat. Once, when Judith came to class dressed as a nun—"It's Halloween," she said to everyone who asked her why. "I don't have a choice"—and called out to Leiland, who was teaching, "I have a question. How do I plié in my habit?", it was Pat who answered for him: "Just keep your knees together, sister.")

But also: Judith and I quickly formed an ad hoc welcoming committee for newcomers to the studio. We did this without ever once discussing it; it came naturally to both of us. People walked in looking wary, nervous—shy—and Judith and I were always the first to speak to them, to ask their names, to introduce ourselves, to introduce them to whoever was around. We asked them about themselves. We did what we could to make them feel included. Our styles were different, though. Judith liked to say, cheerfully, "Watch out, we're a cult! It's dangerous. You'll get addicted," while I played the good mother, assuring them that they'd have fun, that they'd see soon enough why we all spent so much of our time here.

Both styles seemed to work, since everyone who came back after their first class and then kept coming back—becoming regulars, like us—remembered that we'd put them at ease, made them feel at home.

We had made the studio *our* home. I suppose we felt like we were being gracious hosts. Co-hosts. We'd chosen each other. We *were* a pair.

I don't think Judith ever thought about this, any more than I did. I think she took our affinity for granted, and by this I don't mean that she wasn't grateful for it, glad about it. I am confident she was, just as I was.

But there is so much I *don't* know.

For six and a half years, six days a week, Judith and I danced together. I stood behind her at the barre, admiring her back, her épaulement, the grace and self-assurance of her port de bras. When we danced on the diagonal across the room, for years, she always joined the first group (though never claimed the front position, or the one downstage, because while she was confident about the execution of the steps in any given combination, she was never able to remember what the combination *was*). I always hung back to dance in the last or next-to-last group. This gave me time to prepare—to work up my nerve, to practice the combination in my mind—and to watch Judith as she moved across the floor, the back point of the triangle she made with Brad and Rian, or Lauren and Mal.

On Fridays, when there were no classes for us at the studio, we checked in by text (me) or a phone call (Judith). On weekend evenings, after a long afternoon of classes, sometimes we'd go out to dinner (but dinner out with Judith was never a very satisfying enterprise, since she found menus baffling, would ask me to order for her—"Oh, you know what I like!" she'd say, with that little wave of hers—and then ate almost nothing, claiming, always, that she wasn't hungry). We went to the movies only a few times (she pronounced *Once Upon A Time … in Hollywood* boring, and I said, "Boring? With all that gory violence?" and shuddered—I had been enjoying it up until the fight scene near the end—and Judith said, "Should've been more of it and started sooner"—and *Barbie* "utterly stupid"); we went often to the ballet and to dance concerts at the university.

When she was outrageous—just "being Judith," as we'd say—calling out, from where she sat in the anteroom's only chair, "Welcome to Dancers Anonymous" each time the door opened, or making jokes that upset some people (on the day the Proud Boys demonstrated in Columbus, and a lot of us were shaken—they'd marched, fully armed, right by our houses, in the neighborhood most of us lived in—Judith came through the door declaring, "I've decided that I'm going to join the Proud Boys"), I did what I could ("She doesn't mean it, it's meant to be a joke"), then pulled her aside to beg her, once again, to think before she spoke. (And sometimes she would. But she might say something offensive even if she had thought about it first. "Because it was funny," she'd insist afterward.)

She was forever hurting or insulting people without meaning to: choosing as her "gesture" in response to a note plucked on a harp, as we rehearsed a piece we were performing in an art gallery—and others' gestures were wriggles or spins, jazz hands, air guitar, ballet port de bras (you get the picture)—to raise her third finger, which profoundly disturbed the woman she had made the gesture to. ("It was a *joke*," Judith told me later. "Has she no sense of humor?" And when I told her that giving somebody the finger wasn't a *good* joke, and that in that context, especially—of gesture as delicious movement, meant to invite a movement in response—it wasn't funny in the least, she told me I had no sense of humor either.) She'd mock-threaten to sue Russ and Fili—or Scott, who danced with us and was a massage therapist (Judith had gone to see him; she'd told me he had helped her, that he was "a wonder")—or write a bad Yelp review. She was always surprised when people were offended by her jokes.

But she also had no qualms about intentionally insulting some people: those whom she considered humorless, which she believed to be a capital offense—it amused her, she would tell me, to try to get a rise out of them. She told awful jokes, some of them only silly, some absurd, some truly ugly. If anybody told her a joke was offensive, she'd be hurt, then angry. She might accuse her accuser of not being very smart ("and I thought you were," she'd say. "I'm so sorry I was wrong") or of antisemitism ("because my sense of humor is Jewish—and you don't care for that, do you?"). She once tried to hand someone in the studio a book on "Jewish humor" that she'd purchased just for this purpose after he'd taken offense at something she'd said. He politely declined the gift (which Judith complained about, to me, at length).

She was difficult—I recognized that. I'd seen it myself, early on, hadn't I? My patience with her might have been greater than that of some of the others at the studio (and, I would learn, many of her colleagues at the university) because I felt that I knew her heart: I knew she wasn't mean, wasn't malicious, truly thought that she was being funny even when (and perhaps especially when) she did or said something that seemed harsh or callous. My father too hardly ever stopped to think before he spoke, told awful and sometimes offensive jokes, was hurt if people didn't laugh—and even more hurt if they said they were (or even if they didn't say but only seemed to be) offended; he too would sometimes lash out then. But, like Judith, my father wasn't mean. He was kind. He was generous to a fault, and not only to his family. He gave me the down payment for my house and paid for the portion of Grace's tuition that her substantial aid package hadn't covered ("It's called 'family contribution,'" he said when I hesitated to accept this offer, "so what am I, chopped liver?"), but he also helped put my best friend through law school in the 1980s and financed the production of a demo for a young singer he and my mother had met on one of their cruises.

And Judith would give you the shirt off her back. I once witnessed her give someone she'd met for the first time, who'd mentioned that her feet hurt, the socks off her own feet. "Try these," she said. "They're very good compression socks. I just put them on this minute, so they're not sweaty. See if they help you." And if someone said that something she was wearing was pretty—or cool or chic or looked comfortable or warm—she'd order another one just like it as soon as she got home, and a few days later hand it over in the studio's anteroom before class (usually saying something like, "I don't know how or why, but this landed in my mailbox! You should have it").

I'd known her less than a year when she insisted that I make use of her car for a month while she was away on a research project and I was carless in Columbus—Glen was spending the summer as artist-in-residence over 800 miles away. (First she scolded me for letting him have the car—we had just the one—calling me a prisoner of the patriarchy. Then: "What's mine is yours," she said. I had never heard that phrase uttered without irony before.)

I guess what I am saying is that it was easier for me to be patient with her because she reminded me so much of my father. They were both so *immoderate.* When my father liked someone, he would do anything for them (whether they wanted him to or not). He threw himself into solving his friend's problems—legal, medical, financial, psychological—with so much energy and information and enthusiasm, the people he was helping were often disconcerted or chagrined (or both).

I will admit that, in this latter way, I'm the one who's like my father. I'm like him in many ways: I'm social, helpful, garrulous, warm, bossy. A buttinsky. Anxious, eager to please, not easily daunted (unrelenting, actually). I'm always having ideas, big and small, and I'm quick—too quick, sometimes—to put them into action. I'm loyal, a devoted friend, a dedicated fan of everyone I love—unless/until they've done something to hurt me. Then I hold a grudge forever.

I am too easily hurt. I'm not *hardy*. (Although, like my father, I give every appearance of being so.)

Judith was like my father in some of the same ways I am. But she was also like him in some ways I'm not. She might have been the sister I never had.

I wish she'd been my sister.

I wish she'd had my father instead of hers. I wish she'd had a father who, like mine, thought the world of his only daughter.

It was not until after her death, in November 2023, that I knew enough to wish that for her—only after she was gone that I understood how little I had known about her.

Though I can see now that there were things she told me in the last weeks of her life that pointed to some of what I would learn later on. She mentioned these things nonchalantly, as if what she was saying was part of an ongoing conversation, as if they weren't revelations. Her long estrangement from her father, for example, which she spoke of for the first time while we were driving home together after the memorial service for our friend Annie, who had danced with us for years. Judith had done very well that day, saving her complaints ("Why on earth did there have to be so much God in what that guy said?" and "Why was it so long? It just went on and on") until we were walking to my car.

"He's a minister," I said. "That *guy*. That's his job. And the service was long, but none of it was boring, was it? That's unusual in itself."

"I wouldn't know," she said. "I've never been to such a thing before."

That startled me—how does one get to be in her late seventies without a single funeral?—but I let it go. I told her this one had been unique in my experience. It had been both wise and comforting, inclusive, loving, specific to Annie in every way, and filled with wonderful music. I don't much like churches either (honestly, I'm not even all that comfortable in most synagogues), but I'd liked this service. What I'd been thinking during it was: *Everyone deserves a memorial like this one.* To be celebrated, honored, recognized for who they were without a note of falsity, without generalization, beautifully and realistically, with people who knew them well and loved them well speaking eloquently about them. Telling good stories. Letting the rest of us know things we hadn't known before.

"If you say so," Judith said.

I laughed. "Judith, my darling," I said, "must you always search out the negative? Can't you just try to appreciate what was good about it?"

"Oh, yes"—that familiar wave—"I do. And there was a lot that was very nice. It's not my fault that I can't focus on that. Don't you know? The negative searches *me* out." We had reached my car; I had unlocked it. Judith paused before getting in. "It's sometimes a problem," she said—wistfully, I thought. Judith was so rarely wistful.

And then, as we settled in for the drive home, she said, "You know, I didn't even find out about my father's death until afterwards. If there was any kind of service, I wasn't there. I hadn't talked to him in years."

I knew enough to know that I was not supposed to sound surprised, not supposed to make what Judith would derisively call "a big deal" out of this.

I made sure to sound as casual, as matter-of-fact, as she had. "How'd you find out?"

"My brother—my half-brother—Eric, called to tell me."

"Ah," I said. I knew about the half-brother—knew that he existed. I hadn't known his name.

Then I asked her what the cause of the estrangement had been—and it was just as if a door slammed shut between us in the front seat of my ancient Volvo. As if, in saying anything at all about this, she'd forgotten herself briefly, had let a door that had been firmly closed swing open without meaning to.

"Not worth talking about," she said. She said this coldly. She turned her head away, looking out the passenger-side window at the blank suburban landscape.

Also in those last weeks—but of course she could not have known they were her last weeks—she mentioned her half-brother's name again, as well as where he lived, what sort of work he did, and (drily) that he was "born again." She mentioned that they had been talking regularly on the phone "for a while now"; she didn't wait for me to ask but volunteered that in these conversations they mainly argued politics. There was a cousin, too—Jean, in Los Angeles—whom she'd never before spoken of to me. Now she told me (once again as if in passing, as if I already knew) that they talked weekly, that they'd been doing so for years.

After Judith's death, when I talked to Jean myself, she told me it had been her husband, Jack, who'd been Judith's cousin. "But she and I were always close. She was one of my best friends."

I learned, in the days and weeks following her death, that many people had considered Judith one of their best (or even their one best) friend. There was the woman I'd met once, who'd taken an instant, visible dislike to me—she was Judith's friend of over thirty years and worshipped her unreservedly. She had told Judith that she'd been appalled by the "disrespectful" way I talked to her at the dinner party where we'd met—"contradicting and scolding me," Judith reported, "criticizing me, telling me what I should and shouldn't be making jokes about."

We were walking arm in arm—both of us were feeling shaky—across the parking lot of the church where the service for our friend Annie was being held. What had provoked her to tell me what her friend had said was my cautioning her, as we got out of the car, against making any jokes about death today, no matter how nervous she felt.

Now she said, "See? *Some* people find me absolutely delightful precisely as I am. So are you finally convinced I'm perfect?"

"Yes," I said. "I will never again beg you to please count to ten before you speak."

"Excellent!" said Judith. She squeezed my arm tighter. "Do you mean that?"

"I do not," I told her. But I squeezed back. "I love you anyway," I said.

"Ce n'est pas possible," Judith said.

I didn't know if she meant pausing to think before she spoke, or that I loved her. I knew it was better not to ask.

There were neighbors, several former colleagues, childhood and high school friends, a friend from grad school (whom Judith also spoke to once a week, she told me when I called to break the news of Judith's death). There was the person Judith had named her executor and to whom she had left everything she owned. Her name was Lynn, and she lived an hour away, in Yellow Springs. Judith's roommate of the last nine months of her life, Madeline, had Lynn's name and phone number only because, earlier that autumn, she had insisted Judith give her the names of people "other than Michelle" that she "should call if anything were to happen." (Things had been happening for months. But so far Madeline and I had managed on our own.) Judith felt that we were "making much too big a deal" of this, but she gave Madeline her brother Eric's and her friend Lynn's phone numbers anyway, with instructions not to call unless it were a true emergency. When Madeline told me this, it was the first time I'd ever heard of Lynn.

But then Lynn hadn't heard of me, either.

Perhaps Judith did know, somehow—perhaps she had an intuition (not that she believed in intuition) or a premonition (ditto)—that these were her last weeks. She sold her car, a 1999 Nisson Maxima, for a few hundred dollars to an Uber driver as soon as he dropped her off at home, after he'd told her that he needed to find a decent, cheap, used car. She also had a lawyer draw up all the necessary documents she had never bothered with before—will, living will, health care proxy, etc.—something I'd been urging her to do ever since I'd had mine done in the immediate aftermath of the pandemic lockdown.

It's hard for me not to imagine she knew something, or felt something, of what was ahead. Even if she didn't know she knew. Even if she didn't know what to make of what she felt.

She so often didn't know what to make of what she felt.

Gornisht Helfen

Her seizures began four years after we met.

At first it wasn't clear that they were seizures. All she knew was that she'd fall, black out, wake up confused—she only knew she'd fallen because she awakened bruised and on the floor. She'd call 911 herself, or else she'd call a neighbor, then make a trip to the emergency room. At some point after that, she'd call me.

The doctors she saw in the ER, then later the neurologists she saw in their offices, after long waits for appointments, and periodically in days-long hospital stays, had to rule out all the different kinds of strokes, including mini-strokes, or TIAs (transient ischaemic attacks), before a diagnosis of late-onset epilepsy was pronounced. Even then it took some time before it was concluded that the seizures had resulted in the falls and not vice versa. Anti-seizure medication was prescribed.

But the medication nauseated her and made her sleepy and disoriented. She could not stay awake during the day (and then, somehow, the medication also kept her up at night). So she would reduce the dose until she was no longer sleepy in the daytime, slept better at night, and stopped feeling nauseated—until she was alert and once again felt well enough to read and write. And dance.

She still took class every day—still took two, even three, classes in a row. Ballet, then dance karaoke. Ballet, then Fili's "dance party" or dance aerobics.

At some point she'd reduce the dose too much. Then she would have another seizure.

She'd call me to say that she was in the hospital again. Or, before she had a chance to call me, I'd call her—she'd missed a ballet class that night, which usually meant that she was in the hospital.

I'd ask her how she was doing and she'd say, "Oh, they're very impressed with me here. They got me out of bed and asked if I could walk, and instead of walking, I did a grand battement in the hallway. I missed kicking a nurse by only a few inches."

It was in the midst of this—in and out of the hospital, self-adjusting the dose of her meds, arguing with doctors, counting down the weeks (or days) between seizures—that she retired from teaching. She was not given a choice.

Her department chair had presented her with a laundry list of complaints, some of which—"repeated absences," for instance—were the result of her reluctance to tell her chair ("because she already hates me and I know she'd use it as an excuse to fire me") about her diagnosis. Had she invoked the word *disability*, it would likely have protected her—but then again it would not have helped her battle others of the chair's complaints: rudeness, intransigence, combativeness with colleagues, "sarcasm in the classroom," and other, unspecified "concerns about [her] teaching," The latter was disputed by the "expert observer" Judith was required to have sit in on her classes that final semester. "They wanted him to come up with a 'plan for improvement,' but he said there was nothing to improve. He said I was a *wonderful* teacher!" she reported gleefully. But, as my grandmother used to say—and I taught Judith the phrase—gornisht helfen. It didn't help.

Judith and I talked about fighting the enforced retirement—she even consulted a labor lawyer I found for her—but a long, expensive battle with the university (which, the lawyer told her, she would lose, given the mismatch of resources, plus various precedents he cited) seemed like a terrible idea while she was struggling with her health.

She was also struggling to stay cheerful. She never said she was depressed or anxious—that was not her style—but it was clear her world was narrowing. She was forbidden to drive, and (perhaps as another side effect of the medication—her doctors could not be sure) she developed neuropathy in her feet. This not only made it difficult to walk long distances, as she had done easily before, and which made giving up her car a great deal easier, but—much worse, she said—she could no longer rise to relevé. She could no longer dance across the floor. She couldn't jump—which broke her heart. Her favorite part of class was grand allegro.

But still she came to class. She stayed through barre, her feet flat on the floor, her back and arms as elegant as ever, as the rest of us rose to a balance—and then she'd retreat to the anteroom and read scientific papers while we moved off the barre, to center. She kept herself busy reading journal articles about the brain until the next class, which she'd modify as necessary. No toe-pointing, no balances, no jumping.

Her roommate, Madeline, would tell me later that she'd felt like she was watching Judith waging battle between flesh and spirit. That she'd see her at home wincing, looking grim, in pain, and exhausted—and she would see her rallying before her eyes. *Ballet's in half an hour. Pull yourself together.*

She'd be first at the barre, as usual.

Madeline had danced with us since the beginning, although she'd moved away for a time and had only recently returned to Columbus. She was less than half Judith's age (and Judith claimed never to have seen her before when I reintroduced them). Her temperament could not have been more unlike Judith's. She was calm and even-tempered; her speaking voice was perhaps the gentlest I have ever heard.

Their living together worked out remarkably well given that Judith had been living alone in her barely furnished rental for over three decades and didn't want a roommate. What she told everyone at the dance studio was that "Michelle tells me what to do and I do it." It wasn't true—it was ludicrously untrue. But I *had* brokered the connection, which made sense for both of them (Madeline newly divorced and just now back in Columbus, wanting to save up to buy a house, and Judith—"according to Michelle," she liked to say, making it clear she disagreed—not being safe alone). And Madeline was kind, forgiving, sympathetic, and obliging—but not, I sensed, a pushover. She was disinclined to rise to the sort of bait Judith was inclined to dangle. And she was smart (Judith would have tolerated nothing less).

I was relieved that just this once Judith had listened to me.

The only condition Madeline had to meet before she was able to move in was making sure her dog and Judith's got along. After a first try on neutral territory was successful, Judith and Lucy (a fourteen-year-old German shepherd/Lab mix, almost wholly blind and deaf, arthritic) hosted Madeline and Duke Silver (a young, playful, energetic hound/Lab/pit mix) for a sleepover. Duke Silver was respectful of Lucy, and Lucy didn't seem to mind his presence. They were both big, gentle dogs, and despite the many differences between them—like Judith and Madeline—they were perfectly companionable.

Lucy died a month almost to the day before Judith did. And for that last month of her life, when Judith was at home, Madeline told me—as Judith never did—Duke Silver sat beside her if she asked him to. He was her great comfort.

Madeline moved in in February 2023. Each time, after that, when Judith had a seizure, Madeline would call me. Sometimes Judith was aphasic when she came to. Sometimes she said things that made no sense. Madeline and I conferred (*Call 911 or not?*) and usually we'd conclude that it was pointless. "I'll see how she's doing in an hour," Madeline would tell me. "I'll call you back."

Before, whenever Judith had a seizure, she would end up in the hospital all day, and sometimes for several days, while the doctors ordered tests that told them nothing new, then sent her home with stern instructions to take her medication as prescribed. Now, instead, Judith would rest, and slowly she'd be back to herself. By the next day—sometimes even by that evening—she'd be back in a dance class.

When Madeline called me at seven in the morning on the day Judith died, she'd already talked to Lynn and left a message for Eric. The paramedics were already there.

It was Madeline who'd found her, face down on her bed. Only hours before her death she'd taken two dance classes, ballet and karaoke, then texted me to tell me I *had* to come back to class. I hadn't been in class all week (I'd hurt my back, as I so regularly did, and was taking a few days off). She missed me, she said. *So I insist. It's no fun without you.* And then, right away, another text: *No, it's still fun. But NOT AS MUCH FUN without you.*

Then one more, telling me she'd just finished reading a book she wanted to pass along to me. It was called *How to Dance Forever*.

Madeline cracked the lock code on Judith's phone on her first try (it wasn't hard: 1234—something I should have thought to warn Judith against) and passed the phone along to me that afternoon. I did what

I do when slapped—shoved, bitten—by grief. I pitched myself headlong into *tasks*.

My first calls were to anyone who'd sent multiple, increasingly anxious-sounding texts, including Cousin Jean in LA (Judith had missed their scheduled weekly call) and a woman I was startled to learn was Judith's therapist (who'd sent three texts over two hours: *Judith, did you forget you had an appointment this morning?* and then, *It's not like you not to call if you can't make it. Pls. call, I'm getting worried,* and finally, *Now I'm getting *really* worried—PLEASE call me ASAP*). Then I went through her contacts and called everybody else. If I had to leave a message, I said only that I was her friend, calling from Columbus, and asked to be called back. I spent hours—hours over days—on the phone. I wouldn't stop until I had called every last person she'd known and told them she was gone.

I called Lynn too, of course. We made plans to meet the next day at Judith's house, and I learned that she and Lynn had met when she—Lynn—was a child. Judith was in college, glamorous, a decade older; she was dating Lynn's big brother. "I still think of her the way she was then," Lynn said. "Oh, I just so admired and adored her!" Later, after her brother and "Jude" broke up, "we'd become so close, in a big-sister/little-sister way, there was no prying us apart. We've been close ever since." I asked her how long Judith—*Jude*—and her brother were together. Lynn's answer astonished me: they had dated for twenty-five years.

Before we hung up, Lynn asked if I could do one thing for her right now: go over to Judith's house and pick out clothes for Judith's body. The funeral home she had selected had asked her for them. Someone (that turned out to be Lynn, as executor, since there was no family available) was supposed to identify the body before its cremation, and it had to be clothed for that to happen. Could I find something appropriate and bring it to them?

I was in task mode—I didn't hesitate. When I got to Judith's house, Madeline had already laid out some of Judith's favorite dance clothes—a hot pink Athleta yoga top and tie-dyed leggings—and she and I agreed that nothing could be more appropriate. I took them and left. Then I returned to the house and started sorting things.

Lynn had said she wanted nothing, that I should give everything away or throw it out.

When she and I met at the house the next afternoon, I could see right away that she was the other sort of person, the kind who is undone by grief. She kept sitting down, wringing her hands. She'd pick up something—a photograph, a hairbrush, a glass bowl—and sit holding it and staring at it. Her husband was there too, and he would bend down and gently take the object from her hands, rub her shoulder, speak to her softly.

But I was deep into tasks by then. I was taking stock and making piles. I was opening drawers and assessing the need for boxes.

Madeline had cleaned up the horror scene in Judith's bedroom as soon as the medics and police left—they'd been there for hours and hours. She'd already packed up her own things and started making calls about a place to live—she wanted to move out right away (and she did). She too was someone who had to take action, who could not be still when *something happened.*

Lynn and her husband left with only Judith's laptop, once I'd cracked its lock code (it was not much more complex than the phone's 1234) and checked to make sure Judith had saved all the passwords they would need (bank, pension fund, healthcare, social security). I was grateful that it was Lynn and her husband, and not I, who had to deal with all of that—the administrative, bureaucratic tasks—and she was grateful for my offer to deal with the rest of it—"all this *stuff,*" she said.

I managed to persuade her to come back the next day and walk through the house once more, to be certain that there wasn't anything she wanted, before I tackled "all this stuff." I didn't want her to be sorry she had not kept anything of her old friend's.

And she did that. She found a few things she wanted. Photographs, mostly. Whatever jewelry there was (there wasn't much). A handful of keepsakes.

I was well prepared for the disposition of a lifetime's worth of her belongings. I created categories and made lists, tossed things onto piles, filled boxes and bags.

Our dance friends came out in force to help.

Pat and Steve brought everything that had been in the basement up to the first floor, and in the living room Pat sorted them: trash or donate. Li, who'd considered Judith his adoptive "lefty grandma," helped me go through all her clothes: Judith items (the shaggy off-white coat, the down-filled zip-up maxi skirt from Sweden she wore every winter day, dozens of tiny short black dresses and black or black-and-white knit boatneck tops, many pairs of tall black boots, tutus, a purple flamenco skirt, dance gear we'd seen her in a million times, long-unused pointe shoes we had heard her talk about) were packed up for the celebration of her life we were holding at the studio, when I planned to distribute things to anyone who wanted something of hers; warm clothes that we did not associate especially with her, and jeans and sweaters, snow boots, rain boots, hiking shoes (Judith, who hated the outdoors, had hiking shoes?), and other sensible footware and thick socks were bagged and brought to Star House, a drop-in center for homeless teenagers in Columbus; low-heeled pumps, blazers, blouses, and the sort of pants I thought of as trousers went to Dress for Success; and all the rest—dressy, sparkly things we'd never seen her wear, high heels it was hard to imagine she had ever worn, roller blades (with the tags still on), ice skates, and anything else that was neither infused with her personality nor of practical use—was marked for general donation to Out of the Closet, a thrift store that supports the local AIDS healthcare center, or Goodwill.

Madeline took all of Lucy's things—multiple dog beds, bags and cans of food, toys, dishes—to the Humane Society. Brad brought tools and took apart the bed frame; he and someone else—it might have been Tyler—dragged the mattress and box spring downstairs and out for bulk pickup, which I called to arrange. The sofa was dragged out there too.

I put all the scientific papers in bags Madeline hauled out for recycling.

Cheryl, Micki, Cynthia, Tina—oh, so many people, I can't remember everyone—packing, sorting, lifting, hauling. Rolling up ancient, exhausted, dusty rugs. Filling bags and boxes.

Some things, we brought out to the curb. A hat stand, a dresser with drawers that stuck. A folding table. The plastic chairs Judith had used around her dining table. Boxes full of cleaning supplies, car supplies, and other odds and ends that could not be donated because they'd been opened. I put a notice on our neighborhood's Buy Nothing/Sell Nothing Facebook site, and everything was gone by the next day.

The dining table went to Li, who promised to host loud political discussions around it, and the standing desk to Scott, the massage therapist, for his office. Judith's portable ballet barre, the one she used during lockdown, went to the studio to become the "teacher barre"; one of the director's chairs went there too (it's hard to recall now that there was ever a time when our ballet teachers didn't have a place to sit). Fili and Russ took home Judith's bookcases to put in their baby's room, and the books that had been in them, like the "iconic Judith" articles of clothing, were boxed up and stored until the celebration at the studio, when everyone who wanted any of her books could take them.

I set aside the envelopes of photographs Lynn hadn't taken and the photo album and a scrapbook (teenaged Judy!), the correspondence and the notes she'd scrawled on looseleaf paper, her report cards, documents of a great many kinds. These artifacts that had been meaningful enough to her for her to keep had to be *handled*, I felt—looked at, considered, taken seriously. Someone had to do that.

There was no one else to do that.

This Part's for You

Almost everyone I'd called to break the news of Judith's death to wanted to talk for a long time. They all had stories. They all had *different* stories, different pieces of her life they wanted—needed—to tell me about.

Their stories were not only from the different periods of Judith's life, or simply the result of their different roles in it (high school friends telling Judith-as-a-teenager stories, her therapist telling me—was this allowed?—what had been most troubling Judith during the months she had been her client), but also different parts of her biography. It seemed she had told everybody different things about her past.

The things she'd told us weren't contradictory—or they weren't exactly contradictory. It was more like each was a small piece of the whole, so that talking to the people she had left behind was like collecting what might be the truth, but only in small segments. Some of the pieces fit together, but some—most—seemed to fit nowhere. Or else they snapped into place with just one or two other pieces, but then I couldn't figure out where in the puzzle this small constellation of interlocked parts belonged.

And there were, there are, so many *missing* pieces.

Cousin Jean was the first person to tell me anything about Judith's father, Harry. But that wasn't until our third or fourth conversation, and by then I'd already learned some things about him beyond what Judith had told me. I'd seen photographs, which had been buried at the bottom of a stack of journal articles in a file cabinet's bottom drawer. He was young in all of them, and looked a bit like Saul Bellow (handsome in a sort of tough-guy Jewish way). I'd also read Judith's college-era letters to him: a mix of banal news, barely concealed ingratiation, and desperation, especially about money. Every letter begged for help that was not forthcoming.

I'd found two thick stacks of these letters, in manilla envelopes, in another file cabinet, stuffed behind carefully filed research notes, copies of Judith's own scholarly papers and articles and her cv, and forty years' worth of professional correspondence (actual letters, from the age before email, as well as printed-out emails dating back to 1997).

It felt strange, going through my friend's file drawers, reading her letters without her permission. But it would have been worse, it would have been unbearable, if every piece of paper she had saved had been discarded without so much as a glance, as if it all were meaningless.

How could I help thinking of the thousands of my own such papers—two file cabinets and two deep desk drawers and I don't even know how many plastic bins full of them in the closet in my study?

What happens to the things one keeps forever when forever is over?

As I read through all of Judith's papers, looked at all her photographs and scrapbooks and report cards—everything she had seen fit to save—I was thinking about how, once we are gone, our lives become stories, because that's all that's left. I was thinking about meaning, about meaningfulness, and how that doesn't have to, shouldn't, cease after a death. As long as there is someone left to contemplate and tell, to do their best to make sense of it, to carry it with them for the rest of *their* life. To pass it along, and along again.

Jean had nothing good to say about her late husband's Uncle Harry, and she had ample opportunity to think of something, since she and I ended up talking every day for weeks—we seemed to have become friends over the phone, both of us so shaken by Judith's sudden death. And she reminded me of Judith, but with softer edges.

I don't know what or who, if anything, I reminded her of.

But we both missed Judith so, and we both wanted so much to talk about her. We kept finding reasons to check in. I consulted her about certain details of the obituary I was writing (on which Lynn would spend most of the money Judith had in her "estate," because a *New York Times* in-print obituary is absurdly, mind-bogglingly expensive—but I knew that was where Judith would have wanted it to run). The obituary wasn't hard to write once I had gathered all the information (it was just a variation of what I do all day, every day), and I wanted to do it. I felt sure Judith would have counted on me to do this for her, and also that she would not have taken it for granted.

Besides, no one else volunteered, and the thought of no obituary horrified me.

Jean called me on the day it ran in *The Times* and asked if I would place it in the *LA Times* as well. I did, and then I called her back to tell her so. We talked again when it appeared there. And so on. And because neither Lynn nor I knew what to do with Judith's ashes (we couldn't scatter them in a special place because there was no special place—as noted, Judith hated the outdoors—but neither Lynn nor I felt we should keep them, and it seemed morbid to keep an urn in the dance studio), I asked Jean, who eventually came up with a marvelous plan. Judith's ashes are interred at Forest Lawn, in the plot where her cousin Jack, whom she had loved, was buried—and where Jean will be buried too—not far from the remains of Buster Keaton, Liberace, Lucille Ball, Stan Laurel, Steve Allen, and Bette Davis. I think she would have liked that very much. I think it would have made her laugh.

One of Judith's friends, whose relationship with her had been founded on shared politics and activism, told me that what Judith (but she called her Judy) had told her about her early life was that her father and stepmother were under suspicion during the McCarthy years, as were some of their left-wing neighbors, and that "people were always coming around making inquiries about her parents." Another friend, a former student who would later become her colleague, told me that she'd been the one to connect Judith with Lucy, that she'd found her at the Humane Society, where she volunteered as a dog-walker, and felt instantly that "she was the one" for Judith, who'd been looking for a dog after the death of her last one. Judith hadn't told her that Lucy had died, although they'd spoken over the few weeks since it had happened.

This same friend also told me she remembered clearly that when Judith's father died, "she chose not to go to the funeral." She told me that Judith said, "Why should I? He won't know I'm not there." But she hadn't known until I told her that by then it had been years since Judith had last spoken to her father, that she would not have heard about his death if her brother hadn't called her.

One friend told me that her stepmother had been an alcoholic, her father a "grifter who took advantage of people and had no remorse." Another told me that her mother had been an actress, her father a movie producer. I'd never heard such a thing! Another said she'd never known that Judith had a younger brother. "Her father and stepmother had a child together? Was he much, much younger? I feel sure she told me that she was an only child." No, I said, Judith was only ten when Eric was born.

Both of us paused to consider this. Judith did seem like an only child.

Eric and I never did talk on the phone, but we exchanged a stream of messages. (In one, he asked me if Judith had ever married.) I cannot recall now—and I seem to have deleted our message thread—if it was him or somebody else (perhaps the wife of another one of Judith's—and Eric's—cousins) who told me they thought that Harry and his second wife, Judith's stepmother, had been having an affair before the death of her mother.

I wish I'd asked Judith more questions. Even if she had declined to answer, even if my questions had irritated her. It troubles me that she did not feel she could talk more freely to me—if she wanted to, I mean. It troubles me to think she might have wanted to but didn't. It troubles me that I will never know if she wanted to but couldn't.

That I had learned from Lynn that Judith had been part of a couple for twenty-five years but had never spoken of it to me was something

I could not let go of. "Twenty-five years is a big chunk of her life," I told Cousin Jean one night on the phone. "How can it be that she never talked to me about it?"

Jean said, "No, no, it can't have been a twenty-five-year relationship. I remember that boy. It was a long time ago."

I didn't point out that the early 1990s, which must have been when Judith and Lynn's brother split up, *was* a long time ago. (It doesn't seem very long ago to me, either. Jean is close to eighty, I am close to seventy—that's how time works when you get to be this old.)

Judith had spoken to me only of one former boyfriend—"my Swedish boyfriend," she always called him, never mentioning his name—and never in flattering terms. But a friend who had known her during the time they were dating told me Judith had liked him very much, that she was "so happy in those days, when she often traveled to the Karolinska Institute for work and got to spend time with him." She must have told her brother something along those lines too, because he asked, when we first exchanged messages, if I thought he should try to track down "the boyfriend in Stockholm." I said no—Judith had told me last summer that she'd recently declined his request for friendship on Facebook. She was furious that he had asked. "How dare he?" she said. But when I asked her what he'd done to make her so angry, she shook her head. It was ancient history, she said. What did it matter?

There was one story Judith seemed to have told everyone she'd ever known. It was about when she had worked for Joan Rivers, as her daughter Melissa's nanny. Judith was in her twenties; Melissa was a small child. When Judith gave two-weeks' notice—she planned to go to grad school—Joan Rivers said, "Nobody gives me notice," then called the police and told them Judith was a stranger who had broken in. "But the police who came knew her," Judith said, "so they knew how she was. They ignored her screaming and helped me get my belongings together and get out of there." Then, slyly—Judith knew how to tell a story—she would say, "But the policemen weren't really very nice. When I asked if they could please drive me to the bus station, they said, 'What do you think we are, a taxi service?'"

Even this story was told with slight differences, depending upon whom she told it to. In the version she told her friend Daniel, whom she'd known in high school and reconnected with in spring 2020—when a whole group of her high school friends, most of whom hadn't talked to one another in close to sixty years, started meeting weekly over Zoom—the policemen took her to the bus stop after all. "That was when I decided to go to graduate school in epidemiology instead of history," she told Daniel in an email. "I needed to get a job! I thought it would be easier to get a job in epidemiology than in history."

Why she'd thought of epidemiology at all wasn't a part of the story. But Daniel was an epidemiologist—a coincidence that charmed her (she had told me so)—and so it did not occur to him to ask. (I imagine that for him it was an unremarkable decision. We all fill in the gaps in other people's stories with the things we know about ourselves—we do it without even thinking.) I've no doubt that she offered that coda to Daniel *because* he was an epidemiologist—and it might even have been true (who's to say?); she might have told this part to Daniel because she believed that only he would understand it.

I asked her once (because I'd heard the Joan Rivers story enough times to wonder about details she had not included) where the child, Melissa, was while this was happening. How had *she* reacted to it? Was she frightened? Upset? In another room, asleep? Judith was annoyed: that was not important to the story. But she seemed to have registered the question, for the next time I heard her tell it—to someone at the studio who, like me, was a parent—I heard Judith say, "The child was unfazed, obviously. She was as accustomed to her mother's outbursts as the police were."

What I want to say about this is not that it matters to me one way or another if what she told Daniel—or what she told anybody about any part of the Joan Rivers story (though it seems safe to assume she really did work for her after college, half a century ago)—was true. What matters to me is that she told parts of the story only to those whom she felt would appreciate it.

This part is for you, she seems to have thought, *and* this *one is for you.*

What I have come to think is that Judith did this with and about everything. She kept whole parts of her life, her self, for certain people, and other parts for others. Each of us was privy to different parts of her life story.

I suppose we all do this in some way. That is, none of us tell everything there is to tell to everyone we know. But for Judith, this curation rose to an art form.

And then there were the things she seemed to have told no one. The things that no one, now, would ever know.

They Should Know the Truth

Judith talked a lot (just as she had promised early on). She had so much to say, it was hard to imagine she was keeping anything to herself, and because she seemed never to think before she spoke, who would have supposed that she was holding so much back?

I should have supposed. I, of all the people who knew her, should have known better.

I am not a secret-keeper. I actively dislike being secretive, to an extent that certain ex-friends have called pathological. But I am aware that my "I'll tell you anything" persona lets me keep parts of myself, parts I am ashamed of, out of sight. All those true stories I tell about my childhood, youth, parents and grandparents, career misadventures, old boyfriends, failed friendships, crises, and calamities—along with my apparent unshyness and self-confidence—serve *both* to reveal "the real me" and as misdirection from the bits I don't want most people to see. Bits that are dark enough, I guess, that even some people I do let have a look at them can't or won't see them.

Judith did, though. Judith saw—I think she saw, because I unveiled them for her and she didn't look away—my uncertainty, my anxious self-doubt. My longing to be loved "for who I am"—appreciated. Treasured. Needed.

Judith wore her longing to be loved right on her sleeve. I could see it, anyway, after the first weeks of our acquaintance. I did my best to respond to it, in the ways I could: I brought her a container of whatever I'd made for dinner (because Judith didn't cook; before Madeline, who loved to cook, moved in, she ate frozen dinners, or else the same takeout meal from a mediocre restaurant she'd picked and stuck with so she didn't have to think about it—and when I say she didn't cook, I mean she didn't even make herself a hardboiled egg: she bought pre-boiled ones at the supermarket. "People make too big a deal about food," she said). I texted her to ask if she was okay anytime she didn't come to class (she was never okay if she didn't come to class). I invited her to the ballet or the theater even though I knew she would complain, loudly and without concern that a dancer/choreographer/actor/director/writer's spouse or parents or best friend might be seated next to or in front of or behind us (and when I whispered this reminder to her, she'd say, every time, "So what? They should know the truth too!").

Now it seems clear to me that I didn't do enough. That I should have *told* her that I loved her, that her friendship mattered to me. Maybe if I had, maybe if she'd known how much I wanted to know her—to know her the way I wanted to be known—she would not have kept so many secrets.

Did she think of them as secrets? Or only as facts about herself, her life, that weren't worth talking about? But how could that be, when what she hid seems to be everything that made her who she was?

There are so many things I've learned about her only since her death—things I've learned from farflung friends and family, from emails and letters and text messages and phone calls and Facebook DMs. Or that I've gleaned from the stacks and scraps of paper left behind—those thousands of pages she saw fit to keep "forever."

There were things I learned only through my sleuthing on the internet, typing in search terms I knew of only because I'd read through that tower, that monument, of paper. Or because someone had told me something unexpected and specific—something searchable.

Did I become somewhat obsessive about this? Is the essay in your hands now evidence of that?

Am I asking these questions that do not require an answer—questions to which I already know the answer—as another way to honor her memory?

I miss Judith's rhetorical questions.

I miss the sound of her voice, the way she'd preface every question she asked in class with, "I have a question" (she said it so solemnly, with such portentousness—and then almost always it would be rhetorical, a joke, or an absurdity). The variations of her voice when we talked, when it was just us, when she was excited about something. The way she talked to Lucy. The way she had talked to Ella.

The way she talked to me after Ella was gone.

I miss her laugh. I miss going places with her. I miss the way she marveled over things she liked and the way she airily dismissed what she did not. I miss her fierceness.

I miss her defiant, regal presence at the barre.

It's still fun. But it's not as much fun without her.

(Some of) The Rest of the Things I Now Know

Judith's mother's name was Bess, and she was called Bessie (but *Bess* was how she signed her letters). Bess was twenty-three when she married Harry, who was only nineteen.

At the time of Bess's death, Judith was almost four. She was a shy child—Bess mentions this repeatedly in a letter, most likely written in 1948, to Celia, one of her sisters-in-law. The letter bears a truncated date—two dates (it's a stop-and-start letter, begun on September 10, finished on September 12), but not the year. (In September 1948, Judith would have been three and a half. But it's possible that, though shy, she might have been precocious—a year younger than that—when she told her mother, who duly reported it to Celia in this letter, that she planned to marry Michael, Celia's son. Precociousness would not surprise me. Shyness does.)

Harry's second wife, whom Judith took pains to refer to as her stepmother, was named Mary Lou, and it is Mary Lou's, not Bess's, name that is on Judith's birth certificate. (This shocked me, but it shouldn't have. It makes sense that Mary Lou would have adopted Harry's four-year-old when they married.) Eric had been insistent about Mary Lou being Judith's mother. "She was *not* her stepmother, she was our mother," he wrote in response to my fact-checking for the obituary. (At that point, I didn't know her name—I had asked him for it.) I wrote back, "I'm really sorry, Eric. But it mattered to your sister that Bess was her mother, that Mary Lou came later."

It turns out that, strictly speaking, he was right. (Even so, I am not sorry the obituary names Bess as Judith's mother, "who died early in her childhood," and Mary Lou as her stepmother. Along with publishing the obit in *The New York Times*, and holding the celebration of her life at the dance studio, this is one of the few things I feel sure Judith would have wanted.)

Bess and Harry were married for eight years before Judith's birth. Bess was thirty-five at the time of her death. Mary Lou and Harry married only months after Bess's death. Mary Lou was twenty-two.

Mary Lou might have been Harry's secretary. (This I was told by a friend of Judith's of many years, who said she had often mentioned it, rolling her eyes: "After my mother died, my father married his secretary.")

Judith had not, however, suspected—or at least she'd never said she did (unless it was to someone she was not in touch with anymore, like the Swedish ex-boyfriend, whom I would not have contacted)—the possibility of an affair.

Harry left Mary Lou, or she left him (the latter seems less likely, though I have no proof of this, only circumstantial evidence indicting Harry), when Eric was a child. Judith would have been in her teens. The connection between Harry and his son was severed then, and remained so for some time.

Harry married again, quickly. Judith had had a second stepmother! (Or: she had two mothers and a stepmother, depending on who's counting.)

Judith had never spoken of the second stepmother because, for at least thirty years, she must not have thought of her that way—nor had Cyrell, the third wife I hadn't known about, thought of Judith as her stepdaughter. (I know this because I found her obituary online. It mentions a daughter, Lois—a half-sister I had never heard of—and a stepson, Eric. A beloved husband, Harry, who had predeceased her. No other survivors.)

At some point, Judith and Cyrell, who was only ten years older than the stepdaughter who would later be erased from an accounting of her life, *had* had a relationship. I know this because I have read the many letters Judith wrote to her (most often to her and Harry—the salutation usually "Dear Dad & Cyrell" or, sometimes, "Dear Dad & Cyrell & Lois"—but there are two letters addressed to Cyrell alone) from the 1960s and early 1970s, when Judith was in college and studying abroad, and some from the early to mid 1980s.

In 1969, when Judith was in school in England and Eric was a teenager, there was a rapprochement between son and father. Judith mentions it in one of her letters, written on tissue-thin blue airmail paper: how glad she is to hear that Harry and Cyrell "are talking to Eric again, because he is my brother and I love him."

Judith and Mary Lou were estranged "for decades" (as per Eric) but "recreated a relationship" after they saw each other, for the first time in years, in 1999 at Eric's wedding. Harry was also present. (Eric did not mention whether Cyrell and Lois were, and I dared not ask.)

Mary Lou and Judith, once reunited, remained close. When Mary Lou died, she left Judith her car—the 1999 Nissan Maxima Judith drove (and that she lent me for a month in 2018) until she sold it to the Uber driver.

Harry died in 2004, at the age of eighty-six, on the day after Judith's birthday.

Cyrell died in 2012. (Since I hadn't known of her existence until after Judith's death, at first this meant nothing to me. But by the time

I finished reading all of Judith's letters to her, which I suppose must have come into Judith's possession after Harry died—either Eric or Lois must have sent them to her [my money's on Eric]—I felt her death as a blow, even if Judith had made the decision not to feel it at all. Even if, as seems clear, she and Cyrell had not had a relationship for years. Still the fact remains: Harry was married to Cyrell for far longer than he'd been to either one of Judith's mothers, and to judge from the letters Judith wrote, Cyrell had been a part of Judith's family for at least fifteen years. That Judith had never spoken of her second stepmother to some of her closest friends—that she seemed to have made an effort to erase that relationship, just as Cyrell's obituary does—doesn't mean that it was not part of her story.)

Mary Lou remarried at some point. Learning this made me happy for her.

And Cyrell, I learned, had a devoted boyfriend at the time of her death: he posted a long, loving message in the comments space below her obituary. This made me happy too.

Ce n'est pas Possible

One more thing I didn't know until Judith was gone: that she had been prepared for an emergency. For all sorts of emergencies. She had stockpiled bottled water (there were cases stashed in every closet on the first and second stories of her house as well as in the basement), light bulbs—hundreds of them—batteries (a lifetime supply), soap, nonprescription medications of all kinds, toilet paper, cleaning supplies, Scotch tape, paperclips, envelopes of every size, packets of tissues, jugs of windshield washer fluid and of antifreeze, bags (and bags and bags) of rock salt and pet-safe de-icers—everything, really. She was ready, whatever might come.

I will never know the cause of her long estrangement from her father, whom she so often spoke of without telling me, until so near the end, that they had ceased to be in contact many years before his death. I don't know if it was he or she who cut the other off. I only know that she lived most of her life without a parent.

I know that she thought of the mother she could not remember as her mother. I know the enormity of that blow to a four-year-old, even if Judith claimed not to remember anything about it. I know that she thought of Mary Lou as her stepmother, that it didn't matter that she had been adopted, or that she had been told to call her Mother.

So much about Judith—the way she kept herself apart, the way she used humor (and what she thought of as humor that nobody else did) to keep at arm's length even those she loved, the way "the negative search[ed her] out," the way she would so often respond to questions or suggestions (Why not hardboil eggs at home? Why not use a refillable water bottle?) with a sad-sounding, murmured, "Ce n'est pas possible," the way she made herself outrageous and provocative and difficult—oh, so much of who she was and how she was—must have been about her losses.

If Eric or the wives of his and Judith's cousins knew why Judith and her father had stopped speaking, they did not or would not tell me. Jean didn't know the answer—I asked her. I didn't feel that I could ask Eric this question. I did ask another of the cousin-wives, and she said "it could have been for any number of reasons." When I asked, "Like what?", she changed the subject, asking me about the memorial service she'd heard rumors of. Yes, I said, we were planning on a celebration of Judith's life and times—it would not be a *memorial*, I told her, because Judith would have hated that. Would it be possible, she asked, to attend it virtually? I told her it would. And she and her husband, Judith's first cousin Michael—the one she'd planned to marry as a toddler—did attend, via the link I sent to her and everybody else who didn't live in central Ohio. Many other people attended the celebration virtually. But not Judith's brother. I don't know what to make of that.

And I don't know what to make of Cyrell's erasure of Judith from *her* story. Or if it was whoever wrote that (succinct—nothing like Judith's) obituary who made the decision to erase her. (Could it have been Lois, the half-sister I had never heard of?) Had Cyrell and Lois been forced by Judith's father to take sides after their falling out? But eight years had passed since Harry's death. There was no one keeping Lois and Cyrell from Judith if they wanted her to be a part of their lives—unless it was Judith.

In the story I now tell myself about my friend, it is she who ended all communication with her father. She was fed up with him—his faithlessness, his bluster, his selfishness and self-absorption.

When she said, "It's him I take after," it was a dark, awful, self-hating conviction—a confession. But she was not like him, I think. While she might have styled herself to be what she had understood of him throughout her childhood—the loud opinions and the confrontations, the eagerness for a debate—she was loving, loyal, kind. Munificent. Everything there is no evidence her father was.

For the celebration of her life, the main studio room was packed with our dance friends as well as friends from every other part and phase of her life in Columbus, plus her neighbors, former students, colleagues who had loved her. One after another, people rose to tell their Judith stories.

In the smaller second studio, Russ and Fili had our dance film *Spatula* projecting on a loop, as well as our second dance film, *Tenderly*, which we had made once we could dance again indoors in person. Spread out across half of the marly floor and hanging from all the barres were the "iconic Judith" items Li and I had set aside to be distributed; on the other half of the floor were all her books—fanned out, in piles, and in rows propped up against the wall under one of the barres.

There was not a single thing left at the end of the night. People exited the studio wearing her clothes, her boots, her hats, her leopard-printed scarves. Carrying armloads of her books. Pointe shoes dangling by pink ribbons from the crooks of their elbows.

I catch glimpses of these fragments of her life. Fili in the oversized black winter coat, Russ in the leopard-patterned hat. Kiley, across the room from me in intermediate ballet, wearing one of Judith's leotards. Mara teaching her beginner ballet class in one of Judith's Athleta or lululemon yoga tops, or else walking by my house—she lives just up the street—in one of her boat-neck black-and-white knit shirts. Cynthia in the sleek, tight-fitting, black zip-up jacket. Mike, a former grad student of mine who lives two houses down from the house Judith had lived in all those years, reading her copy of Susan Blum's *Ungrading* on his porch when I walk by.

Jennifer has Judith's down-filled maxi-length black skirt. Cheryl has the shaggy Tibetan lamb coat that Judith always told people was fake ("so they won't get mad about it") but which she assured me was real and had been in her possession since the 1960s.

I kept her Apple watch. She'd worn it every day—I don't think I ever saw her without it. She'd answer the phone on it, say, "I'm talking to you on my watch. I'm walking Lucy. Why don't I call you back when I get home?"

I'd never worn a smartwatch—I'd never wanted one. (It took me years to accept that I would probably enjoy having a smartphone.) But I like wearing Judith's. Every time it tells me to stand up and move around—I've been sitting, working, for too long, the watch advises me—I whisper my thanks to her. I *do* need to stand up and move around. I had forgotten to.

It's not like me to do this—to talk to a watch. To talk to someone who's no longer alive. To imagine or even pretend that talking to her watch is talking to her. And yet I do it, every time.

And at least once a week, when I am in dance karaoke or dance party or Russ's Sunday morning "club flow" class, I move in such a way that distresses the watch. The screen lights up. It tells me that it looks like I've had "a hard fall." Call 911? it asks me.

No, I tell Judith, and I x out of the screen. *But thanks.*

I did have a hard fall. But not the kind the watch, her watch—my watch—means.

Anyway, it's summer now. And there is no emergency.

Acknowledgments

Heartfelt thanks to Mike Kardos and Chris Coake, excellent friends and first readers (who, I am honor-bound to mention, were once—long, long ago—my students at Ohio State). Nick White, another former student (indeed, my *grand*student; Mike Kardos was his teacher before I was) and later a dear friend and the best teaching colleague I ever had, read drafts of many of these essays too. Yet another former student, the estimable Nelle Smith, joined the chorus for the final essay/chapter. All of these folks made this book much better. (My advice to other writers looking for their best first readers: Grow your own.)

The brilliant, singular Judith Schwartzbaum—whom I most certainly did not grow myself; who, if I did not by now know better, I might imagine sprang from the seas fully formed—read the dance essays in early drafts and always had interesting, surprising things to say about them, and questions I would not have thought to ask. She had a sharp, exacting literary eye, and was also the most appreciative and generous of readers of my work (after my mother, I hasten to say).

Judith and I would never have met if not for dance. This is true of so many of the people I count among my most treasured friends at this point in my life. I want to thank them all for keeping me company, shoring me up, offering empathy and jokes and news and stories and good will, and leading the way across the floor. (I actually did start listing their names alphabetically, but by the time I got to Mal and Mia, the list was already absurdly long—like the most boring Academy Award acceptance speech ever—plus I began to fear I might unintentionally leave somebody out, the way Dustin Hoffman did in 1988 when he accepted the award for *Rain Man,* and forgot to mention the director of the movie or his co-star, Tom Cruise.) They know who they are. They know, I hope, how much I love them, and that I think of them as family.

Speaking of family: I am grateful beyond measure to E.J. (Hula) Holahan for unmatched love and support, shared joys and griefs, and mischief-making for damn near half a century. And a thousand hugs and kisses, chocolate and champagne and flowers to Russ Lepley and Fili Pelacchi, who turned my life upside down in the best possible way.

To all my other teachers—Leiland Charles, Abby Dorn, Caitlin Valentine, Alyssa Stover, Cherelle Brown, Candice Igeleke, Kelly Hurlburt, Yukina Sato, Mathilde Gilhet, Christina Providence, TyLeigh Baughman, Mara Frazier, Alicia Leigh, Erica Alvarez, and of course Stephanie Henkle—the grandest of grand révérences. And a sheynem dank to David Brown and the Harmony Project, his brainchild, for the inspiration, the music, the opportunity to do good, and everything else, including bringing Eva Tibor, my sister under the skin, into my life.

To Jeri Wolman, may she rest in peace, and Shani Topolosky: a groysn dank fun tifn hartsn mit libshaft, ale mole.

Many thanks to the Ohio Arts Council, the Greater Columbus Arts Council, and the Emeritus Academy of The Ohio State University for their support, to Tessa Kasmar for her magical powers of observation, to Stephanie Rosalia—my retreat-benefactor, fan, and friend—and to all the editors I worked with along the way to this book: Laurel Billings, Hattie Fletcher, Dan Kois, Andrew Snee, Noreen Tomassi, Deborah Way, Bob Wilson, and especially and truly-madly-deeply Barrett Warner. Thanks, too, to Sam Schmidt and Adam Robinson.

And to my bedrock—Sheila Herman, Glen Holland, Grace and Nathan Luttrull, and Scott Herman—I am, as always, more thankful than I can say.

ABOUT THE AUTHOR

Michelle Herman is the author of nine previous books—the novels *Missing, Dog, Devotion*, and, most recently, *Close-Up*; the story collection *A New and Glorious Life*; three earlier collections of essays—*The Middle of Everything, Stories We Tell Ourselves,* and *Like A Song*; and a book for children, *A Girl's Guide to Life*. She taught creative writing for many years at The Ohio State University, where she was a founder of the MFA program in creative writing and founded and directed a graduate interdisciplinary program for artists. Since 2019, she has been dispensing relationship and family advice every Sunday as a columnist for Slate. A New Yorker by birth (and temperament), she lives in Columbus, Ohio, with her husband, the painter Glen Holland.

Author photo copyright © Leiland Charles 2025

www.ingramcontent.com/pod-product-compliance
Lightning Source LLC
Chambersburg PA
CBHW032032290426
44110CB00012B/767